POWERSCORE
TEST PREPARATION

LSAT
LOGIC GAMES
SETUPS
ENCYCLOPEDIA II

**Optimal setups for every LSAT
Logic Game from PrepTest 21 through 40!**

Published by
PowerScore Publishing, a division of PowerScore Incorporated
57 Hasell Street
Charleston, SC 29401

Author: David M. Killoran

Manufactured in Canada
July 2011

ISBN: 978-0-9826618-8-8

PowerScore Publications

PowerScore LSAT Logic Games Bible

The ultimate guide for attacking the analytical reasoning section of the LSAT. *The LSAT Logic Games Bible* features a detailed methodology for attacking the games section, extensive drills, and 30 real LSAT logic games with detailed analyses.

Available on the PowerScore website for $51.99.
Website: www.powerscore.com/pubs.htm

PowerScore LSAT Logic Games Bible Workbook

The *PowerScore LSAT Logic Games Bible Workbook*™ is the ideal companion to the *PowerScore Logic Games Bible*™, providing the opportunity to apply the concepts and approaches presented in the renowned *Games Bible*. *The Logic Games Workbook* contains thirty logic games, reproduced in their entirety from actual released past LSATs, and multiple drills created to reinforce the skills you need to effectively attack the Logic Games section. Each game's answer key presents an ideal setup for the game, with every rule and important logical inference discussed and diagrammed, and all of the questions answered and explained.

Available on the PowerScore website for $29.99.
Website: www.powerscore.com/pubs.htm

PowerScore LSAT Game Type Training

LSAT Game Type Training provides you with the complete text of every LSAT Logic Game from LSAT PrepTests 1 through 20, sorted according to the games classification system used in the *PowerScore LSAT Logic Games Bible*.

Containing 80 different games, including hard-to-find games from the early PrepTests, this book is an ideal training tool to increase your LSAT Logic Games score.

Available on the PowerScore website for $29.99.
Website: www.powerscore.com/pubs.htm

PowerScore LSAT Game Type Training II

LSAT Game Type Training II provides you with the complete text of every LSAT Logic Game from LSAT PrepTests 21 through 40, sorted according to the games classification system used in the *PowerScore LSAT Logic Games Bible*. Containing 80 different games, this book is an ideal training tool to increase your LSAT Logic Games score.

Available on the PowerScore website for $44.99.
Website: www.powerscore.com/pubs.htm

PowerScore LSAT Logical Reasoning Bible

One of the most highly anticipated publications in LSAT history, the *PowerScore LSAT Logical Reasoning Bible*™ is a comprehensive how-to manual for solving every type of Logical Reasoning question. Featuring over 100 real Logical Reasoning questions with detailed explanations, the Bible is the ultimate resource for improving your LSAT Logical Reasoning score.

Available on the PowerScore website for $49.99.
Website: www.powerscore.com/pubs.htm

PowerScore LSAT Logical Reasoning Bible Workbook

The *PowerScore LSAT Logical Reasoning Bible Workbook*™ is an ideal companion to the renowned *PowerScore Logical Reasoning Bible*™, designed specifically to test and reinforce *Logical Reasoning Bible*™ concepts and strategies. The Workbook features a full chapter of reasoning drills, as well as six LSAT Logical Reasoning sections presented in their entirety (over 150 LSAC-released Logical Reasoning questions in all), followed by complete explanations of every stimulus, question, and answer choice.

Available on the PowerScore website for $34.99.
Website: www.powerscore.com/pubs.htm

PowerScore LSAT Logical Reasoning: Question Type Training

LSAT Logical Reasoning: Question Type Training provides you with the complete text of every LSAT Logical Reasoning question from LSAT PrepTests 1 through 20, sorted according to the questions classification system used in the *PowerScore LSAT Logical Reasoning Bible*.

Containing 997 different questions, including hard-to-find questions from the early PrepTests, this book is an ideal training tool to increase your LSAT Logical Reasoning score.

Available on the PowerScore website for $54.99.
Website: www.powerscore.com/pubs.htm

PowerScore LSAT Reading Comprehension Bible

The *Reading Comprehension Bible* provides the complete guide to reading difficult passages, increasing comprehension, understanding argumentation, and effectively attacking different question types. It includes complete explanations of passages and questions drawn from actual LSATs, guides to passage diagramming, and multiple practice drills.

Available on the PowerScore website for $47.99.
Website: www.powerscore.com/pubs.htm

PowerScore LSAT Reading Comprehension: Passage Type Training

LSAT Reading Comprehension: Passage Type Training provides you with the complete text of every LSAT Reading Comprehension section from LSAT PrepTests 1 through 20, sorted according to the passage classification system used in the *PowerScore LSAT Reading Comprehension Bible*.

Containing 80 different passages, including hard-to-find passages from the early PrepTests, this book is an ideal training tool to increase your LSAT Reading Comprehension score.

Available on the PowerScore website for $34.99.
Website: www.powerscore.com/pubs.htm

PowerScore LSATs Deconstructed Series

The *PowerScore LSATs Deconstructed Series*™ offers comprehensive, question-by-question analysis of real LSATs. Each book provides a practice test as well as detailed explanations of every question and answer choice for the Logical Reasoning, Reading Comprehension, and Analytical Reasoning sections of an actual LSAT, administered by the LSAC. The concepts presented in *The PowerScore LSATs Deconstructed* ™ reflect techniques covered in PowerScore's live courses and have consistently been proven effective for thousands of our students.

Available on the PowerScore website for $19.99.
Website: www.powerscore.com/pubs.htm

PowerScore Flashcards

PowerScore Logic Games Bible Flashcards

The Logic Games Bible Flashcards relay and test foundational concepts such as games terminology, game-type recognition, and rule language, as well as advanced conceptual approaches including conditional reasoning, formal logic, and numerical distribution. Mini-challenges allow test takers to develop the skills necessary to create effective diagrams and draw sound logical inferences. Each set includes 140 cards that test the concepts and approaches to logic games taught in the *PowerScore LSAT Logic Games Bible* and in PowerScore LSAT courses.

Available on the PowerScore website for $24.99.
Website: www.powerscore.com/pubs.htm

PowerScore Logical Reasoning Bible Flashcards

The Logical Reasoning Bible Flashcards introduce and test concepts taught in our courses and in PowerScore's LSAT Logical Reasoning Bible. The flashcards cover everything from foundational definitions and question type recognition to more advanced Logical Reasoning skills, including causal reasoning, conditional reasoning, and understanding formal logic. *The Logical Reasoning Bible Flashcards* can be used as a stand-alone study aid, or as an ideal complement to the renowned *Logical Reasoning Bible*.

Available on the PowerScore website for $29.99.
Website: www.powerscore.com/pubs.htm

Tutoring and Admissions Counseling

PowerScore LSAT Private, Virtual, and Telephone Tutoring

PowerScore Private Tutoring gives students the opportunity to work one-on-one with a PowerScore tutor for the most specialized learning experience. Whether you need personalized lesson plans or you want a review on a few concepts, PowerScore can create a tutoring experience that will address all of your LSAT difficulties.

Our tutors have all scored in the 99th percentile on an actual LSAT. Aside from mastering the test themselves, every PowerScore tutor can clearly explain the underlying principles of the LSAT to any student.

PowerScore offers individual tutoring hours or tutoring packages. Please visit www.powerscore.com, or call 1-800-545-1750 for more information.

PowerScore Law School Admissions Counseling

While your LSAT score and GPA will undeniably be major factors during your admissions cycle, to truly separate yourself from the rest of the applicant pool you must assemble the most powerful application folder possible. To do this you must have an outstanding personal statement, top-notch letters of recommendation, and flawless overall presentation.

PowerScore has gathered a team of admissions experts—including former law school admissions board members, top lawyers, and students from top-twenty law schools—to address your admissions counseling and personal statement needs and help you get to where you want to be.

Please visit www.powerscore.com, or call 1-800-545-1750 for more information.

CONTENTS

INTRODUCTION

CHAPTER ONE: DECEMBER 1996 LSAT GAMES

CHAPTER TWO: JUNE 1997 LSAT GAMES

CHAPTER THREE: OCTOBER 1997 LSAT GAMES

CHAPTER FOUR: DECEMBER 1997 LSAT GAMES

CHAPTER FIVE: JUNE 1998 LSAT GAMES

Chapter Six: September 1998 LSAT Games

Chapter Seven: December 1998 LSAT Games

Chapter Eight: June 1999 LSAT Games

Chapter Nine: October 1999 LSAT Games

Chapter Ten: December 1999 LSAT Games

Chapter Eleven: June 2000 LSAT Games

Chapter Twelve: October 2000 LSAT Games

Chapter Thirteen: December 2000 LSAT Games

Chapter Fourteen: June 2001 LSAT Games

Chapter Fifteen: October 2001 LSAT Games

Chapter Sixteen: December 2001 LSAT Games

Chapter Seventeen: June 2002 LSAT Games

CHAPTER EIGHTEEN: OCTOBER 2002 LSAT GAMES

CHAPTER NINETEEN: DECEMBER 2002 LSAT GAMES

CHAPTER TWENTY: JUNE 2003 LSAT GAMES

ENDNOTES

About PowerScore

PowerScore is one of the nation's fastest growing test preparation companies. Founded in 1997, PowerScore offers LSAT, GMAT, GRE, and SAT preparation classes in over 150 locations in the U.S. and abroad. Preparation options include Full-length courses, Weekend courses, Virtual courses, and private tutoring. For more information, please visit our website at www.powerscore.com or call us at (800) 545-1750.

For supplemental information about this book, please visit the *Logic Games Setups Encyclopedia II* website at www.powerscore.com/lgsetups.

About the Author

David M. Killoran is an expert in test preparation with over 20 years of teaching experience and a 99th percentile score on a Law Services-administered LSAT. In addition to having written the renowned *PowerScore LSAT Logic Games Bible*, the *PowerScore LSAT Logical Reasoning Bible*, and many other popular publications, Dave has overseen the preparation of countless students and founded two national LSAT preparation companies.

INTRODUCTION

Introduction

Welcome to the *PowerScore LSAT Logic Games Setups Encyclopedia, Volume 2*. This book provides you with complete setups and explanations for each Logic Game on LSAT PrepTests 21 through 40.

The *Setups Encyclopedia* is intended for anyone studying the LSAT who wishes to improve their Logic Games performance. The book uses the diagramming methodology, approaches, and terminology from the *PowerScore LSAT Logic Games Bible*, and a working knowledge of those techniques will increase the value you derive from the *Setups Encyclopedia*. If you do not currently own a copy of the *PowerScore LSAT Logic Games Bible*, we strongly recommend that you purchase one immediately. If you already own a copy of the *Bible*, we recommend that you complete that book prior to using this book.

Each chapter of this book contains setups, notes, and question explanations for each of the four Logic Games that appears on each released LSAT. This book does *not* contain reproductions of the games themselves. This is because many students already have copies of the games, and adding those games would have added prohibitively to the book's cost. If you do not have all of the games in this book, you can purchase PowerScore's *LSAT Logic Games: Game Type Training II*, which contains the complete text of every LSAT Logic Game from LSAT PrepTests 21 through 40. If you already have many of the games and are just looking for a few select tests, those can often be purchased directly from PowerScore or Law Services.

The LSATs containing the Logic Games covered in this book can be purchased through our website at powerscore.com.

Because access to accurate and up-to-date information is critical, we have devoted a section of our website to *Setups Encyclopedia* students. This free online resource area provides updates to the book as needed, and contains a cross-reference listing the source location of each game in this book. There is also an official book evaluation form that we strongly encourage you to use. The exclusive *LSAT Logic Games Setups Encyclopedia* online area can be accessed at:

www.powerscore.com/lsatbibles

If we can assist you in your LSAT preparation in any way, or if you have any questions or comments about the material in this book, please do not hesitate to contact us via email at lsatbibles@powerscore.com. Additional contact information is provided at the end of this book. We look forward to hearing from you!

A Brief Overview of the LSAT

When you take an actual LSAT, they take your thumbprint at the testing site. This is done in case of test security problems.

The Law School Admission Test is administered four times a year: in February, June, September/October, and December. This standardized test is required for admission to any American Bar Association-approved law school. According to Law Services, the producers of the test, the LSAT is designed "to measure skills that are considered essential for success in law school: the reading and comprehension of complete texts with accuracy and insight; the organization and management of information and the ability to draw reasonable inferences from it; the ability to reason critically; and the analysis and evaluation of the reasoning and argument of others." The LSAT consists of the following five sections:

• 2 Sections of Logical Reasoning (short arguments, 24-26 total questions)
• 1 Section of Reading Comprehension (3 long reading passages, 2 short comparative reading passages, 26-28 total questions)
• 1 Section of Analytical Reasoning (4 logic games, 22-24 total questions)
• 1 Experimental Section of one of the above three section types.

You are given 35 minutes to complete each section. The experimental section is unscored and is not returned to the test taker. A break of 10 to 15 minutes is given between the 3rd and 4th sections.

The five-section test is followed by a 35 minute writing sample.

The Logical Reasoning Section

At the conclusion of the LSAT, and for six calendar days after the LSAT, you have the option to cancel your score. Unfortunately, there is no way to determine exactly what your score would be before cancelling.

Each Logical Reasoning Section is composed of approximately 24 to 26 short arguments. Every short argument is followed by a question such as: "Which one of the following weakens the argument?" "Which one of the following parallels the argument?" or "Which one of the following must be true according to the argument?" The key to this section is time management and an understanding of the reasoning types and question types that frequently appear.

Since there are two scored sections of Logical Reasoning on every LSAT, this section accounts for approximately 50% of your score.

The Analytical Reasoning Section

This section, also known as Logic Games, is probably the most difficult for students taking the LSAT for the first time. The section consists of four games or puzzles, each followed by a series of five to eight questions. The questions are designed to test your ability to evaluate a set of relationships and to make inferences about those relationships. To perform well on this section you must understand the major types of games that frequently appear and develop the ability to properly diagram the rules and make inferences.

The Reading Comprehension Section

This section is composed of three long reading passages, each approximately 450 words in length, and two shorter comparative reading passages. The passage topics are drawn from a variety of subjects, and each passage is followed by a series of five to eight questions that ask you to determine viewpoints in the passage, analyze organizational traits, evaluate specific sections of the passage, or compare facets of two different passages. The key to this section is to read quickly with understanding and to carefully analyze the passage structure.

The Experimental Section

Each LSAT contains one experimental section, and it does not count towards your score. The experimental can be any of the three section types described above, and the purpose of the section is to test and evaluate questions that will be used on *future* LSATs. By pretesting questions before their use in a scored section, the experimental helps the makers of the test determine the test scale.

The Writing Sample

A 35 minute Writing Sample is given at the conclusion of the LSAT. The Writing Sample is not scored, but a copy is sent to each of the law schools to which you apply.

For many years the Writing Sample was administered before the LSAT.

The format of the Writing Sample is called the Decision Prompt: you are asked to consider two possible courses of action, decide which one is superior, and then write a short essay supporting your choice. Each course of action is described in a short paragraph and you are given two primary criteria to consider in making your decision. Typically the two courses of action each have different strengths and weaknesses, and there is no clearly correct decision.

Do not agonize over the Writing Sample; in law school admissions, the Writing Sample is usually not a determining element for three reasons: the admissions committee is aware that the essay is given after a grueling three hour test and is about a subject you have no personal interest in; they already have a better sample of your writing ability in the personal statement; and the committee has a limited amount of time to evaluate applications.

You must attempt the Writing Sample! If you do not, Law Services reserves the right not to score your test.

The LSAT Scoring Scale

Each administered LSAT contains approximately 101 questions, and each LSAT score is based on the total number of questions a test taker correctly answers, a total known as the raw score. After the raw score is determined, a unique Score Conversion Chart is used for each LSAT to convert the raw score into a scaled LSAT score. Since June 1991, the LSAT has utilized a 120 to 180 scoring scale, with 120 being the lowest possible score and 180 being the highest possible score. Notably, this 120 to 180 scale is just a renumbered version of the 200 to 800 scale most test takers are familiar with from the SAT and GMAT. Just drop the "1" and add a "0" to the 120 and 180.

Although the number of questions per test has remained relatively constant over the last eight years, the overall logical difficulty of each test has varied. This is not surprising since the test is made by humans and there is no precise way to completely predetermine logical difficulty. To account for these variances in test "toughness," the test makers adjust the Scoring Conversion Chart for each LSAT in order to make similar LSAT scores from different tests mean the same thing. For example, the LSAT given in June may be logically more difficult than the LSAT given in December, but by making the June LSAT scale "looser" than the December scale, a 160 on each test would represent the same level of performance. This scale adjustment, known as equating, is extremely important to law school admissions offices around the country. Imagine the difficulties that would be posed by unequated tests: admissions officers would have to not only examine individual LSAT scores, but also take into account which LSAT each score came from. This would present an information nightmare.

The LSAT Percentile Table

Since the LSAT has 61 possible scores, why didn't the test makers change the scale to 0 to 60? Probably for merciful reasons. How would you tell your friends that you scored a 3 on the LSAT? 123 sounds so much better.

It is important not to lose sight of what LSAT scaled scores actually represent. The 120 to 180 test scale contains 61 different possible scores. Each score places a student in a certain relative position compared to other test takers. These relative positions are represented through a percentile that correlates to each score. The percentile indicates where the test taker ranks in the overall pool of test takers. For example, a score of 163 represents the 90th percentile, meaning a student with a score of 163 scored better than 90 percent of the people who have taken the test in the last three years. The percentile is critical since it is a true indicator of your positioning relative to other test takers, and thus law school applicants.

Charting out the entire percentage table yields a rough "bell curve." The number of test takers in the 120s and 170s is very low (only 1.6% of all test takers receive a score in the 170s), and most test takers are bunched in the middle, comprising the "top" of the bell. In fact, approximately 40% of all test takers score between 145 and 155 inclusive, and about 70% of all test takers score between 140 and 160 inclusive.

The median score on the LSAT scale is approximately 151. The median, or middle, score is the score at which approximately 50% of test takers have a lower score and 50% of test takers have a higher score. Typically, to achieve a score of 151, you must answer between 56 and 61 questions correctly from a total of 101 questions. In other words, to achieve a score that is perfectly average, you can miss between 40 and 45 questions. Thus, it is important to remember that you don't have to answer every question correctly in order to receive an excellent LSAT score. There is room for error, and accordingly you should never let any single question occupy an inordinate amount of your time.

There is no penalty for answering incorrectly on the LSAT. Therefore, you should guess on any questions you cannot complete.

The Use of the LSAT

The use of the LSAT in law school admissions is not without controversy. It is largely taken for granted that your LSAT score is one of the most important determinants of the type of school you can attend. At many law schools a multiplier made up of your LSAT score and your undergraduate grade point average is used to help determine the relative standing of applicants, and at some schools a sufficiently high multiplier guarantees your admission.

For all the importance of the LSAT, it is not without flaws. As a standardized test currently given in the paper-and-pencil format, there are a number of skills that the LSAT cannot measure, such as listening skills, note-taking ability, perseverance, etc. Law Services is aware of these limitations and as a matter of course they warn all law schools about overemphasizing LSAT results. Still, since the test ultimately returns a number for each student, it is hard to escape the tendency to rank applicants accordingly. Fortunately, once you get to law school the LSAT is forgotten. For the time being consider the test a temporary hurdle you must leap in order to reach the ultimate goal.

For more information on the LSAT, or to register for the test, contact Law Services at (215) 968-1001 or at their website at www.lsac.org.

As you know, the focus of this book is on the Analytical Reasoning section. Each Analytical Reasoning section contains four games and a total of 22-24 questions. Since you have thirty-five minutes to complete the section, you have an average of eight minutes and forty-five seconds to complete each game. Of course, the amount of time you spend on each game will vary with the difficulty and the number of questions per game. For many students, the time constraint is what makes Logic Games the most difficult section on the LSAT, and as we present the explanations in this book, we will discuss occasional time-saving tips and methods for solving questions more quickly.

On average, you have 8 minutes and 45 seconds to complete each game.

Each logic game contains three separate parts: the scenario, the rules, and the questions.

The Scenario

The game scenario introduces sets of variables—people, places, things, or events—involved in an easy to understand activity such as sitting in seats or singing songs. Here is an example of a game scenario:

> Seven comics—Janet, Khan, Leticia, Ming, Neville, Olivia, and Paul—
> will be scheduled to perform in the finals of a comedy competition.
> During the evening of the competition, each comic, performing alone,
> will give exactly one performance.

In the above scenario there are two variable sets: the comics J, K, L, M, N, O, and P, and the seven performance positions, which would be numbered 1 through 7.

Always write down and keep track of each variable set.

In basic terms, the scenario "sets the table" for the game and provides you with a quick picture of the situation to be analyzed. Although many game scenarios simply introduce the variables, on occasion the test makers place numerical information in the scenario, and this information is critical to understanding the possibilities inherent in the game.

Because you cannot afford to misunderstand any of the basics of the game, you must read the game scenario very closely.

The Rules

The second part of every game is the rules—a set of statements that describe and control the relationships between the variables. Here are the rules that accompany the above game scenario:

> Neville performs either second or sixth.
> Paul performs at some time after Leticia performs.
> Janet performs at some time after Khan performs.
> There is exactly one performance between Neville's performance and Olivia's performance, whether or not Neville performs before Olivia performs.

Each of the initial rules in a game applies to each and every question; however, on occasion a question will explicitly suspend one or more rules for the purposes of that question only. These "suspension" questions always occur at the end of the game.

The third and final part of each logic game is a set of approximately five to eight questions that test your knowledge of the relationships between the variables, the structural features of the game, and the way those relationships and features change as conditions in the game change. More on the questions in a moment.

Approaching the Games

As you begin each game you should carefully and completely read through the entire game scenario and all of the rules *before* you begin writing. This initial reading will help you determine the type of game you are facing, as well as what variable sets exist and what relationships govern their actions. This advice will save you time by allowing you to formulate an exact plan of action, and it will save you from diagramming a rule and then re-diagramming if you find a later rule that alters the situation. At this point in the game you must also fix the rules in your memory. Students who fail to identify strongly with the rules inevitably struggle with the questions. It is also important to identify the most powerful rules in a game and to consider how the rules interact with one another. Of course, we will discuss how to do this throughout our analysis.

In general, these are the initial steps you must take to efficiently move through each game:

1. Read through and fix the rules in your mind.
2. Diagram the scenario and the rules.
3. Make inferences.
4. Use the rules and inferences to attack the questions.

The initial rules apply to every question unless otherwise indicated.

Always read through the entire scenario and each rule before you begin diagramming.

One of the goals
of this book
is to help you
understand the
ideal setup for
each game you
encounter.

Your initial reading of the game will also indicate what setup to use to attack the game. Many students are not aware of the best ways to set up logic games, and waste far too much time during the actual exam wondering what approach to take. Because you must read the rules and set up a diagram quickly and efficiently, the key to succeeding on the Logic Games section is to know the ideal approach to every game type before walking into the exam.

Make a main
diagram at the
bottom of the
page.

You should use the space at the bottom of each game page to diagram your initial setup. This setup should include:

1. A list of the variables and their number. For example: J K L M N O P [7]
2. An identification of any randoms in the game (randoms are variables that do not appear in any rules).
3. A diagrammatic representation of the variable sets.
4. A diagrammatic representation of the rules.
5. A list of inferences. Making inferences involves deducing hidden rules or facts from the given relationships between variables. Inferences almost always follow from a combination of the rules or limiting structural factors within the game.

By following the above list and using the scenario and rules from the previous pages, we can produce this game setup:

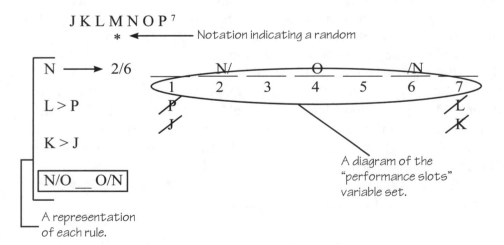

The above setup is linear in nature, on of the most common types of Logic Games.

After making the
initial setup, do
not write on your
main diagram.

Once you have completed your game setup, you should *not* draw or otherwise write on your main diagram again. As you do each question, use the space *next* to the question to reproduce a miniature diagram with the basic structural features of your main diagram. You should *not* use your main diagram for the work of individual questions. For example, if a question introduces the condition that L sits in the third of seven chairs, draw the seven chair spaces next to the question, place L in the third space, make inferences, and then proceed with the question. Refer to your main setup for the details of the relationship between the variables. There are several important benefits that you receive from working next to the question: First, should you need to return to the question later, your work will be readily available and accessible; second, keeping the individual conditions of each question separate from the main setup reduces the possibility that you will mistake a local condition for a global rule; and third, you will be able to more clearly see which conditions produced which results.

Do the work for each question next to that question.

As you complete each question, it is absolutely essential that you *not* erase your previous work. Each question that you complete adds to your repository of game knowledge, and that knowledge can be invaluable when answering other questions. For example, suppose the first question in a game produces a scenario where A is in the first position. Then, the second question asks for a complete and accurate listing of the positions A can occupy. Based on the first question, A can clearly be in the first position, and therefore you can eliminate any answer in the second question which does not contain the first position as a possibility. Thus, the work you do in *some* questions can be used to help answer other questions. This is true as long as the work you are referencing conforms to the conditions in the question you are currently answering. For example, if the third question in the same game states, "If A is in the third position, which of the following can be true?" then you cannot use the information from the first question to help answer the third question because A was in the first position in the first question, and thus does not fit the condition imposed in the third question.

Do not erase unless you make a mistake.

The work done on some questions can be used to help solve other questions.

For students who ignore the above recommendations, the results are often quite negative: confusion, disorganization, constant rereading of the rules, and missed questions. Some students say that they save time by using their main diagram for each question. While they may save a short amount of time, the overall costs always outweigh the benefits, particularly since those same students have a tendency to erase during the game. As we proceed with our analysis of the games section, we will revisit this topic from time to time and ultimately prove the efficacy of our recommendations.

Once you have completed your diagram and made inferences, you will be ready to answer the questions. Keep in mind that each question has exactly the same value and that there is no penalty for guessing. Thus, if you cannot complete the section you should guess on the questions that remain. If you cannot complete an individual question, do not spend an undue amount of time on the question. Instead, move on and complete the other questions.

Games questions are either global or local. Global questions ask about information derived only from the initial rules, such as "Who can finish first?" or "Which one of the following must be true?" Use the rules and your main diagram to answer global questions. Local questions generally begin with the words "if," "when," or "suppose," and occur when the question imposes a new condition in addition to the initial rules, such as "If Laura sits in the third chair, which one of the following must be true?" The additional conditions imposed by local questions apply to that question only and do not apply to any of the other questions. It is essential that you focus on the implications of the new conditions. Ask yourself how this condition affects the variables and the existing rules. For local questions, reproduce a mini-setup next to the question, apply the local condition, and proceed.

Local questions almost always require you to produce a "mini-setup" next to the question.

Within the global/local designation all questions ultimately ask for one of four things: what must be true, what is not necessarily true, what could be true, and what cannot be true. All questions are a variation of one of these four basic ideas. At all times, you must be aware of the exact nature of the question you are being asked, especially when "except" questions appear. If you find that you are missing questions because you miss words such as "false" or "except" when reading, then take a moment at the beginning of the game to circle the key words in each question, words such as "must," "could," etc.

If you frequently misread questions, circle the key part of each question before you begin the game. You will not forget about a word like "except" if you have it underlined!

The key to quickly answering questions is to identify with the rules and inferences in a game. This involves both properly diagramming the rules and simple memorization. If you often find yourself rereading the rules during a game, you are failing to identify with the rules. And do not forget to constantly apply your inferences to each question!

Attacking the Section

The key to optimal performance on Logic Games is to be focused and organized. This involves a number of factors:

1. Play to your strengths and away from your weaknesses

You are not required to do the games in the order presented on the test, and you should not expect that the test makers will present the games in the best order for you. Students who expect to have difficulty on the games section should attack the games in order of their personal preferences and strengths and weaknesses. You can implement this strategy by quickly previewing each of the four games as you start the section. By doing so you can then select a game that you feel is the best fit for your strengths.

2. Create a strong setup for the game

Often, the key to powerful games performance is to create a good setup. At least 80% of the games on the LSAT are "setup games" wherein the quality of your setup dictates whether or not you are successful in answering the questions. Mastering those elements will help you become an expert in handling any type of game.

3. Look to make inferences

There are always inferences in a game, and the test makers expect you to make at least a few of them. Always check the rules and your setup with an eye towards finding inferences, and then use those inferences relentlessly to attack the questions.

4. Be smart during the game

If necessary, skip over time consuming questions and return to them later. Remember that it is sometimes advisable to do the questions out of order. For example, if the first question in a game asks you for a complete and accurate list of the positions "C" could occupy, because of time considerations it would be advisable to skip that question and complete the remaining questions. Then you could return to the first question and use the knowledge you gained from the other questions to quickly and easily answer the first question.

5. Do not be intimidated by size

A lengthy game scenario and a large number of initial rules do not necessarily equal greater difficulty. Some of the longest games are easy because they contain so many restrictions and limitations.

Although test takers have found the first game on many LSATs to be the easiest, there is no set order of difficulty, and you cannot predict where the easiest or hardest game will appear. On some tests the first game has been the hardest and the last game has been the easiest. That said, for the majority of LSATs, the hardest game usually appears second or third, and the easiest game usually appears first.

6. Keep an awareness of time

As stated previously, you have approximately eight minutes and forty-five seconds to complete each game and bubble in your answers. Use a timer during the LSAT so you always know how much time remains, and do not let one game or question consume so much time that you suffer later on.

7. Maintain a positive attitude and concentrate

Above all, you must attack each game with a positive and energetic attitude. The games themselves are often challenging yet fun, and students who actively involve themselves in the games generally perform better overall.

If you do all four games, you have 8 minutes and 45 seconds to complete each game, inclusive of answer transferring. If you do only three games, you have 11 minutes and 40 seconds to complete each game. If you do just two games, you have 17 minutes and 30 seconds to complete each game.

You can do the games out of order and according to your strengths and weaknesses.

There are three parts to every Logic Game: the scenario, the rules, and the questions.

Always read the scenario and rules once through before you begin diagramming.

Fix the rules in your mind.

Make a main diagram for each game. Include the following:
>   List the variables and their exact total number
>   Identify Randoms
>   Diagram the variable sets
>   Diagram the rules
>   Make inferences
>   Identify the powerful rules and variables

Write neatly.

You can do the questions out of order if it saves time or is more efficient.

For local questions, do your work next to the question.

Always look to use your inferences when answering questions.

Do not erase unless you have made a mistake.

Do not forget that work from one question might be useful on other questions.

Maintain a positive attitude, concentrate, and try to enjoy yourself.

Memorize these points! They are basic principles you must know in order to perform powerfully.

Game Setup Usage Notes

The following pages contain game setups organized by chapter. Each chapter contains the setups for the four games from a single LSAT, and the chapters are presented in order according to PrepTest number. Thus, the setups for PrepTest 21, the December 1996 LSAT, are presented first.

The chapters do not have traditional "chapter divider" headings. Instead, each chapter has a numbered tab along the side of the page with the PrepTest number of the games explained in the chapter. Each game is introduced by a header that indicates the exact source and position of the game, for example, "October 1997 Game #1: Questions 1-5." Finally, at the bottom of each right-hand page is a reference to the month and year of the LSAT games in the chapter, for example, "Chapter Eleven: June 2000 Logic Game Setups." In addition, the Table of Contents lists the start page of each chapter. You can quickly find game setups within the book by referring to the side, top, or bottom of each page, or by referring to the Table of Contents.

POWERSCORE

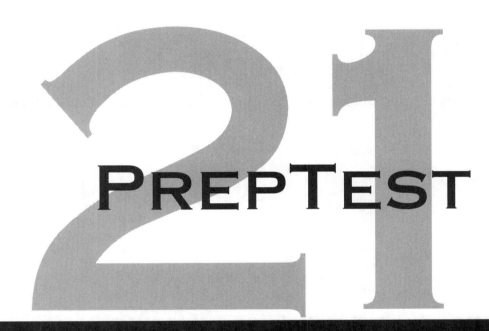

21 PREPTEST

DECEMBER 1996 LOGIC GAMES SETUPS

This is a Grouping: Defined-Moving, Balanced, Numerical Distribution, Identify the Templates game.

This is a deceptively tricky game because it does not at first appear to be controlled by a Numerical Distribution. However, the presence of "singles," "doubles," and "triples" lends a natural numerical base to the game, and ultimately controls all of the possible outcomes. In our diagram, we will use the room capacity as the base, with a single represented by "1," a double represented by "2," and a triple represented by "3." With those designations in mind, here is the initial diagram of the game:

4th: K L ^{2}
3rd: P R ^{2}
2nd: S T V ^{3}

$$\underline{\qquad} \qquad \underline{\qquad} \qquad \underline{\qquad}$$
$$\quad 1 \qquad\qquad 2 \qquad\qquad 3$$

The third and fourth rules are simple block rules, and can be added to the side of the diagram:

4th: K L ^{2}
3rd: P R ^{2}
2nd: S T V ^{3}

$$\underline{\qquad} \qquad \underline{\qquad} \qquad \underline{\qquad}$$
$$\quad 1 \qquad\qquad 2 \qquad\qquad 3$$

$$\boxed{\begin{matrix} K \\ P \end{matrix}} \qquad \boxed{\begin{matrix} \cancel{L} \\ \cancel{R} \end{matrix}}$$

The first and second rules create a number of Not Laws, and when combined with the fourth rule, a number of inferences:

Because no fourth-year student can be assigned to a triple, K and L Not Laws can be placed under the "3." And, because K and P must share a room, a P Not Law also can be placed under the "3." With three of the seven students eliminated from sharing a triple, there are only four possible candidates to live in a triple, meaning *there is at most one triple in this game.*

Because no second-year student can be assigned to a single, S, T, and V Not Laws can be placed under the "1." And, because K and P must share a room, K and P Not Laws also can be placed under the "1." Thus, only L or R can be assigned to a single, meaning that *there are at most two singles in this game.*

Because K and P must share a room, and it cannot be a single or a triple, they must share a double room.

Thus, the game scenario and rules combine to form the following diagram:

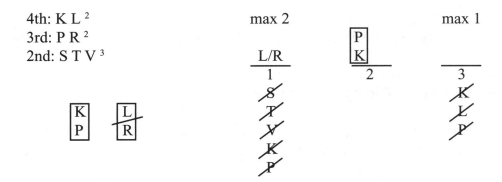

4th: K L ²
3rd: P R ²
2nd: S T V ³

As mentioned before, the Numerical Distribution is hidden in this game. The singles, doubles, and triples form natural numerical limitations within the game, and the assignment of students-to-rooms further limits the possible distributions. In fact, only three distributions of students-to-rooms exist:

Single/Double/Triple Numerical Distributions:

Distribution #1: 1-1-2-3   (two singles, one double, and one triple)

L	R	KP	STV
single	single	double	triple

In this distribution, there are two singles, which must be L and R. K and P are assigned to the sole double, and the remaining three students—S, T, and V—are assigned a triple. This is the only distribution where every student is assigned to a specific room.

Distribution #2: 1-2-2-2   (one single, three doubles, and no triple)

L/R	KP	__ __	__ __	◄——— R/L, S, T, V
single	double	double	double	

In this distribution, there is one single, which must be L or R. K and P are assigned to one double, and the remaining four students—R/L, S, T, and V—are assigned in pairs to the remaining two doubles.

Distribution #3: 2-2-3   (no single, two doubles, and one triple)

KP	L __	R __ __	◄——— S, T, V
double	double	triple	

In this distribution, K and P are assigned to one of the doubles. L, a fourth-year student who cannot be assigned to a triple, must be assigned to a double. Because the third rule stipulates that L and R cannot share the same room, R must then be assigned to the triple. Of the three remaining students—S, T, and V—one is assigned to a double and the other two are assigned to the triple.

Most of the questions can be easily answered by using the distributions above.

Question #1: Global, Could Be True. The correct answer choice is (C)

The only answer which contains any of the allowable distributions is answer choice (C), which is the correct answer choice and reflects Distribution #2 discussed above (the 1-2-2-2 distribution).

Question #2: Local, Could Be True. The correct answer choice is (B)

This local question requires that R be assigned a single, and we also know that K and P always share a double, so the distribution must be either 1-2-2-2, or 1-1-2-3. Answer choice (B) is the correct answer, because it is possible to assign L to a single, and assign the remaining three students (S, T, and V) to a triple. (Note that if the 1-1-2-3 distribution is used, the second single must go to L, because S, T, and V are second-years and thus prohibited from living in singles).

Question #3: Global, Must Be True. The correct answer choice is (B)

The correct answer to this question, answer choice (B), is discussed in our setup. Because K and P must share a room (and therefore cannot be assigned to singles), and K, who is a fourth-year student, cannot be assigned to a triple, the KP block must be assigned to a double.

Question #4: Local, Must Be True. The correct answer choice is (C)

The question stem dictates that R is assigned to a triple. The only scenario where this can occur is under the 2-2-3 distribution. As there are no singles in this distribution, answer choice (C) must be the correct answer choice.

Question #5: Local, Must Be True. The correct answer choice is (A)

If T and V are each assigned to different doubles, and we already know that K and P are assigned to a double, that totals three doubles, leaving only one allowable distribution: 1-2-2-2. Therefore, the correct answer choice is (A).

Question #6: Global, Could Be True. The correct answer choice is (C)

Answer choice (A) is incorrect because L and R are the only two students who can be assigned to a single, and while L is a fourth-year student, R is not.

Answer choice (B) is incorrect because K and L are the only two fourth-year students, and K must share a double with P, a third-year student. Thus, K and L cannot share a room.

Answer choice (C) is the correct answer. L could share a room with a second-year student, as long as that room is not a triple.

Answer choice (D) is incorrect because L cannot room with either third-year student—P always shares with K, and the third rule prohibits L from sharing a room with R.

Answer choice (E) is incorrect because P must share a double with K.

PrepTest 21. December 1996 Game #2:   *7. D 8. A 9. A 10. B 11. A*

This is a Basic Linear: Unbalanced: Overloaded game.

The basic scenario for the game is as follows:

G G G ³
P P P ³
Y Y Y ³

<u>   </u>   <u>   </u>   <u>   </u>
 1   2   3

The first rule is a fairly simple conditional rule:

$$1P \longrightarrow 2Y$$

The second is conditional as well:

$$2G \longrightarrow 1G$$

The third rule features a compound sufficient condition:

$$\begin{matrix} 3P \\ \text{or} \\ 3Y \end{matrix} \longrightarrow 2P$$

The contrapositive of the third rule is particularly important in this game:

$$\cancel{2P} \longrightarrow \begin{matrix} \cancel{3P} \\ \text{and} \\ \cancel{3Y} \end{matrix}$$

When translated using the fact that there are only three colors, this is identical to:

$$\begin{matrix} 2Y \\ \text{or} \\ 2G \end{matrix} \longrightarrow 3G$$

This information can then be added to the first two rules:

Rule #1:

$$[1P \longrightarrow 2Y] \longrightarrow 3G$$

Rule #2:

$$[2G \longrightarrow 1G] \longrightarrow 3G$$

In games such as this one with unusual conditional rules, always consider the contrapositives. For example, question #8 can easily be solved by taking the contrapositive of the second rule:

$$\cancel{1G} \longrightarrow \cancel{2G}$$

Accordingly, if light 1 is Y, then light 2 cannot be G, and the correct answer is (A).

Question #7: Global, Could Be True, List. The correct answer choice is (D)

Answer choice (A) is incorrect because it violates the third rule.

Answer choice (B) is incorrect because it violates both the first and second rules.

Answer choice (C) is incorrect because it violates the first rule.

Answer choice (D) is the correct answer.

Answer choice (E) is incorrect because it violates the third rule.

Question #8: Local, Could Be True, Except. The correct answer choice is (A)

Answer choice (A) is the correct answer. As explained above, if light 1 is not green, then light 2 cannot be green.

Answer choice (B) is incorrect because, as shown in the correct solution to question #7, when light 1 is yellow, light 2 can be purple.

Answer choice (C) is incorrect because, as shown in the correct solution to question #7, when light 1 is yellow, light 3 can be green.

Answer choice (D) is incorrect because when light 1 is yellow, light 3 can be purple under the following hypothetical: Y-P-P.

Answer choice (E) is incorrect because when light 1 is yellow, light 3 can be yellow under the following hypothetical: Y-P-Y.

Question #9: Local, Justify. The correct answer choice is (A)

Note that this is a Justify question, wherein you must supply the answer choice that forces the desired result, which in this case is to have only one possible solution.

Looking over our setup, when we added the contrapositive of the third rule to the original first rule, the following resulted:

$$[\ 1P \longrightarrow 2Y\ ] \longrightarrow 3G$$

Thus, if an answer stipulated that light 1 was purple, that would result in a single color sequence. As it happens, answer choice (A) indicates that light 1 is purple, and answer choice (A) is thus correct.

Note that this question can also be easily solved using hypotheticals.

Question #10: Local, Must Be True. The correct answer choice is (B)

If no green bulbs are selected, then each bulb is either purple or yellow:

$$\frac{P/Y}{1} \qquad \frac{P/Y}{2} \qquad \frac{P/Y}{3}$$

Because the question asks for how many different color sequences are possible, the best approach is to test light 1, first as purple, and then as yellow.

<u>When light 1 is purple:</u>

When light 1 is purple, according to the first rule light 2 must be yellow. But, when light 2 is yellow, from the contrapositive of the third rule, light 3 cannot be purple or yellow, and must be green. But, as this violates the condition in this question stem, this does not allow for a workable solution. Thus, there are no viable solutions when light 1 is purple.

<u>When light 1 is yellow:</u>

When light 1 is yellow, then light 2 can be purple or yellow:

$$\frac{Y}{1} \qquad \frac{P/Y}{2} \qquad \frac{\quad}{3}$$

When light 2 is yellow, from the contrapositive of the third rule, light 3 cannot be purple or yellow, and must be green. But, as this violates the condition in this question stem, this does not allow for a workable solution. Thus, there are no possible solutions when light 1 is yellow, and light 2 is yellow.

When light 2 is purple, then light three can be purple or yellow:

$$\frac{Y}{1} \qquad \frac{P}{2} \qquad \frac{P/Y}{3}$$

When light 3 is purple or yellow, no violations occur, meaning that there are two possible solutions when light 1 is yellow and light 2 is purple. Thus, two is the correct answer, and answer choice (B) is correct.

Question #11: Local, Could Be True. The correct answer choice is (A)

The condition in this question stem stipulates that no color is used twice, and thus each light must be a different color. From a direct application of the rules, this automatically affects the second and third rules:

Because the second rule stipulates that when light 2 is green then light 1 must also be green, which would violate the condition in this question stem, we can determine that light 2 can never be green. This immediately eliminates answer choice (D) from consideration.

In the third rule, when light 3 is purple, then light 2 must also be purple. Accordingly, in this question light 3 can never be purple, and this information can be used to eliminate answer choice (E).

However, the other two incorrect answer choices can also be eliminated by examining the third rule more closely:

In the third rule, when light 3 is yellow, then light 2 must be purple. Answer choice (C), which states that light 1 is purple and light 3 is yellow, would thus cause purple to be used twice (in lights 1 and 2), a violation of the condition in the question stem. Thus, answer choice (C) cannot be true and is incorrect.

From the contrapositive of the third rule, when light 2 is yellow or purple, then light 3 must be green. Answer choice (B), which states that light 1 is green and light 2 is yellow, would thus cause green to be used twice (in lights 1 and 3), a violation of the condition in the question stem. Thus, answer choice (B) cannot be true and is incorrect.

Therefore, answer choice (A) is the correct answer, and is possible under the following solution: G-P-Y.

PrepTest 21. December 1996 Game #3: *12. D 13. D 14. B 15. E 16. E 17. A*

This is an Advanced Linear: Unbalanced: Underfunded game.

Because this game features the days of the week, they should be used as the base, and then a row for the morning interviews and a row for the afternoon interviews should be stacked above the base, making this an Advanced Linear game:

Nonhostile: Q R U X Y Z [6]
Hostile:

H	H
H	H

Afternoon: ___ ___ ___ ___ ___ ___
Morning: ___ ___ ___ ___ ___ ___
         M Tu W Th F Sa

Note that while we use the morning interviews as the bottom row, you could just as easily use the afternoon interviews as the bottom row.

In the diagram there are 12 available interview times (2 times per day over 6 days), but there are only 10 total variables (6 nonhostile and 4 hostile). Further, because two of the nonhostile witnesses are interviewed together, there are 9 variables available for the 12 interview times. Thus, there must be three empty interview times in each solution (these will shown with three "E" variables).

While the nonhostile witnesses are given in standard variable form, the hostile witnesses are bit unusual. They are not specified as variables, but rather as a two-day block (shown above as a block around four Hs). Because interviewing the hostile witnesses takes up two full consecutive days of the week (and X is already assigned to Thursday morning), the hostile witnesses can only be interviewed on Monday and Tuesday, Tuesday and Wednesday, or Friday and Saturday. This point will be discussed in more detail later in this setup discussion.

As mentioned before, the first rule helpfully assigns X to Thursday morning. The second, third, and fourth rules are sequential in nature, and, when combined, create a large chain sequence:

$$
\begin{array}{c}
Y \\
\text{-----------} > Z \\
U > \boxed{Q\ R} > X
\end{array}
$$

This sequence generates a number of Not Laws, which are shown on the final diagram:

Nonhostile: Q R U X Y Z ^{6} E E E

Hostile:

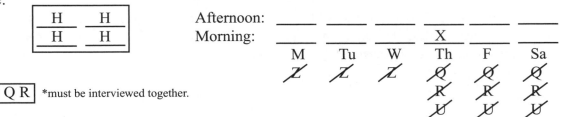

| Q R | *must be interviewed together. |

Y
- - - - - - - - - - - > Z
U > | Q R | > X

The last rule states that Z must be interviewed after X, which is interviewed on Thursday morning. Thus, Z must be interviewed on Thursday afternoon, any time Friday, or any time Saturday. Therefore, if the hostile witnesses are interviewed on Friday and Saturday, Z must be interviewed on Thursday afternoon. Via the contrapositive, if Z (or Y) is interviewed on Friday or Saturday, the hostile witnesses must be interviewed either on Monday and Tuesday or on Tuesday and Wednesday. Essentially, if Z is interviewed on Friday or Saturday, hostile witnesses must be interviewed Tuesday and either Monday or Wednesday. This inference is one of the keys to the game.

Because the hostile witness block has only three options, and there are severe restrictions on the nonhositile witnesses, there is a strong argument to be made that this game should be attacked by Identifying the Templates. While this approach is not necessary to successfully solve this game, it is useful, and so we will show each template below:

Template #1: Hostile witnesses on Monday-Tuesday

In this template, the hostile witness block occupies Monday and Tuesday. Thus, from the second and third rules, U must be interviewed on Wednesday morning, and Q and R must be interviewed on Wednesday afternoon. Y > Z then occupies part of Thursday, Friday, or Saturday:

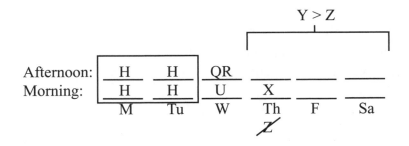

Note that both Y and Z could be interviewed on Saturday, so no global Not Law prohibits Y from being interviewed on Saturday. However, if Y is interviewed on Saturday, it must be in the morning, and Z would be interviewed on Saturday afternoon.

Template #2: Hostile witnesses on Tuesday-Wednesday

In this template, the hostile witness block occupies Tuesday and Wednesday. Thus, from the second and third rules, U must be interviewed on Monday morning, and Q and R must be interviewed on Monday afternoon. Y > Z then occupies part of Thursday, Friday, or Saturday:

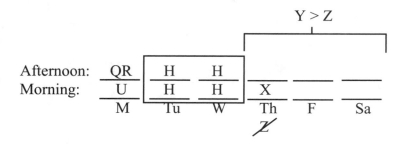

Note that both Y and Z could be interviewed on Saturday, so no global Not Law prohibits Y from being interviewed on Saturday. However, if Y is interviewed on Saturday, it must be in the morning, and Z would be interviewed on Saturday afternoon.

Template #3: Hostile witnesses on Friday-Saturday

In this template, the hostile witness block occupies Friday and Saturday. Thus, from the last rule, Z must be interviewed on Thursday afternoon. The remainder of the sequence occupies part of Monday, Tuesday, or Wednesday:

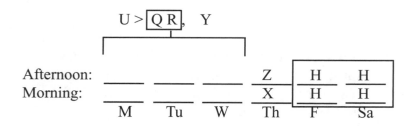

Again, showing these templates is not necessary, but when a significant factor in the game (in this case, the hostile witness block) has limited options, attacking the game with templates is always an option.

Question #12: Global, Could Be True, List. The correct answer choice is (D)

Answer choice (A) is incorrect because U must be interviewed before R.

Answer choice (B) is incorrect because X and Y are not interviewed together.

Answer choice (C) is incorrect because Q must be interviewed before X.

Answer choice (D) is the correct answer choice.

Answer choice (E) is incorrect because Q is interviewed with R, not U.

Question #13: Global, Could Be True, List. The correct answer choice is (D)

Answer choices (A) and (B) are incorrect because Q and R must be interviewed simultaneously, not separately.

Answer choice (C) is incorrect because X is interviewed on Thursday.

Answer choice (D) is the correct answer choice.

Answer choice (E) is incorrect because Z cannot be interviewed on Tuesday.

Question #14: Local, Must Be True. The correct answer choice is (B)

If Y is interviewed at some time after X, then Z must be interviewed on Friday or Saturday. Thus, the hostile witnesses must be interviewed on either Monday-Tuesday or Tuesday-Wednesday. Accordingly, answer choice (B) is correct.

Question #15: Local, Must Be True. The correct answer choice is (E)

Since R is interviewed after Y, and R is interviewed before X, the following chain sequence results:

$$\begin{array}{c} Y \\ \text{----}> \boxed{Q\ R} > X > Z \\ U \end{array}$$

Since Y, U, and the QR block require three separate interview times, three of the six available interview slots during the Monday, Tuesday, and Wednesday scheduling period must be reserved for them. This effectively denies the hostile witnesses sufficient time to be interviewed during the Monday, Tuesday, Wednesday period and so the hostile witnesses must be interviewed on Friday and Saturday. Answer choice (E) is thus correct.

Question #16: Local, Must Be True. The correct answer choice is (E)

The conditions imposed by the question stem force the hostile witnesses to be interviewed on Friday and Saturday, and this forces Z to be interviewed on Thursday afternoon. It follows that answer choice (E) is correct.

Question #17: Local, Could Be True. The correct answer choice is (A)

Answer choice (A) is the correct answer choice.

If Z is interviewed on Saturday morning, then the hostile witnesses must be interviewed on either Monday-Tuesday or Tuesday-Wednesday. This information eliminates answer choice (B).

Answer choice (C) is incorrect because R must be interviewed before X, and thus R cannot be interviewed on Thursday.

Answer choice (D) is incorrect because Tuesday is reserved for interviewing the hostile witnesses.

Answer choice (E) is incorrect because if Y was interviewed before Thursday, there would be insufficient space to interview the hostile witnesses as well as U, QR, and X in the Monday-Wednesday slots.

PrepTest 21. December 1996 Game #4: *18. B 19. C 20. B 21. A 22. E 23. D 24. E*

This is a Basic Linear: Unbalanced: Underfunded game.

This is a difficult game, so do not be upset if you struggled. As mentioned previously in our books and courses, Unbalanced Linear games are typically more difficult than Balanced Linear games. It is incumbent upon you to always keep track of whether or not a game is Balanced, and then use that information to your advantage. For example, if this were the first game in a Logic Games section, the best strategy might be to skip this game and return to it later in the section. There would surely be easier games in the section; you could attack them first, then return to this more difficult game having already answered a number of questions correctly. For those students who took the December 1996 LSAT, it was fortunate that the most difficult game of the test appeared last in the section. Thus, most students had already successfully completed many of the easier questions in the section when they arrived at this game.

Let us take a moment to examine the Underfunded aspect of the game. There are seven products that must fill eight advertising periods (7 into 8). In order to compensate for this shortfall, exactly one of the products is advertised twice. This doubling produces a 2-1-1-1-1-1-1 numerical distribution. Regrettably, we cannot ascertain exactly which product is doubled, and this greatly contributes to the difficulty of the game.

Since the products are advertised over a four-week period, and two products are advertised each week, our linear setup will feature two slots per week, diagrammed in stacks:

$$\frac{\overline{}}{1} \quad \frac{\overline{}}{2} \quad \frac{\overline{}}{3} \quad \frac{\overline{}}{4}$$

Note that you do not want to draw out the 8 spaces on one horizontal line. Having two stacks creates a vertical component and that allows for better representation of the different types of blocks (e.g. the HJ block versus the blocks involving G).

Using this structure, most students diagram the game in a manner similar to the following:

G H J K L M O⁷
   * *

J ⟶ [H J]

Doubled ⟶ 1,4 or 2,4
Product

[G / J] or [G / O]

K ⟶ at least 1 or 2

K̅/ /K̅ O̅ ―
1 2 3 4

Several of the rules are quite tricky. The first rule, which states that "J is not advertised during a given week unless H is advertised during the immediately preceding week," can be partially represented as a block because of the "immediately preceding" qualifier. However, because of the "unless" portion of the rule, the block only occurs when J is present. Hence, the rule is diagrammed as a conditional statement with an arrow. When J is advertised, H must be advertised in the preceding week. This rule automatically means that J cannot be doubled because this would cause H to be doubled as well (and only one variable can be doubled).

However, the normal Not Laws that follow from a block do not occur in this case because of the fact that one of the products is doubled (and thus the problems created by the Underfunded aspect of the game begin). While it is true that J cannot be advertised during week 1, it is *not* true that H cannot be advertised during week 4. Since H could be the doubled product, H could be advertised during week 1 and week 4, for example (J would be advertised during week 2).

The second rule also produces two notable inferences. The rule states that the product that is advertised twice is advertised during week 4, but not during week 3. Thus, the only two options would be to advertise that doubled product on weeks 1 and 4 (1-4) or weeks 2 and 4 (2-4). Because the major point of uncertainty in this game is the doubled product, this information is very valuable. Since the doubled product must be advertised during weeks 1 and 4 or weeks 2 and 4, any variable that appears in week 3 cannot be the doubled product and therefore cannot appear in any week except week 3. By combining this inference with the last rule, we can infer that O cannot be advertised during weeks 1, 2, or 4. The second rule also allows us to infer that any product advertised during weeks 1, 2, or 4 cannot be advertised during week 3, since the doubling does not allow for week 3 to be used. By combining this inference with the rule involving K, we can infer that since K must be advertised during week 1 or 2 at the least, K cannot be advertised during week 3. K could still be advertised during week 4 since K could be the doubled product. Thus, a K Not Law cannot be placed on week 4.

There is still one critical inference yet to be uncovered, but because very few students discover this inference during the setup, we will continue on to the questions now, and then discuss the inference when it arises in question #20. The game diagram above is therefore only partially complete. We will fill in the rest of the diagram as we analyze the questions. We take this approach in an effort to more realistically deconstruct the way most students attack this game, and thereby provide more insightful and useful analysis. Of course it would be preferable for you to discover all inferences in a game before proceeding to the questions, but there will be times when this does not occur. How you react to that situation is just as important as your ability to make initial inferences.

Question #18: Global, Could Be True, List. The correct answer choice is (B)

The most obvious rule to check first, O in week 3, does not eliminate any of the five answer choices. Either the third or fourth rule should be used next because they are the easiest to apply visually. Answer choice (C) can be eliminated because G is not advertised with J or O, and answer choice (D) can be eliminated because K is not advertised during week 1 or 2. Next, apply the first rule, because the application of the first rule requires less work visually than the second rule. Answer choice (A) can be eliminated since J cannot be advertised during week 1, and answer choice (E) can be eliminated because J is advertised during week 2 but H is not advertised during week 1. Thus, answer choice (B) is proven correct by process of elimination. Note also that by applying the rules "out of order," you save time because it is not necessary to apply the second rule, and the second rule would probably have required more processing time than the other rules because it forces variables to be counted.

Question #19: Global, Cannot Be True. The correct answer choice is (C)

This is a question that separates students. Some students recognize the importance of the doubled product during the setup and then apply that knowledge to the rule stating that G must be advertised with either J or O. From this they are able to infer that J and O can never be advertised together: if J and O are advertised together, the pairing of J and O must occur in week 3, but then neither J nor O could be doubled, and one of J and O would have to be doubled in order to go with G. That line of reasoning indicates that answer choice (C) is correct.

For students who did not make that inference during their setup, there were still several steps available to help direct them to the correct answer. First, the correct answer in question #18 proves that H and K can be advertised during the same week, and so answer choice (A) can be eliminated with no work. Always remember to use the hypotheticals produced by earlier questions, especially List questions! Now, assume that none of the remaining answer choices appears noteworthy. The variables that cannot go together are probably prohibited from doing so because of their involvement with other variables. This makes it likely that any answer choice containing a random variable (a variable not cited in any rule) is less likely to be correct. L and M are the two randoms in the game, and answer choices (B), (D), and (E) each contain at least one random. Thus, answer choice (C) appears to be the most likely answer choice to initially analyze. This does not mean that you automatically choose answer choice (C) as the correct answer. It means that you can now closely examine (C) knowing that it has some characteristics that make it more likely to be correct than the other answer choices. Proceed by attempting to make a hypothetical with the two variables in (C). When a workable hypothetical cannot be produced, you will know that answer choice (C) is correct.

Question #20: Global, Must Be True. The correct answer choice is (B)

This is the defining question of the game. From the language in the question, it is clear that one of the five variables listed in the answer choices must always be advertised during the second week, yet prior to this question very few students realize that one of the products must always be advertised during week 2. Answering this question correctly is crucial since this information will definitely impact your ability to answer the subsequent questions both quickly and accurately.

The easiest way to attack this question is to again use the information from the hypothetical created in question #18. From answer choice (B) in that question, it is certain that either J or G must be the product advertised in week 2. Let us stop and take a moment to analyze this critical insight. First, as indicated by the question stem to #20, you now know that one of the products will *always* be advertised on week 2. If you did not discover this inference previously (and most people do not), you know you are missing a key piece of information that will undoubtedly help you solve not only question #20, but other questions as well.

When you know that one of the products must be advertised on week 2, then you can deduce that every single solution to the game will contain that product on week 2. This is a vital point since you can then look at any other hypothetical and immediately know that one of the two products listed on week 2 will be the one that is always on week 2. So, in question #18, when we determine that (B) is the correct answer, we know that either J or G must be the product that is always on week 2, and we can then look at only J or G in question #20. If there were other hypotheticals we could look at those also, and we would see that either J or G would always be present. For example, if another question produced J and K on week 2, this would show G does not have to be on week 2, and G would be eliminated from consideration; since J would be the only common variable between the two hypotheticals, then J would be proven correct. Thus, even though question #18 lists just one possible schedule of ads ("could be" a schedule of ads) it will still contain the product that we know from the wording of question #20 must always be on week 2.

Another way of thinking about questions #18 and #20 would be to say that if a product must always be advertised on week 2, and then if it does not appear on week 2 in one of the solutions, then how can that particular product be the one that is always on week 2? Therefore, any product not on week 2 in the solution to question #18 is immediately eliminated as the product that must always be advertised on week 2 (for example, if (D) was the answer to #20, then L would be in *every* solution to the game. But L is not in the solution to #18, so how could it be L?).

In applying this thinking to similar questions in other games, whenever you encounter a question that indicates that a variable must be in a certain group or position, then every other solution to the game will contain that variable in that position. So, if a question asks, "Which one of the following people must always be in the first group of runners?" and the correct answer to another question indicates that W, X, and Y are the only runners in the first group, then you would automatically know that one of W, X, and Y would have to be the runner that is always in the first group. Similarly, if a question asks, "Which one of the following must always be the third factory inspected?" and the correct answer to another question indicates that P is the third factory inspected, then you would automatically know that P is always the third factory inspected.

Returning to our consideration of G and J from question #18, the fact that one of those two must be the correct answer eliminates answer choices (C), (D), and (E) in question #20, once again demonstrating how important it is for you to answer List questions correctly and then use their information when applicable. Now that the contenders have been narrowed to two, you can easily make a hypothetical that proves or disproves one of the answers. Let us begin by attempting to prove that G does not have to be advertised in week 2 (it is almost always easier to disprove a Must Be True statement than prove it). The following hypothetical proves that answer choice (A) is incorrect:

$$
\begin{array}{cccc}
\dfrac{\text{K}}{\text{H}} & \dfrac{\text{L}}{\text{J}} & \dfrac{\text{G}}{\text{O}} & \dfrac{\text{M}}{\text{H}} \\
1 & 2 & 3 & 4
\end{array}
$$

Since answer choice (A) can be disproved, it follows that answer choice (B) is correct and J must be advertised during week 2. We can then infer that H must be advertised during week 1 (Why must H be advertised during week 1? Because in this question we discover that J must be advertised during week 2. Adding that piece of information to the first rule of the game then leads us to the inference that H must be advertised during week 1).

Adding these new inferences and Not Laws, we arrive at the following optimal setup for the game:

Note that H cannot be advertised in weeks 2 or 3 due to the second rule (that is, if H is the doubled variable it would have to be in 1-4). J cannot be doubled since that would also require H to be doubled—a violation of the rules. Therefore, J can be eliminated from weeks 1, 3, and 4. Since G must be advertised with either J or O, and J and O cannot be doubled, G must be advertised during week 2 or 3, and thus G cannot be advertised during weeks 1 or 4.

The above setup is optimal and should be used for all subsequent questions. Of course, you would want to check the previous questions to make sure you have not made any errors.

Perceptive students may have noticed another way to disprove answer choice (A) in this question. If G is advertised during week 2, then automatically J must also be advertised during week 2, since G must be advertised with either J or O, and O cannot be advertised during week 2. Since selecting answer choice (A) would automatically make answer choice (B) correct, answer choice (A) must be incorrect since there can be only one correct answer.

An additional note on the difficulty of this game: the importance of the inference contained in this question is reflected in the very nature of the questions themselves. Six of the seven questions in this game are Global, which means that most of the questions are based on information derived from the initial setup. If you miss this one key inference or never answer this question, you are automatically at a disadvantage in answering the rest of the questions. In other words, if you skip this question, you are passing on a chance to discover a major inference that applies to every other question.

Question #21: Global, Cannot Be True. The correct answer choice is (A)

If a product is advertised during two weeks, then, according to the second rule, that product must be advertised during week 4. In the optimal setup created in question #20, it was established that neither G, J, or O could be advertised in week 4. Consequently, answer choice (A) must be correct.

Question #22: Local, Must Be True. The correct answer choice is (E)

This is the only Local question of the game. Given the information in the question stem, according to the second rule L must be advertised during week 4:

Since only G, K, and M are available to fill the second advertising slot in week 4, it can be inferred

---

that either G, K, or M must be advertised with L. It follows that either answer choice (A), (D), or (E) is correct. Since G must be advertised along with J or O, G must be advertised in week 2 or 3, and thus G cannot be advertised with L. Consequently, answer choice (A) can be eliminated. Since L is the doubled product and K must then be advertised in week 1 or 2 only, it follows that K cannot be advertised with L, and answer choice (D) can be eliminated. Answer choice (E) is thereby proven correct by process of elimination.

Note how much easier this question is to solve with the knowledge that J must be advertised during week 2.

Question #23: Global, Could Be True. The correct answer choice is (D)

This question can effectively be attacked by applying the Not Laws from the optimal setup. The Not Laws show that there are restrictions on the placement of G, H, J, K, and O, eliminating answer choices (A), (B), (C), and (E). Accordingly, answer choice (D) is correct.

Question #24: Global, Could Be True. The correct answer choice is (E)

Answer choice (A) can be eliminated since G must be paired with either J or O. Answer choice (B) can be eliminated because if J and H were paired, then H would appear in both weeks 1 and 2, a violation of the rules. Answer choices (C) and (D) can be eliminated since neither H nor K can be advertised during week 3. Thus, answer choice (E) is proven correct by process of elimination.

Note that only answer choice (E) contains one of the randoms of the game. As briefly mentioned in question #19, randoms are more likely to be able to be paired with other variables, and you can use that information to select likely contenders for the correct answer choice. Do not use randoms to automatically choose an answer, just use them to help determine which answer choices to look at first.

POWERSCORE®

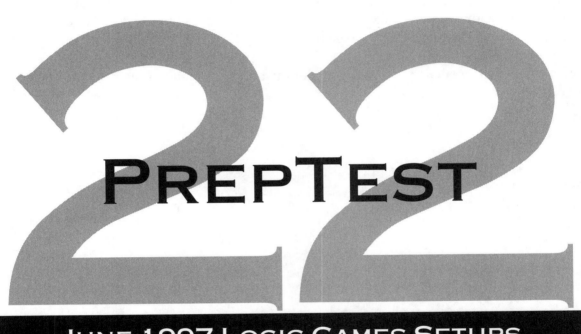

22

PREPTEST

JUNE 1997 LOGIC GAMES SETUPS

This is a Grouping: Defined-Moving, Balanced game.

Although the number of variables—sponsors in this case—being placed is Defined at seven, the number of spaces per table is not precisely defined, and therefore the game is Moving. This type of uncertainty almost always increases the difficulty of a game because it introduces another element that must be tracked during the game. In addition, each of the seven sponsors will be seated at one of the three tables and thus the game is Balanced. Therefore, the game is Defined-Moving, Balanced.

The first rule establishes that each table must have at least two sponsors seated at it, and since there are a total of seven sponsors, it can be deduced that one of the three tables will have three sponsors seated at it and the other two tables will each seat two sponsors. This is a 3-2-2 numerical distribution. In this case, the 3-2-2 distribution is considered "unfixed," since the three sponsors could be seated at either table 1, table 2, or table 3. In some games "fixed" distributions occur, and these fixed distributions are generally a benefit since they limit the possibilities within a game.

The other rules of the game are relatively straightforward, and the initial setup should appear similar to the following:

K L M P Q V Z ^{7}
                    *

Honors: K L M
Speech: M P Q

L
V

3-2-2 distribution:

___ ___ ___
 1   2   3

Since K, L, and M must sit at either table 1 or table 2, they cannot sit at table 3. Since V must sit at the same table as L, it follows that V cannot sit at table 3. Since K, L, M, and V cannot sit at table 3, only P, Q, and Z can possibly sit at table 3. Clearly then, table 3 is extremely restricted. As in any game, always examine the points of restriction since they often yield powerful inferences. In this case, since table 3 must have at least two sponsors, and only P, Q, and Z can possibly sit at table 3, at least two of the P, Q, Z group must always sit at table 3. Therefore, if a question states that one of the P, Q, Z group is seated at table 1 or table 2, then the remaining two sponsors must *automatically* be seated at table 3. Furthermore, any arrangement that attempts to seat two of the P, Q, or Z group at table 1 or table 2 will violate the rules and thus cannot occur. Ultimately, this simple analysis has uncovered the most important inference of the game. To reiterate, since table 3 has only three available sponsors to fill at least two seats, if any one of the sponsors is seated elsewhere, the remaining two sponsors must be seated at table 3. This is a variation of the type of inferences common when a dual-option is present, and you can expect at least one or two of the questions to directly test your knowledge of this inference.

Question #1: Global, Could Be True, List. The correct answer choice is (D)

As in many games, the first question in this game is a List question. The optimal attack for List questions is as always to apply one rule at a time to each of the five answer choices, eliminating answer choices from consideration until only one answer choice remains. In choosing the first rule to apply, try to choose a rule that can be easily applied from a visual standpoint. In this game, the LV block and the Not Laws on table 3 are the easiest to apply. The 3-2-2 distribution, although not difficult to apply, is more time consuming than the other two rules and thus should be applied last.

Applying the LV block rule eliminates answer choice (C). Applying the Not Laws on table 3 eliminates answer choices (A) and (B), as well as (C) again. Finally, applying the 3-2-2 numerical distribution rule eliminates answer choice (E). Answer choice (D) is thus proven correct by process of elimination.

Question #2: Global, Could Be True, List. The correct answer choice is (C)

From our earlier analysis of table 3 we know that answer choice (C) is correct.

Question #3: Local, Must Be True. The correct answer choice is (E)

If K and M are assigned to different tables, one must be assigned to table 1 and the other must be assigned to table 2. Since we cannot be certain which is assigned to table 1 or table 2, it is best to display this situation as a dual option and then Hurdle the Uncertainty:

$$
\frac{\overline{K/M}}{1} \quad \frac{\overline{M/K}}{2} \quad \frac{\overline{}}{3}
$$

Since the LV block must be seated at either table 1 or table 2, it follows that table 1 or table 2 must have three sponsors seated at it. Therefore, table 3 can only have two sponsors seated at it and answer choice (E) is proven correct. Answer choice (D) is incorrect since it is possible for three sponsors to sit at table 1. Answer choices (A) and (C) are both incorrect since the LV block can sit at either table 1 or table 2, as can K or M. Thus, although many combinations of K, M, and the LV block are possible, none must occur. Answer choice (B) is incorrect since L and Q can never sit together given the condition in the question stem.

Question #4: Local, Could Be True. The correct answer choice is (B)

If Q is assigned to table 1, P and Z must be assigned to table 3:

$$
\frac{\overline{Q}}{1} \quad \frac{\overline{}}{2} \quad \frac{\begin{matrix} Z \\ P \end{matrix}}{3}
$$

Since the question stem also states that table 1 has three sponsors, the numerical distribution is now fixed at 3-2-2:

$$
\frac{\overline{}}{Q \atop 1} \quad \frac{\overline{}}{2} \quad \frac{\begin{matrix} Z \\ P \end{matrix}}{3}
$$

Since the four remaining unseated sponsors are K, M, L, and V, two of that group must sit at table 1 and the other two must sit at table 2. Because L and V must sit together as a block, it follows that K and M must also sit together as a block. Thus, the KM block and the LV block cannot sit together:

This information is sufficient to prove answer choice (B) correct.

Question #5: Local, Could Be True, Except. The correct answer choice is (E)

Remember, a Could Be True EXCEPT question asks for what Cannot Be True. This is the first question to address the "speech" subgroup established in the initial conditions of the game. Since M, P, and Q form the speech subgroup, and M cannot be seated at table 3, it follows that the one sponsor seated at table 3 who gives a speech must be either P or Q. Additionally, since at least two sponsors from the group P, Q, and Z must be seated at table 3, we can Hurdle the Uncertainty and infer that Z must be seated at table 3:

Thus, answer choice (E) is correct.

Question #6: Local, Could Be True, List. The correct answer choice is (B)

This is the first question to address the "honors" subgroup established in the initial conditions of the game. The conditions in the question stem establish the following 2-3-2 fixed numerical distribution setup:

Fixed Numerical Distribution 2-3-2:

Honors block →

Since table 1 can only have one sponsor from the honors subgroup, answer choice (A) can be eliminated. Conversely, answer choices (C), (D), and (E) can be eliminated since table 1 must have exactly one sponsor from the honors subgroup, and none of these answer choices meet that criterion. Alternately, answer choices (D) and (E) can be eliminated since they contain two sponsors from the P, Q, and Z group that must supply table 3 with two sponsors. By process of elimination, answer choice (B) is proven correct.

Question #7: Global, Justify. The correct answer choice is (B)

Justify questions, which appear infrequently in the Logic Games section, require you to select an answer choice that, when added to the initial rules of the game, forces the condition requested in the question stem to occur. In this case, the answer choice must force a situation in which no possible hypothetical can meet all of the conditions of the game. Since we know table 3 is the most restricted point in the game, it is a good bet that the answer choice will in some way affect the sponsors available to meet the table 3 requirements. This occurs in answer choice (B), which places P and Q at tables 1 or 2, leaving only Z to fulfill the requirement that two sponsors sit at table 3.

This question also provides an excellent example of the technique of using hypotheticals from other questions to eliminate incorrect answer choices. For example, answer choice (A) states that "At most two sponsors are seated at table 1." From question #6 we know that this scenario produces several workable hypotheticals. Since any workable hypothetical would conflict with the desired result of question #7, answer choice (A) must be wrong. Answer choice (D) can be eliminated by the same process. Answer choice (D) states, "Exactly three of the sponsors are seated at table 1." The information in the stem from question #4 and also answer choice (D) in question #1 shows that this occurrence also allows several workable hypotheticals. Thus, answer choice (D) is incorrect. Answer choice (E) can be eliminated by examining the hypotheticals from question #3 as well as answer choice (D) in question #1. Remember, when a working hypothetical from another question meets the required conditions of a particular question, that hypothetical can be used to eliminate wrong answers or confirm the correct answer.

This game is representative of the type of Grouping games that frequently appear on the LSAT. There are two powerful lessons to learn from this game. First, always examine the restricted points in a game. In a Grouping game this often means examining the available variables for a particular group, or examining the variables that cannot be placed together. Second, always examine any rule that deals with numbers. Often these numerical rules introduce a controlling factor into a game, such as a Numerical Distribution.

PrepTest 22. June 1997 Game #2: *8. B 9. B 10. D 11. B 12. B 13. A 14. A*

This is an Advanced Linear: Unbalanced: Underfunded game.

The initial diagram for this game appears as follows:

Sessions: M O R S ⁴
Psychologists: T V W ³
Nurses: F J L ³

Psych: ___ ___ ___ ___   T V W = 2-1-1

Nurse: ___ ___ ___ ___   F J L = 2-1-1

Session: ___ ___ ___ ___   M O R S
      1   2   3   4

Because each psychologist must teach at least once, and the three psychologists must fill four teaching spaces, one of the psychologists must teach twice. The same is true for the nurses. Thus, because the nurse variable set and the psychologist variable set are underfunded, one variable in each set must be used twice, leading to a 2-1-1 distribution for each set.

The second rule helpfully establishes that L teaches on day 3:

Sessions: M O R S ⁴
Psychologists: T V W ³
Nurses: F J L ³

Psych: ___ ___ ___ ___   T V W = 2-1-1

Nurse: ___ ___ L ___   F J L = 2-1-1

Session: ___ ___ ___ ___   M O R S
      1   2   3   4

Note that L could teach twice, so this placement does *not* eliminate L from further consideration on the others days.

The third rule establishes two not-blocks. These will be shown vertically as our diagram has a vertical aspect:

These not-blocks allow for an immediate inference: because T cannot teach with F or L, T must teach with J:

```
┌───┐
│ T │
│ J │
└───┘
```

The fourth rule adds S to the block just created:

```
┌───┐
│ T │
│ J │
│ S │
└───┘
```

The fifth rule adds another variable to the block above, creating a powerful super-block:

```
┌─────┐
│ T   │
│ J   │
│ S M │
└─────┘
```

Because T is tied to J, and J is tied to S, and S is only be taught once, it follows that T and J can only teach once. Thus, psychologist V or W must teach twice, and nurse F or L must teach twice.

The size of the block also creates placement issues. Because L must teach on day 3, the TJSM block must be scheduled for either days 1 and 2 or days 2 and 3. Thus, T, J, and M cannot be scheduled for day 3, and T, J, S, and M cannot be scheduled for day 4. These inferences directly help answer questions #9 and #10. Additionally, S or M must be taught on day 2, and R or O must be taught on day 4. These inferences help answer question #14.

The final diagram for the game is as follows:

Sessions: M O R S [4]
Psychologists: T V W [3]
Nurses: F J L [3]

Psych: ___ ___ ___ ___ $T V W = 2\text{-}1\text{-}1_T$

Nurse: ___ ___ L ___ $F J L = 2\text{-}1\text{-}1_J$

Session: ___ S/M ___ R/O   M O R S

1	2	3	4
M̶		S̶	M̶
		J̶	S̶
		L̶	J̶
			L̶

```
┌───┐  ┌───┐
│ T̶ │  │ T̶ │
│ L̶ │  │ F̶ │
└───┘  └───┘

┌─────┐
│ S M │
└─────┘

┌─────┐
│ T   │
│ J   │
│ S M │
└─────┘
```

Question #8: Local, Could Be True. The correct answer choice is (B)

The question stem creates an RL block. Because from the second rule L must teach on day 3, R must also be scheduled for day 3:

Sessions: M O R S [4]
Psychologists: T V W [3]
Nurses: F J L [3]

	1	2	3	4	
Psych:	___	___	___	___	T V W = 2-1-1
Nurse:	___	___	L	___	F J L = 2-1-1
Session:	___	___	R	___	M O R S

At this point, the TJSM block must be placed on days 1 and 2 as there is no room for it to be placed elsewhere:

Sessions: M O R S [4]
Psychologists: T V W [3]
Nurses: F J L [3]

	1	2	3	4	
Psych:	T	___	___	___	T V W = 2-1-1
Nurse:	J	___	L	___	F J L = 2-1-1
Session:	S	M	R	___	M O R S

Session O must be taught on day 4, as that is the only remaining day with no session. Additionally, because R can only be taught once, we can infer that L only teaches once. Because L teaches only once, and as discussed previously J cannot teach twice, F *must* be the nurse who teaches twice. Since J teaches on day 1 and L teaches on day 3, it follows that F must teach on day 2 and day 4:

Sessions: M O R S [4]
Psychologists: T V W [3]
Nurses: F J L [3]

	1	2	3	4	
Psych:	T	___	___	___	T V W = 2-1-1
Nurse:	J	F	L	F	F J L = 2-1-1
Session:	S	M	R	O	M O R S

Since F does not appear in answer choices (C), (D), and (E), they can be eliminated. Answer choice (A) can be eliminated because F and T cannot teach together from the third rule (and because T must teach on day 1 only). Answer choice (B) is thus proven correct by process of elimination.

Question #9: Global, Cannot Be True, FTT. The correct answer choice is (B)

The Not Laws created by the super-block easily answer this question. S can never be scheduled for day 3 and thus answer choice (B) is correct.

Question #10: Global, Could Be True. The correct answer choice is (D)

Again, the Not Laws created by the super-block easily answer this question. Only answer choice (D) could be true.

Question #11: Local, Must Be True. The correct answer choice is (B)

If S is scheduled for day 2, then T, J, and S must fill day 2 and M must be taught on day 3. Since L also teaches on day 3, L must be scheduled to teach M, and answer choice (B) is correct.

Question #12: Local, Could Be True. The correct answer choice is (B)

If O and R are scheduled for consecutive days, those days must be day 3 and day 4. Thus T, J, and S must be scheduled for day 1, and M must be scheduled for day 2. Answer choices (C), (D), and (E) can be eliminated since they contain either J, or T, or both. Answer choice (A) can be eliminated since F and L are both nurses and two nurses can never teach together. Thus, it follows that answer choice (B) is proven correct by process of elimination.

Question #13: Global, Could Be True, List. The correct answer choice is (A)

Answer choices (B) and (D) can be eliminated because J is scheduled for day 4, an impossibility since J must be scheduled for day 1 or 2 only. Answer choice (C) is incorrect because J cannot teach twice. Answer choice (E) is incorrect because L is not scheduled for day 3. Thus, answer choice (A) is correct.

Question #14: Local, Must Be True. The correct answer choice is (A)

If O is scheduled for day 3, then the TJSM block must be on days 1 and 2, and the dual option for the day 4 session indicates that R must be taught on day 4:

Sessions: M O R S ^{4}
Psychologists: T V W ^{3}
Nurses: F J L ^{3}

Psych:	T	___	___	___	T V W = 2-1-1
Nurse:	J	___	L	___	F J L = 2-1-1
Session:	S	M	O	R	M O R S
	1	2	3	4	

Thus, answer choice (A) is correct.

This is an Advanced Linear: Balanced game.

The setup to this game requires some manipulation. Since each of the paintings has two characteristics, oil or watercolor and nineteenth-century or twentieth-century, each of the paintings requires two separate spaces to represent these characteristics. In a normal linear game this could easily be represented by double-stacking the characteristics above each painting. However, since the paintings themselves are stacked into two rows, this would cause unnecessary confusion. Thus, we have chosen to represent the characteristics of each painting side-by-side. For example, 19O would represent a nineteenth-century oil painting, and 20W would represent a twentieth-century watercolor. The diagram and rules are then relatively easy to represent:

Minimum requirements:

This game uses several two-value systems. Since each painting must be either an oil or watercolor, but not both, if a painting is not a watercolor then it must be an oil, and if a painting is not an oil then it must be a watercolor. The same type of reasoning can be applied to the nineteenth- and twentieth-century paintings. This leads to several powerful inferences in question #15.

Question #15: Local, Must Be True. The correct answer choice is (E)

The question stem states that all of the nineteenth-century paintings are watercolors, which can be diagrammed as:

$$19 \longrightarrow W$$

The contrapositive of this rule would be:

$$\cancel{W} \longrightarrow \cancel{19}$$

However, because of the two-value system, if a painting is not a watercolor then it must be an oil, and if a painting is not a nineteenth-century painting then it must be a twentieth-century painting. Thus, the contrapositive above can be more effectively diagrammed as:

$$O \longrightarrow 20$$

Applying both of these statements to the original diagram leads to the following setup:

19 W	20 O
1	2	3

	20	
4	5	6

However, this does not take into account the second, third, and fifth rules. When those rules—which dictate what type of paintings are adjacent to each other—are taken into account, the diagram fills out considerably:

19 W	19 W	20 O
1	2	3

	20	20 O
4	5	6

Painting 6 cannot be a nineteenth-century painting since that would violate the rule that states that a nineteenth-century painting must be next to or below another nineteenth-century painting. Thus, painting 6 is a twentieth-century painting, and answer choice (E) is correct.

Question #16: Global, Could Be True. The correct answer choice is (D)

If there are only two watercolors, then according to the third rule they would have to be next to or across (above or below) from each other. The only answer choice that allows for such an arrangement is answer choice (D), which is the correct answer.

Question #17: Local, Must Be True. The correct answer choice is (C)

If there are exactly three oils, in order to conform to the second rule they must be paintings 1-2-3, paintings 2-3-6, or paintings 3-5-6. Thus, the watercolors must be paintings 4-5-6, paintings 1-4-5, or paintings 1-2-4. Accordingly, painting 4 must always be a watercolor and it follows that answer choice (C) is correct.

Question #18: Local, Cannot Be True, FTT. The correct answer choice is (E)

Because there are *exactly* two oils, they must be paintings 2 and 3 or paintings 3 and 6. Thus, it follows that paintings 1, 4, and 5 are watercolors. Similarly, since there are only two nineteenth-century paintings, they must be paintings 1 and 2 or paintings 2 and 3. Thus, it follows that paintings 4, 5, and 6 are twentieth-century paintings:

$$
\begin{array}{ccc}
\dfrac{\quad\text{W}\quad}{1} & \dfrac{19\quad}{2} & \dfrac{\quad\text{O}}{3} \\[2em]
\dfrac{20\;\;\text{W}}{4} & \dfrac{20\;\;\text{W}}{5} & \dfrac{20\quad}{6}
\end{array}
$$

Consequently, since painting 4 must be a twentieth-century painting, answer choice (E) cannot be true and is correct.

Question #19: Global, Could Be True. The correct answer choice is (A)

Each answer choice specifies that exactly three of a certain type of painting is under analysis. Because of the second, third, and fifth rules, these three paintings must be contiguous, and so the correct answer must contain two paintings either adjacent (such as 3-6 or 4-5), or at most two spaces away (such as 2-4 or 1-3). Accordingly, answers (B), (C), and (D) can be eliminated immediately. Answer choice (E) can be eliminated because painting 5 would have to be from the nineteenth-century, yet the rules specify that painting 5 is from the twentieth-century. Thus, answer choice (A) is correct.

This is a Grouping: Defined-Fixed, Unbalanced: Overloaded game.

This game is quite difficult, in part because of the extra juggler available to fill the two groups, and in part because of the assignment of positions within each group.

The initial diagram for the game appears as follows:

G H K L N P Q⁷

```
      R  ____      ____

      M  ____      ____

      F  ____      ____
          1         2
```

The first rule establishes that G and H, if they are assigned to team, must be assigned to the front position. This means that G and H cannot be assigned to the middle or rear position on either team, inferences which can be shown as side Not Laws:

G H K L N P Q⁷

```
      R  ____      ____    G̸ H̸

      M  ____      ____    G̸ H̸

      F  ____      ____
          1         2
```

Note that this also means that G and H cannot be assigned to the same team, which will be shown in the final setup with a not-block.

The second rule establishes that K, when it is assigned to a team, must be assigned to the middle position. This results in K Not Laws on the front and rear positions:

G H K L N P Q⁷

```
      R  ____      ____    G̸ H̸ K̸

      M  ____      ____    G̸ H̸

      F  ____      ____    K̸
          1         2
```

The third rule indicates that L, if assigned, must be assigned to team 1. Thus, L cannot be assigned to team 2, and this is shown with a Not Law *under* the team 2 column:

G H K L N P Q ⁷

```
R    ____        ____     G̶ H̶ K̶

M    ____        ____     G̶ H̶

F    ____        ____     K̶
      1            2
                  L̶
```

Note that the rear position on team 2 is now so limited that only N, P, or Q could be assigned to it. This can be shown with a triple-option:

G H K L N P Q ⁷

```
R    ____      N/P/Q     G̶ H̶ K̶

M    ____        ____     G̶ H̶

F    ____        ____     K̶
      1            2
                  L̶
```

The fourth and fifth rules establish three global not-blocks:

The triple-option, the prior Not Laws, and these not-blocks can also be used to draw several interesting inferences:

1. P cannot be assigned to the front or middle position on team 2 because then there would be no juggler for the rear position on team 2 (the not-blocks would eliminate N and Q from being on team 2).

2. If N is assigned to the front or middle position on team 2, then Q must be assigned to the rear position on team 2 (the PN not-block eliminates P from consideration).

3. If Q is assigned to the front or middle position on team 2, then N must be assigned to the rear position on team 2 (the PQ not-block eliminates P from consideration).

Regrettably, these inferences do not play a significant role in the game.

The sixth rule presents an annoying conditional relationship that references exact team positions for H and Q:

$$H_{2F} \longrightarrow Q_{1M}$$

Because H must be in the front position for team 1 or 2 if assigned, the contrapositive is also useful:

$$\cancel{Q}_{1M} \longrightarrow H_{1F}$$

Thus, if Q is assigned to any position other than the middle position of team 1, and H is assigned, H must be assigned to the front position on team 1.

The prior information can be assembled to create the final setup for the game:

G H K L N P Q [7]

Note also that if any one juggler is unassigned, then the remaining six jugglers *must* all be assigned.

Question #20: Global, Could Be True, List. The correct answer choice is (E)

Answer choice (A) is incorrect because K and N cannot be assigned to the same team per the fourth rule.

Answer choice (B) is incorrect because K must be assigned to a middle position in accordance with the second rule.

Answer choice (C) is incorrect because according to the third rule, if L is assigned, L must be assigned to team 1.

Answer choice (D) is incorrect because from the fifth rule P and Q cannot be assigned to the same team.

Answer choice (E) is the correct answer choice.

Question #21: Local, Could Be True, List. The correct answer choice is (E)

If H is assigned to team 2, then from the final rule Q must be assigned to the middle position on team 1. This fact eliminates answer choices (A), (B), and (C). Answer choice (D) can be eliminated since from the first rule G cannot be assigned to the rear position on either team. Accordingly, answer choice (E) is correct.

Question #22: Global, Could Be True, List. The correct answer choice is (E)

This extremely difficult question forces you to account for the variables remaining for team 2. In answer choices (A) and (C), the variables remaining for team 2 include pairs of variables which cannot go together according to the rules:

Answer choice (A): When G, K, and L are assigned to team 1, then H, N, P, and Q are the jugglers available to be assigned to team 2. But, from the fifth rule P and Q cannot be assigned to the same team, so the pool is actually H, N, and P/Q. However, if H is assigned to team 2, then Q must be assigned to the middle position on team 1 per the sixth rule. As that is not the case in this answer choice, H cannot be assigned to team 2. Consequently, there are not enough jugglers available for team 2, and this answer choice cannot occur.

Answer choice (C): When L, K, and Q are assigned to team 1, then G, H, N, and P are the jugglers available to be assigned to team 2. But, from the first rule G and H cannot be assigned to the same team, and from the fourth rule N and P cannot be assigned to the same team, so the pool is actually just G/H and N/P. Consequently, there are not enough jugglers available for team 2, and this answer choice cannot occur.

In answer choices (B) and (D), the variables remaining for team 2 include H and L, but as L cannot be on team 2, H must be on team 2, and assigning H to team 2 forces Q into the middle position on team 1, which does not appear in either answer choice. Thus, both answer choices are incorrect.

Answer choice (B): When G, K, and P are assigned to team 1, then H, L, N, and Q are the jugglers available to be assigned to team 2. But, from the third rule, L cannot be assigned to team 2, so the pool is actually H, N, and Q. However, if H is assigned to team 2, then Q must be assigned to the middle position on team 1. As that is not the case in this answer choice, H cannot be assigned to team 2. Consequently, there are not enough jugglers available for team 2, and this answer choice cannot occur.

Answer choice (D): When Q, K, and P are assigned to team 1, then G, H, L, and N are the jugglers available to be assigned to team 2. But, from the third rule, L cannot be assigned to team 2, so the pool is actually G, H, and N. However, if H is assigned to team 2, then Q must be assigned to the middle position on team 1. As that is not the case in this answer choice, H cannot be assigned to team 2. Consequently, there are not enough jugglers available for team

2, and this answer choice cannot occur.

Thus, as the first four answer choices have been eliminated, answer choice (E) must be correct.

Overall, this is a very hard question.

Question #23: Local, Could Be True. The correct answer choice is (E)

Similar to question #22, this question frequently forces you to account for the variables remaining for team 2.

The question stem establishes that G is assigned to team 1, and from the first rule we know that G must be in the front position. But, by itself, this information does not serve to immediately impact any of the answer choices. Thus, we must look more closely at each answer.

Answer choice (A): Because G must be assigned to the front position per the first rule, H cannot be assigned to the same team, and thus this answer choice is incorrect.

Answer choice (B): When G, K, and L are assigned to team 1, then team 2 must be composed of three members from the group of H, N, P, and Q. But, from the contrapositive of the sixth rule, since Q is not on team 1, H cannot be on team 2, leaving only N, P, and Q available for team 2. But, the fifth rule prohibits P and Q from being on the same team (or, alternately, from the fourth rule N and P cannot be on the same team), and so there are not enough jugglers available to form a viable group for team 2, and this answer choice cannot occur.

Answer choice (C): When G, K, and P are assigned to team 1, then team 2 must be composed of three members from the group of H, L, N, and Q. But, from the contrapositive of the sixth rule, since Q is not on team 1, H cannot be on team 2, and team 2 must then be composed of L, N, and Q. However, from the third rule, if L is assigned, L must be assigned to team 1, and so there are not enough jugglers available to form a viable group for team 2. Thus, this answer choice is incorrect.

Answer choice (D): When G, L, and N are assigned to team 1, then team 2 must be composed of three members from the group of H, K, P, and Q. But, from the contrapositive of the sixth rule, since Q is not on team 1, H cannot be on team 2, and team 2 must then be composed of K, P, and Q. But, the fifth rule prohibits P and Q from being on the same team, and so again there are not enough jugglers available to form a viable group for team 2, and this answer choice cannot occur.

Thus, answer choice (E) is the credited response.

Question #24: Local, Must Be True. The correct answer choice is (D)

From our initial analysis of the game, we determined that only N, P, or Q could be the juggler assigned to the rear position on team 2. Thus, answer choices (A) and (B) can be eliminated.

Considering the conditions in the question stem, when G is assigned to team 1, then from the first rule G must be in the front position, and when K is assigned to team 2, from the second rule K must be assigned to the middle position:

G H K L N P Q [7]

```
R    ____        P/Q
                 ____

M    ____        K
                 ____

F    G           ____
     ____
     1           2
```

With G and K assigned, and L eliminated from being on team 2 due to the third rule, only H, N, P, and Q are available to be assigned to the remaining two positions on team 2. Of course, from the fourth rule, N cannot be on the same team as K (who is already on team 2), and so N can be eliminated from consideration for team 2 (hence, N is not shown as an option for the rear position on team 2 in the diagram above). Thus, only H, P, and Q remain to be assigned to the two available spaces on team 2. However, from the fifth rule P and Q cannot be assigned together, and so by Hurdling the Uncertainty we can deduce that H *must* be assigned to team 2. And, from the first rule, H must be assigned to the front position on team 2. Thus, according to the last rule, Q must be assigned to team 1 in the middle position. With Q removed from team 2 consideration, P must be assigned to the final position on team 2, the rear position:

G H K L N P Q [7]

```
R    L/N         P
     ____        ____

M    Q           K
     ____        ____

F    G           H
     ____        ____
     1           2
```

Answer choice (D) is thus proven correct.

Interestingly (in a demented way), this game ends with three vicious questions that require you to closely examine the variables *remaining* for assignment. Since it is so easy to get caught up in which variables have been placed, these three questions serve as a good reminder that in Grouping games it is always important to examine the variables yet to be placed. Many of the most difficult Grouping game questions have hinged upon recognition of this fact.

POWERSCORE®

23

PREPTEST

OCTOBER 1997 LOGIC GAMES SETUPS

This is a Basic Linear: Balanced game

This game provides an excellent start to this game section. The seven music pieces are placed in linear order, with each music piece occupying one track, and with all tracks occupied. Thus, this is a Basic Linear: Balanced game. These games are often the easiest for the typical test taker, and you should look to attack these games aggressively whenever you encounter one.

The initial base diagram is as follows:

F G H J K L M ^{7}

1	2	3	4	5	6	7

The first and second rules establish that F must be second and that J cannot be seventh:

F G H J K L M ^{7}

	F					
1	2	3	4	5	6	7
						J̶

The third rule establishes a GH not-block. Because this block rotates, no inferences can be drawn:

G̶H̶
H̶G̶

The fourth and fifth rules establish a basic chain sequence:

$$H > L > M$$

As with all sequences of this type, six Not Laws are produced. But, because of the presence of F in the second track, one of the M Not Laws moves over to the third track:

F G H J K L M [7]

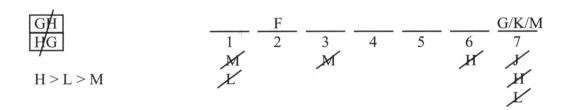

GH
HG

H > L > M

          F
1 2 3 4 5 6 7

As the Not Laws begin to accumulate, always remember to check any space that seems overly restricted. In this case, the seventh track cannot be J, H, or L, and it also cannot be F (because F is second). Thus, the seventh track can only be G, K, or M:

F G H J K L M [7]

GH
HG

H > L > M

          F   G/K/M
1 2 3 4 5 6 7

Also, check any variables that appear in more than one rule. L has already been addressed, but H appears in both the third and fourth rules. G, the other variable in the third rule, can be used to "push" H around, especially since H is at the front of a chain sequence. For example, consider the possible placements of G, and how that affects H. If G is first, then there is no effect, because G would be isolated from H. Similarly, if G is sixth or seventh, H's position at the head of the chain sequence would again insulate H from G. But, as G is moved into the middle of the linear setup, more problems begin to arise for the placement of H. For example, when G is the third track, H must be the first or fifth track. When G is placed fourth, H must be the first track, and when G is fifth, then H must be the first or third track. These inferences while seemingly difficult to draw, actually result from a very simple process:

1. Identify any two rules that have a variable in common.

2. Consider the effects of combining those two rules. In this case, H is pushed forward in the setup because of the sequence, and G then serves to repel H from certain specific tracks. The combination results in significant limitations on H's overall possible placements.

The only variable that does not appear in any rule is K, which is a random and is designated with an asterisk under K.

When all of the information above is combined, the following setup results:

F G H J K L M [7]
*

GH / HG

H > L > M

$$\begin{array}{ccccccc}
\underline{} & \underline{F} & \underline{} & \underline{} & \underline{} & \underline{} & \underline{G/K/M} \\
1 & 2 & 3 & 4 & 5 & 6 & 7
\end{array}$$

Under 1: M̶, L̶
Under 3: M̶
Under 6: H̶
Under 7: J̶, H̶, L̶

$G_3 \longrightarrow H_{1/5}$
$G_4 \longrightarrow H_1$
$G_5 \longrightarrow H_{1/3}$

Question #1: Global, Could Be True, List. The correct answer choice is (B)

The best strategy on List questions is to use the individual rules of the game to eliminate incorrect answer choices.

Answer choice (A) can be eliminated because, as stipulated in the first rule, F must be second (and thus cannot be first).

Answer choice (B) is the correct answer.

Answer choice (C) can be eliminated because J cannot be seventh according to the second rule.

Answer choice (D) can be eliminated because from the third rule G and H cannot be consecutive.

Answer choice (E) can be eliminated because as indicated by the fourth rule, H must be in some track before L.

Question #2. Local, Must Be True. The correct answer choice is (D)

The conditions in the question stem combine the last rule with J and K, creating the following chain:

$$\begin{array}{c}
J \\
H > L > M > - - - - \\
K
\end{array}$$

Because there are four variables after H, H cannot fill any of the final four tracks, and thus H must be first, second, or third. But, because F is always second, we can determine that H is first or third, and that H is immediately before or immediately after F. Thus, answer choice (D) is correct.

Question #3. Global, Could Be True, List. The correct answer choice is (B)

From the Not Laws we know that neither L nor M can be the first recording, and this information eliminates answer choices (C), (D), and (E).

The difference between answer choices (A) and (B) is that (B) contains H whereas (A) does not. As shown in question #2, H can be first, and so the correct answer choice is (B).

Note also that answer choice (E) can be eliminated because it does not contain G, which we know can be first from the hypothetical produced in question #1.

Question #4. Global, Must Be True, Minimum. The correct answer choice is (C)

The last two rules combine to create the chain sequence: H > L > M. Because H and L must both come before M, and F must be second, the earliest track that M can fill is the fourth position. Answer choice (C) is thus correct.

Question #5. Local, Could Be True, Except, Suspension. The correct answer choice is (D)

The condition in the question stem suspends the third rule and replaces it with a GH block, creating the following chain:

$$\boxed{GH} > L > M$$

Since G and H form a block that cannot come before F due to space limitations, the following setup results:

Because J or K must come immediately ahead of F, they cannot be consecutive, and thus answer choice (D) is correct in this Cannot Be True question (remember, Could Be True Except is identical to Cannot Be True).

This is a Grouping: Undefined game.

This game is difficult for two primary reasons. First, the number of applicants interviewed and hired is Undefined. As mentioned elsewhere, Undefined grouping games are generally harder than Defined grouping games because Undefined games have a relatively greater number of solutions, and the lack of certainty in the setup forces the test taker to remember extra elements throughout the game. Second, the two groups are linked. Generally, Grouping games feature separate groups with no true interrelation. For example, a game might feature children in separate canoes. Once a child has been placed in one canoe, he or she is then prevented from being in the other canoe and can be taken out of the variable pool. In this game, however, applicants who are hired must first "pass through" the interview group. Thus, an applicant who is placed into the interview group may or may not proceed to the hiring group. This effectively keeps variables "alive" even though they have already been placed once.

The basic scenario for the game appears as follows, with the relationship between Hired and Interviewed shown with an arrow indicating if an applicant is hired, they must have been interviewed first.

F G J K L M O [7]

$$\overline{\qquad\qquad}\qquad\qquad\overline{\qquad}$$
Interviewed ◄——— Hired

Thus, to be hired, an applicant must be interviewed. The contrapositive of that rule indicates that if an applicant is not interviewed, then they cannot be hired. So, any Not Law that appears under the Interviewed group will automatically result in the same Not Law appearing under the Hired group.

The third rule establishes that F is interviewed, which can be shown directly on the diagram:

F G J K L M O [7]

$$\overset{F}{\overline{\qquad\qquad}}\qquad\qquad\overline{\qquad}$$
Interviewed ◄——— Hired

The remaining rules are conditional in nature. When diagramming these rules, use subscript designations for interviewing (I) and hiring (H):

First rule: $G_I \longrightarrow J_I$

Second rule: $J_I \longrightarrow L_I$

Fourth rule: $F_H \longrightarrow K_I$

Fifth rule: $K_H \longrightarrow M_I$

Sixth rule:
$$\begin{array}{c} M_H \\ + \\ L_I \end{array} \longrightarrow O_H$$

The first two rules can also be combined to form a conditional chain:

$$G_I \longrightarrow J_I \longrightarrow L_I$$

Note the importance of L in the above chain: if L is not interviewed (and thus not hired), then neither G nor J can be interviewed or hired.

It is also important to keep in mind the contrapositive of each rule. For example, the contrapositive of the fifth rule would state that "if M is not interviewed then K is not hired." Thus, in a question like #8, where M is not interviewed, you immediately know that K cannot be hired. Remember, when conditional statements are presented in a form that is in any way unusual, always take the contrapositive.

The information above can be used to form the final diagram for the game:

F G J K L M O [7]

$G_I \longrightarrow J_I \longrightarrow L_I$

$F_H \longrightarrow K_I$

$K_H \longrightarrow M_I$

$$\begin{array}{c} M_H \\ + \\ L_I \end{array} \longrightarrow O_H$$

$$\frac{F}{\text{Interviewed}} \longleftarrow \text{Hired}$$

Question #6: Global, Could Be True, List. The correct answer choice is (C)

The first applicant to check is F, which according to the third rule must be interviewed. However, F appears in every answer choice, so this process does not eliminate any answer choices. Regardless, always make sure to check the basic requirements of the game, however simple.

Because the question stem specifies that you are seeking an answer choice that is a complete list of interviewed applicants, the remaining applicants in each answer choice are the only other applicants that are interviewed. Thus, you should check the rules for references to interviewing. The first two rules both feature stipulations regarding interviewing in both the sufficient and necessary conditions, and so they are the most logical rules to start with.

From the first rule, when G is interviewed, J must be interviewed, and so any answer choice that contains G but not J will be incorrect. This information eliminates answer choices (A) and (D).

From the second rule, when J is interviewed, L must be interviewed, and so any answer choice that contains J but not L will be incorrect. This information eliminates answer choices (B) and (E).

Consequently, answer choice (C) is proven correct by process of elimination.

Question #7: Global, Could Be True. The correct answer choice is (E)

Answer choice (A) can be eliminated because according to the third rule F must be interviewed.

Answer choice (B) can be eliminated because from the second rule when J is interviewed, L must also be interviewed.

Answer choices (C) and (D) can be eliminated because when G is interviewed, both J and I must also be interviewed. Since F is always interviewed, when G is interviewed at least three other applicants must also be interviewed.

Answer choice (E) is thus proven correct by process of elimination.

Question #8: Local, Must Be True. The correct answer choice is (E)

If M is not interviewed, then from contrapositive of the fifth rule, K is not hired. Because from the third rule F must be interviewed, answer choice (E) must be true and is therefore correct.

Answer choice (A) is incorrect because although K cannot be hired, it is possible for K to be interviewed.

Answer choice (B) is incorrect because although K can be interviewed, K does not have to be interviewed.

Answer choice (C) is incorrect because it is possible for F to be hired.

Answer choice (D) is incorrect because while it is possible for F to be hired, F does not have to be hired.

Answer choice (E) is the correct answer choice as explained above.

Question #9: Local, Could Be True, List. The correct answer choice is (E)

The question stem specifies that six applicants are interviewed and three applicants are hired. In addition to F, since G must be interviewed, from the first two rules J and L must also be interviewed:

F G J K L M O [7]

$$\underline{F} \quad \underline{G} \quad \underline{J} \quad \underline{L} \quad \underline{} \quad \underline{} \qquad \underline{} \quad \underline{} \quad \underline{}$$

Interviewed ← Hired

Since F, G, J, and L take up four of the six interview spaces, only two of K, M, and O can be interviewed:

F G J K L M O [7]

$$\underline{F} \quad \underline{G} \quad \underline{J} \quad \underline{L} \quad (K,M,O) \qquad \underline{} \quad \underline{} \quad \underline{}$$

Interviewed ← Hired

The information above is all that can be determined from the conditions in the question stem.

Answer choices (A), (B), and (D) can all be eliminated by applying the last rule that states when "M is hired, and L is interviewed, O is hired." Because M appears in each of those three answer choices but O does not appear in any of those answer choices, they are all incorrect.

Answer choice (C) is incorrect because it does not allow each hired applicant to be interviewed. The answer lists K, L, and O as the hirees, and so each must be interviewed. L was already established as being interviewed, and K and O must then occupy the remaining two spaces in the interview group, and M is left out of the interview group. This presents a problem because according to the fifth rule, when K is hired then M must be interviewed. Thus, this answer creates an unworkable group and is incorrect.

Thus, answer choice (E) is proven correct by process of elimination.

Question #10: Local, Must Be True, Except. The correct answer choice is (B)

If everyone that is interviewed is hired, then F must be hired because F is always interviewed. Additionally, the question stem states that L is hired, meaning that L must have been interviewed:

F G J K L M O [7]

$$\frac{F \quad L}{Interviewed} \longleftrightarrow \frac{F \quad L}{Hired}$$

From the fourth rule, when F is hired then K is interviewed, and so K must be hired as well. From the fifth rule, when K is hired then M is interviewed, so M must be hired too:

F G J K L M O [7]

$$\frac{F \ L \ K \ M}{Interviewed} \longleftrightarrow \frac{F \ L \ K \ M}{Hired}$$

Finally, because M is hired and because the question states that L is hired (meaning L is interviewed), then from the last rule O is hired:

F G J K L M O [7]

$$\frac{F \ L \ K \ M \ O}{Interviewed} \longleftrightarrow \frac{F \ L \ K \ M \ O}{Hired}$$

Thus, F, K, M, and O are all hired, which eliminates answer choices (A), (C), (D), and (E) from consideration. Answer choice (B) is therefore the correct answer choice.

Question #11: Local, Cannot Be True, FTT. The correct answer choice is (B)

The question stem stipulates that exactly four applicants are hired, which means that *at least* four applicants are interviewed:

F G J K L M O [7]

$$\underset{\text{Interviewed}}{\overset{F}{\underline{\quad}\ \underline{\quad}\ \underline{\quad}\ \underline{\quad}}} \longleftarrow \underset{\text{Hired}}{\underline{\quad}\ \underline{\quad}\ \underline{\quad}\ \underline{\quad}}$$

If O is not interviewed, then O is not hired:

F G J K L M O [7]

$$\underset{\text{Interviewed}}{\overset{F}{\underline{\quad}\ \underline{\quad}\ \underline{\quad}\ \underline{\quad}}} \longleftarrow \underset{\text{Hired}}{\underline{\quad}\ \underline{\quad}\ \underline{\quad}\ \underline{\quad}}$$
$$\underset{\not\!O}{} \qquad\qquad \underset{\not\!O}{}$$

From the contrapositive of the last rule, when O is not hired, then M is not hired *or* L is not interviewed (or hired, then). But, consider what would happen if L is not interviewed: from the contrapositives of the first two rules, J could not be interviewed, and G could not be interviewed. That would mean that O could not be hired, L could not be hired, J could not be hired, and G could not be hired, leaving only three applicants available to be hired, violating the stipulation in this question that exactly four people are hired. Thus, L *must* be interviewed, and, correspondingly (to meet the contrapositive of the sixth rule) M cannot be hired. Thus answer choice (B), M is hired, cannot be true and is the correct answer.

This is a Grouping: Defined-Fixed, Unbalanced: Overloaded game.

This is a very challenging game. The first indication of difficulty is the Subdivided selection pool—the researchers are either anthropologists or linguists. The second source of difficulty is that there are six researchers selected, but seven available researchers, leading to an Unbalanced scenario. Finally, the fact that each team includes at least one anthropologist and at least one linguist further adds to the information you must track.

The initial scenario appears as follows:

Anthro: F J M ^{3}
Ling: N O R S ^{4}

$$\text{Anthro} = \underline{\quad} \quad \underline{\quad}$$

$$\text{Ling} = \underline{\quad} \quad \underline{\quad}$$
$$\qquad\quad 1 \qquad 2$$

Thus, each team includes either one or two anthropologists and either one or two linguists.

The first two rules establish negative grouping rules, which will be shown as vertical not-blocks:

F̸/S   N̸/R

The third rule establishes two more negative grouping rules:

M̸/R   M̸/S

Because M appears in both blocks, the researchers that can be included with M are limited. Because M is an anthropologist, and each team must have an anthropologist and a linguist, if M is included on a team, then N or O must also be included the same team (because R and S are unavailable):

$$M \longrightarrow N/O$$

The final rule is conditional:

$$J_1 \longrightarrow R_2$$

Because R appears in two of the other rules, take a moment to consider the implications of this rule. When J is included on team 1, then R must be included on team 2. But, because R cannot be included on a team with M, and each team must have at least one anthropologist, if J is included on team 1, then R and F (the only remaining anthropologist) must be included on team 2:

$$[\, J_1 \longrightarrow R_2 \,] \longrightarrow F_2$$

Via the same reasoning, if R is included on team 1 (and from the rules then J and M cannot be the anthropologists on team 1), then F must also be included on team 1.

$$R_1 \longrightarrow F_1$$

The information derived so far can be added together to create the final diagram:

Anthro: F J M [3]
Ling: N O R S [4]

Anthro = ____   ____

____   ____

Ling =

____   ____
  1   2

$$[\, J_1 \longrightarrow R_2 \,] \longrightarrow F_2$$

$$R_1 \longrightarrow F_1$$

$$M \longrightarrow N/O$$

Question #12: Global, Could Be True, List. The correct answer choice is (C)

Answer choice (A) is incorrect because from the second rule no team includes both N and R.

Answer choice (B) is incorrect because team 1 violates the first rule by including both F and S.

Answer choice (C) is the correct answer.

Answer choice (D) is incorrect because team 2 does not include an anthropologist, a violation of one of the conditions in the game scenario.

Answer choice (E) is incorrect because team 1 includes J, but team 2 does not include R, a violation of the last rule.

Question #13: Local, Must Be True. The correct answer choice is (A)

During the analysis of the final rule, we concluded that if J is on team 1, then R and F must be on team 2:

Anthro: F J M ^{3}
Ling: N O R S ^{4}

$$
\begin{array}{ccc}
\text{Anthro} = & \underline{\quad J \quad} & \underline{\quad F \quad} \\
 & \underline{\qquad} & \underline{\qquad} \\
\text{Ling} = & \underline{\qquad} & \underline{\quad R \quad} \\
 & 1 & 2 \\
 & & \cancel{N} \\
 & & \cancel{M} \\
\end{array}
$$

Hence, answer choice (A) is correct.

Question #14: Local, Could Be True. The correct answer choice is (D)

If N is on team 1, then from the second rule R cannot be on team 1. Accordingly, answer choice (C) can be eliminated.

Because team 1 must also include at least one anthropologist (F, J, or M), and answer choice (E) does not contain an anthropologist, answer choice (E) can be eliminated.

Answer choice (A) can be eliminated because if J is on team 1 then F must be on team 2 (see the previous question).

Answer choice (B) is very tricky to analyze, but it can be eliminated because if J and O are on team 1, then R and F must be on team 2 (as shown during the setup and in the previous question). But if R and F are on team 2, then from the first and third rules neither S nor M can be on team 2 and ultimately there are not enough researchers available to complete team 2. Thus, answer choice (B) can be eliminated.

The correct answer choice is (D).

Question #15: Local, Could Be True. The correct answer choice is (C)

If F and M are on the same team, then from the first and third rules that team will not include R, nor will it include S. The FM team still needs a linguist, however, and this would have to be either N or O. Additionally, since each team must include an anthropologist, whichever team does *not* include the FM block must include J, the only remaining anthropologist. Because placing J on team 1 results in R and F being included on team 2, we can determine that J cannot be on team 1 in this question. Thus, J must be on team 2, and the FM block must be on team 1.

Only one of the answer choices could be true, and the others should be ruled out:

Answer choice (A) is incorrect because J cannot be on team 1. If J is on team 1, then R must be on team 2 (based on the last rule of the game). Since the FM block cannot be teammates with R, they would have to go to team 1, and then team 1 would have no linguists, and team 2 would have no anthropologists.

Answer choice (B) is incorrect for a similar reason. If R is on team 1, J cannot be on team 1 based on the game's last rule. Because of the fourth rule, the FM block also must avoid R, leaving no anthropologists available for team 1.

Answer choice (C) is the correct answer choice.

Answer choices (D) and (E) are both incorrect because if there is an NO block, it must be on the team that does not include the FM block (each team has only three spaces available, and the two blocks would combine to produce four researchers). The FM team still needs a linguist, but there is none that is allowable—N and O must be on the other team, and the global rules prohibit R and S from being on the FM team.

Question #16: Global, Could Be True, Except. The correct answer choice is (B)

The correct answer choice is (B), because, as discussed in question #15 above, if FM is on team 2, that forces the only remaining anthropologist, J, on to team 1. But if J is on team 1, then R is forced into team 2, and R can never be placed with M.

Question #17: Global, Could Be True. The correct answer choice is (A)

Answer choice (A) is the correct answer choice, because it is the only viable setup among the choices provided:

Answer choice (B) is incorrect, because if F is on team 2, then team 1 must have M, since the team needs an anthropologist and J is to remain unassigned. With M on one team, and F on the other, S is prohibited from both teams; without J and S, there cannot be enough researchers to complete the two teams.

Answer choice (C) is incorrect, as we should recognize from question #16: F and M cannot be together on team 2.

Answer choice (D) can be ruled out, because if J is on team 1, R must be on team 2. But team 2 also needs an anthropologist; if F must be unassigned, this leaves M as the only option—but M cannot be placed on the same team as R.

Answer choice (E) cannot be true, because J on team 1 forces R to team 2, and the rules prohibit R and N from being placed on the same team.

Question #18: Local, Must Be True. The correct answer choice is (B)

If M is on team 2, then from the third rule neither R nor S can be on team 2:

Anthro: F J M ^{3}
Ling: N O R S ^{4}

Anthro = ____   M

Ling = ____   ____
          1   2
                  R̶
                  S̶

Accordingly, answer choices (D) and (E) can be eliminated.

Because R cannot be on team 2, via the contrapositive of the fourth rule it follows that J cannot be on team 1. Because M is on team 2 and J cannot be on team 1, it follows that F must be on team 1:

Anthro: F J M [3]
Ling: N O R S [4]

$$\text{Anthro} = \quad \underline{\text{F}} \qquad \underline{\text{M}}$$

$$\underline{\quad} \qquad \underline{\quad}$$

$$\text{Ling} = \quad \underline{\quad} \qquad \underline{\quad}$$
$$\qquad\qquad\quad 1 \qquad\qquad 2$$
$$\qquad\qquad\quad \cancel{J} \qquad\qquad \cancel{R}$$
$$\qquad\qquad\qquad\qquad\qquad\quad \cancel{S}$$

Accordingly, answer choice (A) can be eliminated.

Because F is on team 1, from the first rule S cannot be on team 1. Because S cannot be on team 1 or team 2, and is thus sidelined for this question, we can infer that every other researcher must be included on a team. Accordingly, since J cannot be on team 1, J must be on team 2 and answer choice (B) is proven correct.

This is a Pattern game.

From the nature of the rules, you should deduce that this is a Pattern game. Pattern games are characterized by rules that control the placement of variables without actually placing the variables. This leads to setups that are largely devoid of concrete information. Here is the initial game scenario:

Q R S T U [5]

	1	2	3	4	5
Meeting 1:	___	___	___	___	___
Meeting 2:	___	___	___	___	___
Meeting 3:	___	___	___	___	___

Because the setup contains no "starting point" for analysis, the best approach is to review the rules in order to ensure a complete understanding of the game. As is often the case in Pattern games, the rules are difficult to diagram. However, it is important to symbolize the rules in some way since the focus of the game will be on their application. Fortunately, in this game the rules are relatively simple and thus easy to remember.

Here is the full setup to the game, followed by a discussion of the rules:

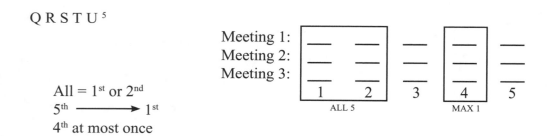

Q R S T U [5]

All = 1st or 2nd

5th ——→ 1st

4th at most once

The first rule states that "Each candidate must speak either first or second at at least one of the meetings." This rule is represented off to the side of the diagram, and also as a block around the first two positions. Because there are three meetings, it follows that there are six available spaces for the candidates to meet this requirement. Since there are five candidates, each of whom must appear once in these six spaces, it can be inferred that exactly one candidate must appear twice within the first two speaking spaces of all three meetings, and the rest of the candidates appear only once. This is an unfixed numerical distribution of 2-1-1-1-1 for the six spaces that represent the first and second speaking slots of the three meetings. Essentially, this rule means that if one speaker speaks within the first two slots at two of the meetings, then the remaining slots must be filled with the rest of the speakers. For example, if Q speaks first at meeting 1 and second at meeting 2, then R, S, T, and U each speak once in the remaining first or second positions of the meetings. This inference comes into play on all of the questions, particularly questions #20 and #21.

The second rule states that "Any candidate who speaks fifth at any of the meetings must speak first at at least one of the other meetings." This is a powerful rule because it establishes a constant connection between the first and fifth spaces. Because the fifth space cannot be filled by the same candidate at all three meetings (that candidate would have to speak first at at least one of the meetings), it follows that there are always two or three different speakers speaking fifth slot in the three total meetings. If there are three different candidates speaking in the fifth slot, then those same three candidates will also speak in the first slot at a meeting in a different order. If there are two different candidates speaking in the fifth slot, then those same two candidates will speak in the first slot, with either another candidate in the remaining first slot or with one of the two candidates doubling up. Therefore, please note that if two different candidates fill all three of the fifth speaking slots, it is possible for a candidate to speak first at a meeting and not speak fifth (to think that if a candidate speaks first at a meeting that he or she must then speak fifth at another meeting would be to make a Mistaken Reversal). For example, if the fifth speaker at each of the three meetings, is R, R, and T respectively, then the first speaker at each of the three meetings could be T, Q, and R respectively.

Although the above explanation is complex, the application of the rule is much easier. Essentially, any candidate placed into the first or fifth slot immediately becomes subject to this rule. Combined with the first rule, slots one, two, and five appear to be the most controlling slots, thereby the most important ones.

Question #19: Global, Could Be True, List. The correct answer choice is (D)

In Pattern games always be sure to do List questions first, in order to establish a workable hypothetical. The easiest rule to apply from a visual standpoint is the last rule, "No candidate can speak fourth at more than one of the meetings." Answer choice (C) violates this rule and is thus incorrect. The next easiest rule to apply is probably the first rule. Answer choice (A) violates this rule (R does not appear) and is therefore incorrect. Finally, applying the second rule eliminates answer choices (B) and (E). Answer choice (D) is proven correct by process of elimination.

Question #20: Local, Could Be True, List. The correct answer choice is (D)

This is the first local question of the game. If R speaks second at meeting 2 and first at meeting 3, then according to our analysis of the first rule R cannot speak first or second at meeting 1. Accordingly, answer choices (B), (C), and (E) can be eliminated. The difference between the remaining two answer choices is whether R can speak third at meeting 1. Since there is no constraint on speaking third, and no violation caused by R speaking third, it follows that answer choice (D) is correct. Note that this answer choice reflects the fact that just because a candidate speaks first does not mean that candidate has to speak fifth. The second rule as stated and diagrammed can be paraphrased as "if a candidate speaks fifth at a meeting, then at some other meeting they must speak first."

Question #21: Local, Could Be True. The correct answer choice is (B)

The information in the question stem produces the following setup:

Meeting 1:	R	U	S	T	Q
Meeting 2:	Q	R	U	S	T
Meeting 3:	T	S			
	1	2	3	4	5

Since R, Q, and U speak first or second at meetings 1 and 2, T and S must speak in the first two slots of meeting 3. Since T speaks fifth at meeting 2, and fourth at meeting 1, T must speak first at meeting 3, and it follows that S must speak second at meeting 3. Accordingly, answer choices (A), (C), and (D) can be eliminated. Answer choice (E) can also be eliminated since if U spoke fifth, U would have to speak first at another meeting and that is not possible in this situation. Thus, answer choice (B) is correct.

In this question, the second rule often gives rise to a Mistaken Reversal. Remember, the second rule means that if a speaker speaks fifth at one of the meetings, then that speaker must speak first at one of the other meetings ($5^{th} \longrightarrow 1^{st}$). Many students wrongly interpret this rule to mean that if a speaker speaks first at one of the meetings that speaker must speak fifth at another meeting ($1^{st} \longrightarrow 5^{th}$). While that interpretation may sound logical, that is not actually what the second rule says, and it does not have to be true. For example, the following hypothetical for meeting 3 in this question satisfies all the rules: T-S-R-U-Q. Note that, with this hypothetical in question #21, anyone who speaks fifth (Q and T) also speaks first (in meetings 2 and 3). R, who speaks first at meeting 1, does not speak fifth at any meeting, and this is acceptable under the wording of the second rule.

Question #22: Local, Must Be True. The correct answer choice is (E)

If R speaks first at meetings 1 and 2, and S speaks first at meeting 3, then, according to our analysis of the second rule, R must speak fifth at meeting 3 and S must speak fifth at meetings 1 and 2. It follows that answer choice (E) is correct.

Specifically, in question #22, we know that:

Meeting 1:	R				
Meeting 2:	R				
Meeting 3:	S				
	1	2	3	4	5

So, from the question stem we already know which speakers are first at each meeting. That brings up an interesting situation for the other speakers. For example, could T speak fifth at one of the meetings, say the meeting 1? No, because then there would be no meeting where T could speak first (those positions are already taken by R or S), and that would violate the second rule. The same situation would apply to Q and U, and so T, Q, and U can never speak fifth in the scenario presented in question #22. Hence, R and S must fill all of the fifth speaking spaces, and that means we can infer that S speaks fifth at meetings 1 and 2, R speaks fifth at meeting 3:

Meeting 1:	R	—	—	—	S
Meeting 2:	R	—	—	—	S
Meeting 3:	S	—	—	—	R
	1	2	3	4	5

This scenario proves answer choice (E) is correct.

Question #23: Global, Could Be True. The correct answer choice is (C)

From our discussion of the first rule, answer choices (A) and (B) can be eliminated. Answer choice (D) can be eliminated because if T always speaks after both S and U, T could never speak first or second, a violation of the first rule. Answer choice (E) can be eliminated since if T always speaks before R and U, then T would speak first at least twice, but could never speak fifth, which would ultimately cause a violation of the first rule. Thus, answer choice (C) is proven correct by process of elimination. Here is a hypothetical that satisfies all of the rules of the game and the condition in answer choice (C):

Meeting 1:	R	T	U	S	Q
Meeting 2:	S	R	T	U	Q
Meeting 3:	Q	U	R	T	S
	1	2	3	4	5

Note that Q and S are the only candidates who speak 5th. Since they both speak 1st at some point, the second rule is satisfied.

Question #24: Local, Must Be True. The correct answer choice is (A)

If S, T, and U speak second, then Q and R must each appear in the first speaking slot at least once. Because of this, either Q or R must speak in the fifth slot at one of the meetings, and it follows that answer choice (A) is correct. From a structural standpoint, answer choices (D) and (E) are very unlikely to be correct since they deal with the third and fourth slots.

Remember, in Pattern games the setup is generally easy to create, and therefore you have a greater amount of time to analyze the rules and ascertain their relationship to the pattern of the game (there are exceptions though!). And with the knowledge that Pattern games produce few inferences, you should not be unduly concerned when your setup seems relatively empty. Also, when in doubt, do the List questions first, or try a hypothetical to help gain an understanding of the nature of the game.

POWERSCORE®

24 PREPTEST

DECEMBER 1997 LOGIC GAMES SETUPS

This is a Grouping: Defined-Moving, Balanced, Numerical Distribution, Identify the Possibilities game.

This game features seven flavorings included in two dishes (7 ——▶ 2). The first rule establishes a limitation on the number of flavorings in the appetizer (a maximum of 3), and thus the stage is set for a Numerical Distribution. Initially, the following distributions appear possible:

Appetizer-Main Dish Numerical Distributions:

Appetizer	Main Dish
0	7
1	6
2	5
3	4

However, the second and third rules create two not-blocks (more on these in a moment), and because every flavoring must be used, these two rules mean that the appetizer cannot have 0 or 1 flavorings. Thus, there are only two possible fixed distributions in the game:

Appetizer-Main Dish Numerical Distributions:

Appetizer	Main Dish
2	5
3	4

To recount, the 0-7 and 1-6 distributions are impossible because they would force either F and N, or S and T, or both together.

The second and third rules establish two not-blocks:

Essentially, each block results in a space in each dish being "reserved" for the members of each pair:

$$\frac{\text{F/N} \quad \text{N/F}}{\frac{\text{S/T} \quad \text{T/S}}{\text{A} \qquad \text{M}}}$$

The fourth rule creates a block:

```
┌───┐
│ G │
│ N │
└───┘
```

By combining the second and fourth rules, the additional inference that F and G cannot be included in the same recipe together can be drawn:

L and P do not appear in any of the rules, meaning they are randoms. That will be shown on the next diagram with asterisks. At this point, the diagram would appear as follows:

F G L N P S T [7]
   *   *

Appetizer-Main Dish Numerical Distribution:

Appetizer	Main Dish	
2	5	(2 possibilities)
3	4	(6 possibilities)

Because of the numerical distribution and the restrictive nature of the rules, this game can be attacked by Identifying the Possibilities:

2-5 Dist Possibility:	3-4 Dist Possibility #1:	3-4 Dist Possibility #2:

```
          P
          L
          G
     F    N
    S/T  T/S
     A    M
```

```
               L/P
        P/L    N
         F     G
        S/T   T/S
         A     M
```

```
                 L
         N       P
         G       F
        S/T     T/S
         A       M
```

There are only eight solutions to this game:

Appetizer-Main Dish Numerical Distributions and Possibilities:

Appetizer	Main Dish	
2	5	(2 possibilities)
3	4	(6 possibilities)

Question #1: Global, Could Be True, List. The correct answer choice is (D)

Answer choice (A) is incorrect because if the main dish recipe has three flavorings, then the appetizer recipe would have four flavorings, and from the first rule the appetizer recipe can only have at most three flavorings.

Answer choice (B) is incorrect because F and N cannot be included the same recipe per the second rule.

Answer choice (C) is incorrect because from the third rule exactly one of S or T must be included in the main-dish recipe.

Answer choice (D) is the correct answer.

Answer choice (E) is incorrect because from the third rule S and T cannot be included in the same recipe.

Question #2: Local, Must Be True. The correct answer choice is (A)

If F is included in the main-dish recipe, only the 3-4 Dist Possibility #2 applies. In that template, G is in the appetizer recipe, and so answer choice (A) is correct.

Alternatively, if F is in the main-dish recipe, then from the second rule N must be included in the appetizer recipe. Since N and G must be in the same recipe per the last rule, G must be included in the appetizer recipe as well.

Question #3: Global, Could Be True, List. The correct answer choice is (A)

Answer choice (A) is the correct answer. As shown in the 2-5 Dist Possibility, F and S can be the only two flavorings in the appetizer recipe.

Answer choice (B) is incorrect because from the third rule either S or T must be included in the appetizer recipe.

Answer choice (C) is incorrect because F and N cannot be included the same recipe per the second rule.

Answer choice (D) is incorrect because from the last rule N and G must be included in the same recipe.

Answer choice (E) is incorrect because from the first rule the appetizer recipe includes at most three flavorings.

Question #4: Local, Must Be True. The correct answer choice is (B)

The question asks for a flavoring that must be included in the contestant's main-dish recipe. When L and P are included in the same recipe, they must be in the main dish recipe, and thus L or P would be a correct answer. L appears in answer choice (B), and therefore (B) is correct.

Question #5: Local, Could Be True, List, Suspension. The correct answer choice is (C)

With the last rule suspended, the setup appears as follows:

F/N	N/F
S/T	T/S
A	M

This setup provides sufficient information to attack the questions.

Answer choice (A) is incorrect because from the third rule either S or T must be included in the main-dish recipe.

Answer choice (B) is incorrect because from the second rule either F or N must be included in the main-dish recipe.

Answer choice (C) is the correct answer.

Answer choice (D) is incorrect because from the third rule both S and T cannot be included in the main-dish recipe.

Answer choice (E) is incorrect because from the second rule both F and N cannot be included in the main-dish recipe.

This is a Basic Linear: Balanced game.

This is the easiest game of the test, and the basic scenario is as follows:

J K L M N O P ^{7}

$$\overline{\quad}\;\overline{\quad}\;\overline{\quad}\;\overline{\quad}\;\overline{\quad}\;\overline{\quad}\;\overline{\quad}$$
$$\;\;1\quad\;2\quad\;3\quad\;4\quad\;5\quad\;6\quad\;7$$

The first rule creates a KJ block, and creates two Not Laws:

J K L M N O P ^{7}

| K J |

$$\overline{\quad}\;\overline{\quad}\;\overline{\quad}\;\overline{\quad}\;\overline{\quad}\;\overline{\quad}\;\overline{\quad}$$
$$\;\;1\quad\;2\quad\;3\quad\;4\quad\;5\quad\;6\quad\;7$$
$$\;\;\cancel{J}\qquad\qquad\qquad\qquad\qquad\cancel{K}$$

The second rule creates a M > P sequence; again, two Not Laws result:

J K L M N O P ^{7}

| K J |

M > P

$$\overline{\quad}\;\overline{\quad}\;\overline{\quad}\;\overline{\quad}\;\overline{\quad}\;\overline{\quad}\;\overline{\quad}$$
$$\;\;1\quad\;2\quad\;3\quad\;4\quad\;5\quad\;6\quad\;7$$
$$\;\;\cancel{J}\qquad\qquad\qquad\qquad\qquad\cancel{K}$$
$$\;\;\cancel{P}\qquad\qquad\qquad\qquad\qquad\cancel{M}$$

The third rule is conditional:

$$L_3 \longrightarrow N_5$$

The fourth rule is also conditional, but the presence of a negative in the sufficient condition makes this rule trickier to interpret than most other conditional rules. The diagram of the rule, and its contrapositive are as follows:

$$\cancel{P}_2 \longrightarrow P_5$$

$$\cancel{P}_5 \longrightarrow P_2$$

Thus, if P is not second then P is fifth, and if P is not fifth then P is second. Therefore, P must always be second or fifth, which can be shown on our diagram with a split option. P's placement also affects M via the second rule, and M cannot be fifth or sixth:

J K L M N O P [7]

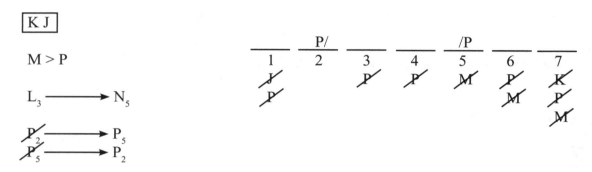

The last rule produces a situation where P must perform on either the second day or the fifth day. This rule, in combination with the third rule, produces the following inferences:

Inferences: $P_5 \longrightarrow \cancel{L}_3$

$$L_3 \longrightarrow \begin{array}{c} P_2 \\ \text{and} \\ N_5 \end{array} \longrightarrow M_1 \longrightarrow K_6 \, J_7 \longrightarrow O_4$$

The second inference is quite powerful; when L performs third, the entire schedule is determined: M-P-L-O-N-K-J. This inference is tested in question #7.

Question #6: Global, Could Be True, List. The correct answer choice is (A)

Answer choice (A) is the correct answer.

Answer choice (B) can be eliminated because from the second rule P's performance must be after M's performance.

Answer choice (C) can be eliminated because according to the last rule P's performance must be second or fifth.

Answer choice (D) can be eliminated because from the first rule J's performance must be immediately after K's performance.

Answer choice (E) can be eliminated because per the third rule when L performs third, N must perform fifth.

Question #7: Local, Must Be True. The correct answer choice is (B)

This question tests the inference chain discussed in the game setup: when L performs third, the entire schedule is determined: M-P-L-O-N-K-J. Consequently, answer choice (B) is correct.

Question #8: Local, Could Be True. The correct answer choice is (C)

The condition in the question stem produces the following setup:

	M	P	L/O	O/L	N	K	J
KJ in 6-7:							
KJ in 3-4	M	P	K	J	N	L/O	O/L
	1	2	3	4	5	6	7

As shown by the diagram above, L could perform fourth, and hence answer choice (C) is correct. In considering this answer choice, some students eliminate it because they make a Mistaken Reversal of the third rule. Just because N performs fifth does not mean that L performs third, and so answer choice (C) cannot be eliminated on the basis of the third rule.

Question #9: Local, Could Be True. The correct answer choice is (E)

If M is scheduled for the second performance, then from the last rule P must be scheduled for the fifth performance (and L cannot be scheduled for the third performance). This information eliminates answer choices (C) and (D).

Answer choices (A) and (B) can be eliminated because with P performing fifth, the KJ block *cannot* be placed so J is sixth or K is fourth. Hence, answer choice (E) is correct.

Question #10: Local, Cannot Be True. The correct answer choice is (A)

The condition in the question stem creates a KJL block. Under this arrangement, if J is scheduled second, then L is scheduled third and the following scenario results:

K	J	L		N		
1	2	3	4	5	6	7

In this scenario, there is no room for P, and thus the hypothetical fails. Therefore, J cannot be scheduled second.

This is an Advanced Linear: Balanced game.

Whereas the first two games on this test are fairly reasonable, this game is considerably harder. This occurs because the Advanced Linear element is paired with a subdivided selection pool (introductory and advanced). The initial scenario appears as follows:

Int: F G H ^{3}
Adv: X Y Z ^{3}

Rosenberg: ____ ____ ____ ____ ____ ____

Juarez: ____ ____ ____ ____ ____ ____
              1   2   3   4   5   6

The first constraint in the game is stated at the end of the game scenario, and stipulates that no textbook is evaluated by both reviewers during the same week:

$$\begin{array}{|c|} \hline T \\ \hline T \\ \hline \end{array}$$

In the above diagram, "T" stands for textbook, indicating that the same textbook cannot be evaluated by both evaluators during the same week.

The first rule establishes that R cannot evaluate an introductory textbook until J has evaluated that textbook. This should be shown as a sequence, with subscripts for "introductory":

$$J_I > R_I$$

The A and I subscripts are the easiest way to keep track of the advanced and introductory textbooks since there are already two stacks for Rosenberg and Juarez.

Of course, under this rule, R cannot evaluate an introductory textbook during week 1, and J cannot evaluate an introductory textbook during week 6. Thus, because each textbook is either introductory or advanced, we can infer that R evaluates an advanced textbook during week 1, and J evaluates an advanced textbook during week 6:

Int: F G H [3]
Adv: X Y Z [3]

$J_I > R_I$

Rosenberg: $\underline{X/Y/Z_A}$ _____ _____ _____ _____ _____

Juarez: _____ _____ _____ _____ _____ $\underline{X/Y/Z_A}$
            1   2   3   4   5   6

The second rule is also sequential, and can be diagrammed as follows:

$$R_A > J_A$$

This rule is really the reverse of the first rule. Under this condition, J cannot evaluate an advanced book during week 1, and R cannot evaluate an advanced book during week 6. Thus, J must evaluate an introductory book during week 1, and R must evaluate an introductory book during week 6:

Int: F G H [3]
Adv: X Y Z [3]

$J_I > R_I$

$R_A > J_A$

Rosenberg: $\underline{X/Y/Z_A}$ _____ _____ _____ $\underline{F/G/H_I}$

Juarez: $\underline{F/G/H_I}$ _____ _____ _____ $\underline{X/Y/Z_A}$
            1   2   3   4   5   6

The third rule indicates that R cannot evaluate any two introductory textbooks consecutively:

This initiates the Separation Principle, and thus for R, the advanced textbooks must separate the introductory textbooks. Because R cannot evaluate any two introductory books consecutively, and because J must evaluate any introductory book before R evaluates it, R must evaluate the introductory textbooks second, fourth, and sixth. Correspondingly, R must evaluate the advanced textbooks first, third, and fifth. Thus, R's sequence of evaluating textbooks must be A-I-A-I-A-I:

Int: F G H [3]
Adv: X Y Z [3]

$J_I > R_I$

$R_A > J_A$

$\boxed{R_I / R_I}$

Rosenberg: $\underline{X/Y/Z_A}$ $\underline{F/G/H_I}$ $\underline{X/Y/Z_A}$ $\underline{F/G/H_I}$ $\underline{X/Y/Z_A}$ $\underline{F/G/H_I}$

Juarez: $\underline{}_{F/G/H_I}$ $\underline{}_{2}$ $\underline{}_{3}$ $\underline{}_{4}$ $\underline{}_{5}$ $\underline{}_{X/Y/Z_A}$

$\quad\quad\quad\quad\quad$ 1 $\quad$ 2 $\quad$ 3 $\quad$ 4 $\quad$ 5 $\quad$ 6

The final rule states that J must evaluate X during week 4, which can be shown directly on the diagram. In addition, because X is an advanced textbook, and from the second rule J cannot evaluate an advanced textbook until R has evaluated it, R must evaluate X first or third, and cannot evaluate X fifth (again, R's even-numbered book evaluations must be introductory books, so X could not be second, fourth, or sixth). Accounting for this information results in the following diagram:

Int: F G H [3]
Adv: X Y Z [3]

$\boxed{\begin{array}{c} T \\ T \end{array}}$ (crossed)

$J_I > R_I$

$R_A > J_A$

$\boxed{R_I / R_I}$

Rosenberg: $\underline{X/Y/Z_A}$ $\underline{F/G/H_I}$ $\underline{X/Y/Z_A}$ $\underline{F/G/H_I}$ $\underline{Y/Z_A}$ $\underline{F/G/H_I}$

Juarez: $\underline{F/G/H_I}$ $\underline{}$ $\underline{}$ $\underline{X_A}$ $\underline{}$ $\underline{Y/Z_A}$

$\quad\quad\quad\quad\quad$ 1 $\quad$ 2 $\quad$ 3 $\quad$ 4 $\quad$ 5 $\quad$ 6

Note that, due to the second rule, whatever advanced textbook R evaluates in week 5 will be the advanced textbook J evaluates in week 6. This relationship is also true in the reverse: whatever advanced textbook J evaluates in week 6 will be the advanced textbook R evaluates in week 5 (otherwise, the textbook reviewed by R in week 5 would have to be reviewed by J in an earlier week, a violation of the second rule). As this relationship goes both ways, so it will be shown with a double arrow.

Similarly, due to the first rule, whatever introductory textbook R evaluates in week 2 will be the introductory textbook J evaluates in week 1. This relationship also reverses, and so it will also be shown with a double arrow.

These relationships can be shown on the main diagram with arrows, leading to the final diagram:

Int: F G H ^{3}
Adv: X Y Z ^{3}

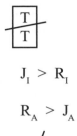

J$_I$ > R$_I$

R$_A$ > J$_A$

R$_I$/R$_I$ (crossed out box)

Rosenberg: $\underline{X/Y/Z_A}$ $\underline{F/G/H_I}$ $\underline{X/Y/Z_A}$ $\underline{F/G/H_I}$ $\underline{Y/Z_A}$ $\underline{F/G/H_I}$

Juarez: $\underline{F/G/H_I}$ _____ _____ $\underline{X_A}$ _____ $\underline{Y/Z_A}$
          1   2   3   4   5   6

While R has a fairly limited number of ordering options, J still has a number of options for ordering the introductory and advanced textbooks. For example, J could evaluate the advanced textbooks 2-4-6, 3-4-6, or 4-5-6. However, as each textbook is placed, the interrelationship of the rules and variable sets will quickly limit the number of remaining options.

Question #11: Global, Could Be True, List. The correct answer choice is (B)

Answer choice (A) is incorrect because according to the fourth rule, J must evaluate X during week 4.

Answer choice (B) is the correct answer.

Answer choice (C) is incorrect because from the third rule R cannot evaluate two introductory books consecutively, and in this answer R evaluates G and H consecutively.

Answer choice (D) is incorrect because from the first rule R cannot evaluate an introductory textbook until J has evaluated it, and in this answer R evaluates F before J evaluates F.

Answer choice (E) is incorrect because from the second rule J cannot evaluate an advanced textbook until R has evaluated it, and in this answer J evaluates Y before R evaluates Y.

Question #12: Local, Must Be True. The correct answer choice is (A)

If J evaluates H during week 3, and R evaluates G during week 6, the initial setup appears as follows:

Rosenberg: _____$_A$ _____$_I$ _____$_A$ _____$_I$ _____$_A$ $\underline{G_I}$
Juarez: _____$_I$ _____ $\underline{H_I}$ $\underline{X_A}$ _____ _____$_A$
            1   2   3   4   5   6

In order to conform to the first rule, R must then evaluate H during week 4, forcing F to be the textbook R evaluates during week 2. J must then evaluate F during week 1:

$$
\begin{array}{c|cccccc}
\text{Rosenberg:} & \underset{A}{} & \underset{I}{F} & \underset{A}{} & \underset{I}{H} & \underset{A}{} & \underset{I}{G} \\
\text{Juarez:} & \underset{I}{F} & & \underset{I}{H} & \underset{A}{X} & & \underset{A}{} \\
\hline
& 1 & 2 & 3 & 4 & 5 & 6
\end{array}
$$

Consequently, answer choice (A) is correct.

Question #13: Local, Must Be True. The correct answer choice is (D)

If J evaluates Z during week 2, then J must evaluate Y during week 6. Accordingly, R must evaluate Y during week 5, X during week 3, and Z during week 1:

$$
\begin{array}{c|cccccc}
\text{Rosenberg:} & \underset{A}{Z} & \underset{I}{} & \underset{A}{X} & \underset{I}{} & \underset{A}{Y} & \underset{I}{} \\
\text{Juarez:} & \underset{I}{} & \underset{A}{Z} & \underset{I}{} & \underset{A}{X} & \underset{A}{} & \underset{A}{Y} \\
\hline
& 1 & 2 & 3 & 4 & 5 & 6
\end{array}
$$

Hence, answer choice (D) is correct.

Question #14: Global, Must Be True. The correct answer choice is (B)

As discussed during the setup, R must conform to an A-I-A-I-A-I lineup. Hence, R must evaluate an advanced textbook during week 3, and answer choice (B) is correct.

Question #15: Local, Could Be True. The correct answer choice is (E)

If R evaluates X during week 1 and F during week 2, the setup appears as:

$$
\begin{array}{c|cccccc}
\text{Rosenberg:} & \underset{A}{X} & \underset{I}{F} & \underset{A}{} & \underset{I}{} & \underset{A}{} & \underset{I}{} \\
\text{Juarez:} & \underset{I}{} & & & \underset{A}{X} & & \underset{A}{} \\
\hline
& 1 & 2 & 3 & 4 & 5 & 6
\end{array}
$$

However, several inferences can be drawn from the above information:

1. In order to conform to the first rule, J must evaluate F during week 1.

2. Due to the effects of the second rule, the textbook evaluated by R during week 3 must be evaluated by J after week 3. Since J evaluates X during week 4, that means that only weeks 5 and 6 are

available for that textbook to be evaluated. And, because J's week 6 is already occupied by whatever book R evaluates during week 5, we can determine that the textbook evaluated by R during week 3 will be evaluated by J during week 5:

$$
\begin{array}{lcccccc}
\text{Rosenberg:} & \underline{X_A} & \underline{F_I} & \underline{Y/Z_A} & \underline{}_I & \underline{Z/Y_A} & \underline{}_I \\
\text{Juarez:} & \underline{F_I} & \underline{} & \underline{} & \underline{X_A} & \underline{Y/Z_A} & \underline{Z/Y_A} \\
& 1 & 2 & 3 & 4 & 5 & 6
\end{array}
$$

Thus, J must evaluate G and H, not necessarily in that order, during weeks 2 and 3:

$$
\begin{array}{lcccccc}
\text{Rosenberg:} & \underline{X_A} & \underline{F_I} & \underline{Y/Z_A} & \underline{}_I & \underline{Z/Y_A} & \underline{}_I \\
\text{Juarez:} & \underline{F_I} & \underline{(G_I,} & \underline{H_I)} & \underline{X_A} & \underline{Y/Z_A} & \underline{Z/Y_A} \\
& 1 & 2 & 3 & 4 & 5 & 6
\end{array}
$$

Consequently, answer choice (E) could be true and is correct.

Question #16: Global, Must Be True, List. The correct answer choice is (A)

As referenced earlier, J's advanced textbook review options are 2-4-6, 3-4-6, or 4-5-6. Thus, J's complete review options are:

I-A-I-A-I-A

I-I-A-A-I-A

I-I-I-A-A-A

Only week 1 appears in all three possibilities, and thus answer choice (A) is correct.

Question #17: Global, Could Be True. The correct answer choice is (D)

Answer choice (A) is incorrect because J must evaluate an advanced textbook during week 6.

Answer choice (B) is incorrect because J must evaluate an introductory textbook during week 1.

Answer choice (C) is incorrect because R must evaluate an advanced textbook during week 3.

Answer choice (D) is the correct answer.

Answer choice (E) is incorrect because R must evaluate X before week 4, and thus cannot evaluate X during week 5.

This is a Grouping: Defined-Fixed, Unbalanced: Overloaded, Numerical Distribution game.

Here is the initial scenario for the game:

Anti: F G H ^{3}
Diet: M N O ^{3}
Phys: U V W ^{3}

____ ____ ____ ____ ____
            Five Treatments

Because there are three different types of treatments, subscripts should be used to help track each treatment group.

The first rule establishes that all three antibiotics cannot be prescribed:

$$\boxed{F \cancel{G} H}$$

The second rule reserves exactly one of the five treatments for a dietary regimen:

Anti: F G H ^{3}
Diet: M N O ^{3}
Phys: U V W ^{3} Diet | ____ ____ ____ ____

$\boxed{F \cancel{G} H}$

These first two rules indicate that a Numerical Distribution is present. In fact, there are only two possible numerical distributions of the three treatment groups to the five prescriptions in this game:

Dietary	Antibiotic	Physical
1	1	3
1	2	2

The third, fourth, fifth, and sixth rules are each conditional in nature:

3. $F_A \longrightarrow O_D$

4. $W_P \longleftrightarrow\!\!\!| \longrightarrow F_A$

5. $\begin{matrix} N_D \\ + \\ U_P \end{matrix} \longrightarrow \cancel{O}_A$

6. $V_P \longrightarrow \begin{matrix} H_A \\ + \\ M_D \end{matrix}$

Note that rule 3 presents the contrapositive in order to eliminate the negative terms.

There are a number of powerful inferences that can be drawn from the rules:

Second and Third Rules Combined

The second rule indicates that exactly one dietary regimen is prescribed. The third rule indicates that if F is prescribed, then O—a dietary regimen—must be prescribed. Hence, if F is prescribed, no other dietary regimen besides O can be prescribed, and thus F cannot be prescribed with M or N.

Second and Last Rules Combined

The last rule indicates that if V is prescribed, then both H and M are prescribed. As M is a dietary regimen, if V is prescribed then no other dietary regimen besides M can be prescribed, and thus V cannot be prescribed with N or O.

Second, Third, and Last Rules Combined

From the second rule, only one dietary regimen can be prescribed. The third rule indicates that if F is prescribed, then O—a dietary regimen— is prescribed. The last rule states that if V is prescribed, then H and M—a dietary regimen—is prescribed. Thus, F and V cannot be prescribed together as they both require different dietary regimens.

By applying the five negative grouping inferences explained above, the following answer choices can be eliminated:

Question #18: Answers (A), (B), and (C)
Question #19: Answers (A), (B), and (C)
Question #20: Answers (B) and (D)
Question #21: Answers (A), (B), (C), and (D)
Question #22: Answers (A), (C), and (E)

Many of the remaining answers can be eliminated by a simple application of the rules.

This is the final setup for the game:

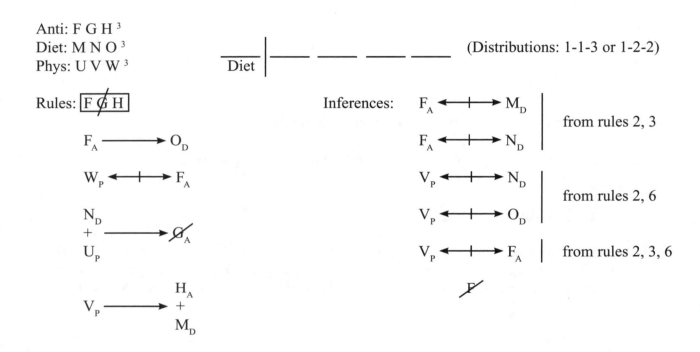

Anti: F G H ^{3}
Diet: M N O ^{3}
Phys: U V W ^{3}

(Distributions: 1-1-3 or 1-2-2)

In fact, due to the many rules and restrictions, there are only five solutions to this game:

1-1-3 distribution:	M-H-U-V-W
1-2-2 distribution:	M-G-H-U-V
	M-G-H-V-W
	M-G-H-U-W
	O-G-H-U-W

A student who identified each of these five possibilities could easily destroy the game. However, because the game can so easily be solved by using the inferences, and identifying the possibilities is somewhat time-consuming, we do not feel it is necessary to identify the possibilities.

Question #18: Global, Could Be True, List. The correct answer choice is (E)

Answer choice (A) is incorrect because F and V cannot be prescribed together.

Answer choice (B) is incorrect because F and V cannot be prescribed together, and also because two dietary regimens cannot be prescribed.

Answer choice (C) is incorrect because F and M cannot be prescribed together, and also because two dietary regimens cannot be prescribed.

Answer choice (D) is incorrect because from the fifth rule if N and U are prescribed, then G cannot be prescribed.

Answer choice (E) is the correct answer choice.

Question #19: Global, Could Be True, List. The correct answer choice is (E)

Answer choice (A) is incorrect because F and W cannot be prescribed together.

Answer choice (B) is incorrect because F and V cannot be prescribed together.

Answer choice (C) is incorrect because F and W cannot be prescribed together.

Answer choice (D) is incorrect because if V is selected then H and M must be selected, which can not occur because only one more treatment is prescribed.

Answer choice (E) is the correct answer choice.

Question #20: Local, Must Be True. The correct answer choice is (E)

If O is prescribed, then from the second rule M and N cannot be prescribed. Accordingly, answer choices (A) and (C) can be eliminated. Also, from our discussion of inferences, we learned that O and V cannot be prescribed together. Consequently, answer choices (B) and (D) can be eliminated. Thus, answer choice (E) is correct.

Question #21: Local, Could Be True. The correct answer choice is (E)

The initial list of inferences eliminates each of the four incorrect answer choices because each pair in answers (A) through (D) is a pair of treatments that cannot be prescribed together. Note that this is true regardless of whether G is prescribed. Therefore, answer choice (E) is correct.

Question #22: Global, Could Be True, List. The correct answer choice is (D)

Again, most of the incorrect answer choices are eliminated by the initial inferences.

Answer choice (A) is incorrect because F and M cannot be prescribed together.

Answer choice (B) is incorrect because F and W cannot be prescribed together.

Answer choice (C) is incorrect because V and N cannot be prescribed together.

Answer choice (D) is the correct answer choice.

Answer choice (E) is incorrect because V and N cannot be prescribed together.

Question #23: Global, Cannot Be True. The correct answer choice is (C)

This is an interesting question because it reveals that at least one of the treatments can never be prescribed. If you did not discover which treatment was unprescribable, then use hypotheticals created during the game to attack this question. For example, the hypothetical from question #18 shows that G, U, and W can be prescribed, and thus answer choices (A), (D), and (E) can be eliminated. The choice is then down to M or N, and you could quickly make a hypothetical to prove or disprove one of the two answers (or, perhaps, you could use the partial hypothetical from question #19 to realize that M can be prescribed). In any event, do not panic if you reach a global question such as this one—relax and use your prior work to quickly solve the question. Note also that this question shows that you do not have to make every inference initially to succeed in a game!

POWERSCORE®

25

PREPTEST

JUNE 1998 LOGIC GAMES SETUPS

This is a Grouping: Partially Defined game.

This game is classified as Partially Defined because each committee must have at least three members, but can have more. At first glance, the game appears as if it may be difficult. However, as you work through the questions, the game turns out to be fairly reasonable.

This game also serves as a useful reminder that you cannot assume that variables are always placed in just one group. No rules establish that a volunteer is a member of only one committee, but the last two rules explicitly allow for volunteers to be members of both committees. The first rule also allows for the possibility that not every volunteer must be a member of a committee (and the fourth rule suggests this as well).

Accounting for the game scenario and the first rule, the initial setup is as follows:

F G H J K L M ^{7}

$$\frac{\quad}{\underset{P}{\quad}} \quad \frac{\quad}{\underset{T}{\quad}}$$

The remaining four rules are fairly simple, and result in the following diagram:

F G H J K L M ^{7}
* *   *

F ◄——┼——► K

K ———► J

M must be used

at least 1 member in common

$$\frac{\quad}{\underset{P}{\quad}} \overset{at}{\longleftrightarrow} \frac{\quad}{\underset{T}{\quad}}$$
1st 1

↖ or ↗
M

Three of the seven volunteers—G, H, and L—are randoms, and so your focus must be on the four non-random volunteers.

Also, please note that you *cannot* make the inference that F and J do not serve on the same committee together. The relationships are not presented in a manner that allows you to make that connection (the arrow between K and J would have to be reversed in order to draw that inference).

Question #1: Global, Could Be True, List. The correct answer choice is (B)

Answer choice (A) is incorrect because M is not a member of either committee, a violation of the fourth rule.

Answer choice (B) is the correct answer.

Answer choice (C) is incorrect because according to the third rule if K is on a committee then J must be on that same committee, and the composition of the trails committee violates the rule.

Answer choice (D) is incorrect because the trails committee has only two members, a violation of the first rule.

Answer choice (E) is incorrect because F and K are both members of the planting committee, a violation of the second rule.

Question #2: Local, Could Be True. The correct answer choice is (B)

The condition in the question stem establishes the following setup:

$$\begin{array}{cc} \underline{M} & \\ \underline{L} & \underline{J} \\ \underline{H} & \underline{H} \\ \underline{F} & \underline{G} \\ P & T \end{array}$$

The question then proceeds to ask for the variable that could be replaced by K without creating a violation.

Answer choice (A) is incorrect because K cannot substitute for any member of the planting committee; if K is a member without the presence of J, the third rule would be violated.

Answer choice (B) is the correct answer. Removing G from the trails committee and replacing it with K would not cause any violations.

Answer choice (C) is incorrect because from the last rule the two committees must have at least one member in common, and H is the only member in common.

Answer choice (D) is incorrect because K cannot substitute for any member of the planting committee; if K is a member without the presence of J, the third rule would be violated.

Answer choice (E) is incorrect because, again, K cannot substitute for any member of the planting committee; if K is a member without the presence of J, the third rule would be violated. In addition, M must appear on at least one of the committees and so removing M would violate the fourth rule.

Question #3: Local, Must Be True. The correct answer choice is (D)

The condition in the question stem establishes that the planting committee has exactly three members: G, H, and L. The trails committee can also have these three members, which maximizes the number of members in common. But, the trails committee must also have M as a member in order to satisfy the fourth rule, leading to the following setup for this question:

$$
\begin{array}{cc}
 & \text{M} \\
\text{L} & \text{L} \\
\text{H} & \text{H} \\
\text{G} & \text{G} \\
\hline
\text{P} & \text{T}
\end{array}
$$

Note that the setup for the trails committee contains the *minimum* number of members; there could be other members of the trails committee. The planting committee is complete.

Answer choices (A) and (B) are incorrect because the question stem stipulates that the two committees have "as many members in common as the conditions allow," which in this instance is three members.

Answer choice (C) is incorrect because if two committees have "as many members in common as the conditions allow," which in this instance is three members, then in order to conform to this answer (which stipulates an equal number of members on each committee), M would not be on a committee, causing a violation of the fourth rule.

Answer choice (D) is the correct answer, and is proven by the setup to the question.

Answer choice (E) is incorrect because this answer would force the trails committee to have just one member, a violation of the first rule.

Question #4: Local, Must Be True. The correct answer choice is (E)

The presence of K on each committee forces J to also to be a member of each committee per the third rule. This gives the planting committee a total of three members, closing it off to further members according to the condition in the question stem. From the fourth rule, then, M must be a member of the trails committee:

$$
\begin{array}{cc}
 & \text{M} \\
\text{J} & \text{J} \\
\text{L} & \text{L} \\
\text{K} & \text{K} \\
\hline
\text{P} & \text{T}
\end{array}
$$

As in question #3, the setup for the trails committee contains the *minimum* number of members; there could be other members of the trails committee. The planting committee is complete.

Answer choice (E) is proven correct by our analysis above. Note that answer choices (A) and (B) could never occur because each committee contains K, and F cannot be a member of the same committee as K per the second rule. Answer choices (C) and (D) could never occur because the question stem stipulates that the planting committee has exactly three members, and as discussed above those three members must be K, L, and J.

Question #5: Global, Must Be True, Maximum. The correct answer choice is (D)

The question asks you to maximize the number of members each committee has in common. There are seven volunteers in total, but we know that no committee can have seven members because from the second rule F and K cannot be on the same committee. Thus, answer choice (E) is immediately eliminated.

If we remove either F or K from a committee and thereby avoid violating the second rule, the two possible groupings of the remaining six volunteers would be:

G H J K L M (all but F)

or

F G H J L M (all but K)

Could either of these groups of six volunteers exist as the exact membership of *both* committees? Yes, both could—none of the other rules are negative grouping rules, and two committees of six identical members would fulfill all of the rules requiring membership. Thus, six members in common is possible, and answer choice (D) is correct.

This is a Grouping: Defined-Moving, Balanced game.

This game is difficult because there are three variable sets: the tourists, the guides, and the languages:

Tourists: H I K L M N ^{6}

Guides: V X Y Z ^{4}

Languages: F R S T ^{4}

Of these three groups, the guides are the most logical base because the tourists are assigned to the guides. Because the languages are combined with the guides, the most efficient way to handle the languages is to attach them as subscripts to each guide. This allows you to track which guide speaks which language, and what possible languages each tourist can speak:

Tourists: H I K L M N ^{6}

Guides: V X Y Z ^{4}

Languages: F R S T ^{4}

$$\overline{\quad}\ \ \overline{\quad}\ \ \overline{\quad}\ \ \overline{\quad}$$
$$V_F \quad X_{TS} \quad Y_{FT} \quad Z_{SR}$$

The first two rules assign specific tourists to specific guides:

Tourists: H I K L M N ^{6}

Guides: V X Y Z ^{4}

Languages: F R S T ^{4}

$$\begin{array}{cccc} & & I & \\ & & H & L \\ \overline{\quad} & \overline{\quad} & \overline{H} & \overline{\quad} \\ V_F & X_{TS} & Y_{FT} & Z_{SR} \end{array}$$

Note that only K, M, and N remain to be assigned at this point, although the languages spoken by each tourist are not fully established.

The final rule is conditional:

$$K_X \longrightarrow M_{V/Y}$$

Note that only V and Y speak French, and so if M is to speak French, he must be assigned to V or Y.

With six tourists assigned to the four guides, and each guide assigned at least one tourist, there are two numerical distributions involving tourists to guides (6 into 4):

$$2 - 2 - 1 - 1$$
or
$$3 - 1 - 1 - 1$$

Because Y already has the assignment of H and I, we can infer that Y always has either two or three tourists, depending on the distribution:

$$2_Y - 2 - 1 - 1$$
or
$$3_Y - 1_V - 1_X - 1_Z$$

These distributions help quickly answer questions such as #6, #7, and #8. Remember: *always* pay attention to the numbers in a game; you will be rewarded.

The prior information can be combined to produce the final setup for this game:

Tourists: H I K L M N [6]
                  *

Guides: V X Y Z [4]

Languages: F R S T [4]

$$K_X \longrightarrow M_{V/Y}$$

$$\begin{array}{cccc} & & \dfrac{\text{I}}{\dfrac{\text{H}}{\ }} & \\ \overline{\ } & \overline{\ } & \overline{Y_{FT}} & \dfrac{L}{Z_{SR}} \\ V_F & X_{TS} & & \end{array}$$

$$2_Y - 2 - 1 - 1$$
           or
$$3_Y - 1_V - 1_X - 1_Z$$

Question #6: Global, Could Be True, Except. The correct answer choice is (C)

For answer choice (C) to occur, there would have to be three tourists assigned to Z. However, as discussed above, in the 3-1-1-1 distribution, the 3 must be assigned to Y. Hence, answer choice (C) cannot occur and is thus correct.

Question #7: Global, Must Be True. The correct answer choice is (A)

Again, the distribution possibilities show that every guide except Y must be assigned fewer than three of the tourists, and hence answer choice (A) is correct.

Question #8: Global, Could Be True, Except. The correct answer choice is (B)

Answer choice (B) would create a distribution of 3-2-1-0, which is not possible as discussed previously. Hence, answer choice (B) is correct.

Question #9: Local, Must Be True. The correct answer choice is (E)

According to the condition in the question stem, K and L speak the same language. Since L speaks Spanish or Russian, K must speak Spanish or Russian, and it follows that K must be assigned to X or Z. Because every guide must be assigned at least one tourist, this leaves only M or N to be assigned to V. Since V speaks French, it follows that M or N must speak French, and thus answer choice (E) is correct.

Question #10: Local, Must Be True, Maximum. The correct answer choice is (B)

According to the condition in the question stem, N and L speak the same language. The correct answer is three, which can be achieved either of two ways:

1. Under the 3-1-1-1 distribution, all three tourists assigned to Y speak Turkish.

    Since L speaks Spanish or Russian, N must speak Spanish or Russian, and it follows that N must be assigned to X or Z. Since the question asks you to maximize the number of Turkish speakers, and Y speaks Turkish, we want to satisfy all conditions while at the same time maximizing Y. Thus, N should be assigned to X (where N will speak Spanish, the same as L), and then K or M can be assigned to V, thereby satisfying the "one tourist to each guide minimum." Thus, we can achieve a 3-1-1-1 distribution with Y being assigned three tourists. Answer choice (B) is therefore correct.

2. Under the 2-2-1-1 distribution, the two tourists assigned to Y speak Turkish, and the one tourist assigned to X speaks Turkish.

    If L and N are both assigned to Z, they can both speak Spanish or Russian. H and I are already assigned to Y, and they can speak Turkish. K and M are then be assigned to V and X, one to each, and the one assigned to X can speak Turkish. Thus, three tourists speak Turkish, and answer choice (B) is therefore correct.

Question #11: Local, Could Be True. The correct answer choice is (E)

The condition in the question stem sets up a 2-2-1-1 distribution:

$$
\begin{array}{cccc}
 & & I & \\
 & & \overline{H} & \overline{L} \\
\overline{} & \overline{} & & \\
V_F & X_{TS} & Y_{FT} & Z_{SR}
\end{array}
$$

As always, K, M, and N remain to be assigned, one of which will be assigned to V (and thus speak French) and the other two will be assigned to X (and speak Turkish or Spanish). As such, only answer choice (E) could be true, and is therefore correct.

Question #12: Local, Must Be True. The correct answer choice is (E)

As H and I are already assigned to Y, and must therefore speak French or Turkish, M and N must also speak French or Turkish. Therefore, M and N must together be assigned to V or X:

Possibility #1: M and N assigned to V (where both speak French)

$$
\begin{array}{cccc}
N & & I & \\
\overline{M} & & \overline{H} & \overline{L} \\
\overline{V_F} & \overline{X_{TS}} & \overline{Y_{FT}} & \overline{Z_{SR}} \\
 & K & &
\end{array}
$$

Possibility #2: M and N assigned to X (where both speak Turkish)

$$
\begin{array}{cccc}
 & N & I & \\
 & \overline{M} & \overline{H} & \overline{L} \\
\overline{K} & & & \\
V_F & X_{TS} & Y_{FT} & Z_{SR}
\end{array}
$$

In each instance, H, I, M, and N speak the same language (French in Possibility #1, Turkish in Possibility #2). As shown in Possibility #2, answer choice (E) could be true and is correct.

This is a Grouping: Defined-Moving, Balanced, Identify the Templates game.

This is a challenging game because it combines so many different elements: grouping, sequencing, and a two-value system. The initial scenario appears as follows:

K L M O P S ^{6}

$$\overline{} \quad \overline{}$$
$$\text{G} \qquad \text{T}$$

This is a two-value system, and all players must play one of two alternate sports (or values): golf or tennis. Thus, if a player is not playing golf, he or she *must* play tennis, and if a player is not playing tennis, he or she *must* play golf. When we examine the final three rules, the presence of this system will have significant effects.

The first two rules helpfully assign two of the people to specific sports:

K L M O P S ^{6}

$$\frac{\text{L}}{\text{G}} \quad \frac{\text{O}}{\text{T}}$$

The third rule establishes that L is the highest ranked golf player, which will be designated with a subscript "1." O's tennis ranking is not established:

K L M O P S ^{6}

$$\frac{\text{L}_1}{\text{G}} \quad \frac{\text{O}}{\text{T}}$$

The last three rules are conditional, and each addresses player sport assignments and rankings:

$$M_G \longrightarrow P_G + S_G \qquad (\text{Golf: } M > P > S)$$

$$M_T \longrightarrow S_T \qquad\qquad (\text{Tennis: } O > S > M)$$

$$P_T \longrightarrow K_T \qquad\qquad (\text{Tennis: } K > O > P)$$

Applying the two-value system to the contrapositive of each of these rules leads to several interesting statements:

Contrapositive of rule #4: P_T or S_T ⟶ M_T

Contrapositive of rule #5: S_G ⟶ M_G

Contrapositive of rule #6: K_G ⟶ P_G

Since when M plays golf then S must also play golf (rule #4), and when S plays golf then M must also play golf (contrapositive of rule #5), we can infer that S and M always play the same sport. Thus, S and M form a block within the game, and this is one of the critical inferences of the game.

Because this block must be placed into either the golf group or the tennis group, two basic templates apply in the game:

Template #1: SM play golf   Template #2: SM play tennis

K? $\dfrac{S}{P}$ KP? $\dfrac{M}{S}$
            $\overline{\underset{\overline{G}}{L_1}}$ $\overline{\underset{T}{O}}$ $\overline{\underset{\overline{G}}{L_1}}$ $\overline{\underset{T}{O}}$

        (golf: L > M > P > S)   (tennis: O > S > M)

In template #1, K is the only variable yet to be placed and there are no restrictions on its placement.

In template #2, K and P are the only variables yet to be placed. According to the rules, if K plays golf, then P plays golf, and if P plays tennis then K plays tennis.

These two basic templates provide a solid base with which to attack the questions. The biggest issue then becomes the ordering of the players within each sport.

Question #13: Global, Could Be True. The correct answer choice is (C)

Answer choice (A) is incorrect because, as discussed in the setup, M and S must always play the same sport.

Answer choice (B) is incorrect because from the last rule when P plays tennis then K plays tennis.

Answer choice (C) is the correct answer.

Answer choice (D) is incorrect because from the last rule when P plays tennis he must rank lower than O.

Answer choice (E) is incorrect because from the fifth rule when M and S play tennis, S must rank higher than M.

Question #14: Global, Could Be True, Except. The correct answer choice is (A)

This is a tricky question, and probably the hardest question of the game. The question is very difficult if you do not infer that S and M must play the same sport.

Because M and S must play the same sport, when S plays tennis, M must also play tennis. When M plays tennis, the fifth rule is enacted, and that rule indicates that when M plays tennis, S always ranks higher than M. Thus, because M and S would always play tennis together, S could never be the lowest-ranking tennis player, and answer choice (A) is correct.

Note that O (as referenced in answer choice (C)), could be the lowest-ranking tennis player if S and M (and therefore P) play golf.

Question #15: Global, Could Be True, List. The correct answer choice is (D)

The question asks for a viable list of tennis players, *in the correct ranking order*. From the first rule, O plays tennis, and so answer choice (E), which does not contain O, can be eliminated.

From the fifth rule, when M plays tennis, O must rank higher than S, who must rank higher than M (O > S > M). This information eliminates answer choice (C), as the players violate the ranking order.

From the last rule, when P plays tennis, K must play tennis. This eliminates answer choice (A), which does not include K. Further, from the same rule, when P plays tennis, K must rank higher than O, who must rank higher than P (K > O > P). This information eliminates answer choice (B), as the players violate the ranking order.

Thus, answer choice (D) is proven correct by process of elimination.

Question #16: Local, Must Be True, Except. The correct answer choice is (C)

If S plays golf, then Template #1 applies. As shown in template #1, K can play either golf or tennis, and thus K and M do not have to play the same sport, and answer choice (C) is correct.

Question #17: Local, Must Be True. The correct answer choice is (B)

If O is the highest-ranked tennis player, then, from the last rule P must play golf otherwise K would rank higher than O. From the second rule L plays golf, so P and L must play the same sport and answer choice (B) is correct.

Question #18: Local, Could Be True, Except. The correct answer choice is (C)

The condition in the question stem establishes that P and S do not play the same sport. Because M and S must play the same sport, we can infer than P and M do not play the same sport, and answer choice (C) cannot be true and is correct.

This is an Advanced Linear: Balanced game.

This game features three variable sets: the sequence of the songs (1-7), the seven song names, and the ballad/dance tune characterization of each song. As the sequence of the songs has an inherent order, that should be used as the base, and then the song names and ballad/dance type should be stacked above, creating an Advanced Linear scenario:

Ballads: F G H [3]
Dance: R S V X [4]

Ballad/Dance: ____ ____ ____ ____ ____ ____ ____

Song: ____ ____ ____ ____ ____ ____ ____
       1   2   3   4   5   6   7

The first rule enacts the Separation Principle™. The Separation Principle applies when variables involved in not-blocks are placed into a limited number of spaces. In this case, no dance tune can be played immediately after another dance tune, and thus each dance tune must be separated, in this case by the ballads. And, because there are four dance tunes and only three ballads, the dance tunes must be played 1-3-5-7, and the ballads must be played 2-4-6. Combining these two sequences, the songs must be played in this order: D-B-D-B-D-B-D.

Because understanding this idea is critical to success on this game (and any game that features the Separation Principle) let's explore this concept a bit more closely. For example, suppose two boys are placed into three chairs, with a rule that the two boys cannot sit next to one another. The minimum amount of room needed to comply with the not-block rule is:

$$\boxed{\text{B} \underline{\quad} \text{B}}$$

Since the minimum requirement happens to be the same as the number of available chairs (or spaces), the boys are forced into chairs 1 and 3:

$$\frac{\text{B}}{1} \quad \frac{\quad}{2} \quad \frac{\text{B}}{3}$$

Now suppose we expand the scenario to four boys being placed into seven chairs, still with the rule that no boys can sit next to each other. The minimum space required by the not-block rule is:

$$\boxed{B \ \underline{\quad} \ B \ \underline{\quad} \ B \ \underline{\quad} \ B}$$

Again, the minimum requirement happens to be identical to the number of available spaces, and the boys are forced into chairs 1, 3, 5, and 7:

B		B		B		B
1	2	3	4	5	6	7

This scenario is, of course, identical to the one in this game, with the boys representing the dance tunes. Thus, we can fill in the ballad/dance tune stack on our diagram, along with the corresponding Not Laws for each type (this is not necessary to do when you diagram the game, but we will show them here as it reveals how powerful this rule is):

Ballads: F G H [3]
Dance: R S V X [4]

$\boxed{D\!\!\!/D}$

Ballad/Dance:	D	B	D	B	D	B	D
Song:							
	1	2	3	4	5	6	7
	F̶	R̶	F̶	R̶	F̶	R̶	F̶
	G̶	S̶	G̶	S̶	G̶	S̶	G̶
	H̶	V̶	H̶	V̶	H̶	V̶	H̶
		X̶		X̶		X̶	

The second rule is a simple sequential rule:

$$H > V$$

This rule eliminates V from being played first, which can be shown as a Not Law. H cannot be played last, but that was already known from the prior rule. The Not Laws shown on the prior diagram will be removed; their placement above was for demonstration purposes only.

Ballads: F G H [3]
Dance: R S V X [4]

$\boxed{D\!\!\!/D}$

H > V

Ballad/Dance:	D	B	D	B	D	B	D
Song:							
	1	2	3	4	5	6	7
	V̶						

The third rule establishes that V and S are separated by exactly one song, creating a split-block:

$$\boxed{\text{S/V \_\_ V/S}}$$

S and V are both dance tunes, meaning they must be played 1-3, 3-5, or 5-7. However, V cannot be played first from the second rule, slightly limiting the options for this block. More on this in a moment.

The fourth rule establishes another block:

$$\boxed{\begin{array}{c} \text{F S} \\ \text{S F} \end{array}}$$

Again, no Not Laws can be drawn directly from this block because it rotates.

The final rule is an unusual conditional rule, which can be diagrammed as:

$$\boxed{\text{R/F}} \longrightarrow G > R$$

Thus, if F is not played immediately after R, then G must be played earlier than R. By the contrapositive, if G is not played earlier than R (and thus G is played later than R), then F must be played immediately after R.

At this point, all of the rules have been diagrammed. From an inference standpoint, there are some possible linkage inferences because V appears in the second and third rules, and S appears in the third and fourth rules. Let's examine those connections more closely:

In a very tricky inference, we can deduce that S cannot be played first. If S is played first, then from the fourth rule F must be played second, and from the third rule V must be played third. However, this creates a violation of the second rule stating that H must be played before V. Thus, an S Not Law can be placed under the first song.

In addition, because neither S nor V can be played first, we can infer that either R or X is played first.

Finally, because the SV split-block must now be played 3-5 or 5-7, we can determine that the fifth song is S or V.

These inferences can be shown on the final diagram, along with the fact that X is a random, which is shown on the diagram with an asterisk.

Ballads: F G H [3]
Dance: R S V X [4]

	Ballad/Dance:	D	B	D	B	D	B	D
D/D̸	Song:	R/X				S/V		
		1	2	3	4	5	6	7

H > V

S/V __ V/S

F S
S F

R̸/F̸ ———→ G > R

Question #19: Global, Must Be True, List. The correct answer choice is (E)

Answer choice (A): This answer choice violates the fourth rule.

Answer choice (B): This answer choice violates the last rule.

Answer choice (C): This answer choice violates the third rule.

Answer choice (D): This answer choice violates the second rule.

Answer choice (E): This is the correct answer choice.

Question #20: Global, Must Be True. The correct answer choice is (D)

From our discussion of the Separation Principle, we can determine that answer choice (D) is correct.

Question #21: Global, Could Be True. The correct answer choice is (A)

The fourth song in the sequence must be a ballad, and therefore the fourth song must be F, G, or H. Only answer choice (A) is a ballad, and so answer choice (A) is correct.

Note how easy this question is once you identify that the Separation Principle is present in this game.

Question #22: Global, Could Be True. The correct answer choice is (A)

The first song in the sequence must be a dance song, and of the dance songs only R or X can be the first song. Thus, answer choice (A) is correct.

Question #23: Local, Must Be True. The correct answer choice is (A)

The sixth song in the sequence is a ballad, and so the correct answer cannot be (C), (D), or (E).

If the third song in the sequence is S, then from the third rule V must be fifth (remember, V cannot be first due to the second rule). From the second rule H must be played earlier in the sequence than V, and so H cannot be sixth. Thus, answer choice (B) can be eliminated, and answer choice (A) is proven correct by process of elimination.

Question #24: Local, Could Be True. The correct answer choice is (D)

The fifth song in the sequence must be a dance tune, and so answer choices (A), (B), and (C) can be eliminated.

If you made the inference that S or V must be played fifth, then you would select answer choice (D) as correct. However, for demonstration purposes, let's proceed as if you did not make that inference during the setup of the game.

Without the inference that S or V must be played fifth, the difference between (D) and (E) is not immediately discernible, so make a hypothetical for one of the two answers in order to determine which is correct.

Answer choice (E) cannot work because it creates the following problematic hypothetical:

$$\frac{S}{1} \quad \frac{F}{2} \quad \frac{V}{3} \quad \frac{G/H}{4} \quad \frac{X}{5} \quad \frac{H/G}{6} \quad \frac{R}{7}$$

This hypothetical violates the second rule of the game. Accordingly, answer choice (D) is correct.

Again, note the massive impact that the ballad/dance tune separation has on this game. If you identified that inference, then question #20 is easily answered, and 12 of the next 20 answers (on questions #21-24) can be effortlessly eliminated. As is often the case in Logic Games, if you can draw one or two key inferences, the game becomes much more manageable. The lesson is clear: study these ideas and make sure that you can recognize them every time they appear.

POWERSCORE®

26

PREPTEST

SEPTEMBER 1998 LOGIC GAMES SETUPS

This is an Advanced Linear: Balanced game.

In this Balanced game there are three variable sets: the four majors, the four nonmajors, and the four laboratory benches. Since the laboratory benches have a sense of order, they should be selected as the base. A diagram similar to the following should be created:

Nonmajors: V W X Y [4]
Majors: F G H J [4]

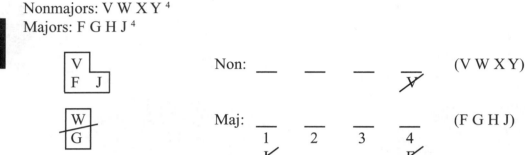

The second rule can be somewhat confusing. "Lower-numbered" means one number is less than another; for example, 2 is less than 3. Do not confuse the meaning of this rule with ranking-type games where 1 is ranked higher than 2, etc. (games like this *do* occur on the LSAT). When the rule discusses "lower-numbered" or "higher-numbered" elements, it means actual numerical value and 1 is always lower than 2, 2 is always lower than 3, 3 is always lower than 4, and so on. Thus the rule is properly diagrammed as an FJ block. Applying the basic principle of linkage to the second and third rules produces the VFJ super-block. This super block is clearly one of the keys to the game since it has a limited number of placement options.

In fact, the game is made somewhat easier by the fact that there are only two "active" formations to track: the VFJ super-block and the GW not-block. The first rule is essentially dead since it is incorporated into the main setup. With only two active rules to consider, you should always be looking to apply them as you attack the questions.

Note that due to the two blocks in this game, G must be assigned to a bench with X or Y, which is shown above in block form.

Question #1: Global, Could Be True, List. The correct answer choice is (C)

This question is rather irritating because of the layout chosen by the test makers. It would have been much easier had they separated the benches with some space instead of lining them up. However, as usual, apply the List question technique.

Answer choice (A) can be eliminated because bench 2 contains two majors, a violation of the rules (and, of course, bench 4 contains two nonmajors).

Answer choice (B) is incorrect because F and V are not assigned to the same bench, a violation of the third rule.

Answer choice (C) is the correct answer.

Answer choice (D) is incorrect because it violates the second rule.

Answer choice (E) is incorrect because G and W are assigned to the same bench, a violation of the fourth rule.

Question #2: Local, Must Be True. The correct answer choice is (B)

If V is assigned to bench 2, then, by application of the super-block, F must be assigned to bench 2, and J must be assigned to bench 3. Then, when W is assigned to bench 4, this affects G, who can no longer be assigned to bench 4, or benches 2 and 3 since they are taken by F and J. Therefore, G must be assigned to bench 1:

$$
\begin{array}{ccccc}
\text{Non:} & \underline{} & \underline{V} & \underline{} & \underline{W} \\
\text{Maj:} & \underline{G} & \underline{F} & \underline{J} & \underline{H} \\
& 1 & 2 & 3 & 4 \\
& & & & \cancel{G}
\end{array}
$$

Since G must be assigned to bench 1, answer choice (B) is proven correct. Additionally, when G is assigned to bench 1, H is forced into bench 4. The last two variables, X and Y, create a dual option that rotates between benches 1 and 3.

Question #3: Local, Must Be True. The correct answer choice is (A)

The question stem contains the unusual condition that majors G and H cannot be consecutive, creating a GH not-block. The key to the question is realizing that since G and H are majors, their placement will have a direct effect on the other two majors, F and J, who happen to be in a block configuration. Since the VFJ super-block can only be assigned to three positions—benches 1 and 2, benches 2 and 3, or benches 3 and 4—it makes sense to quickly examine the effect these placements have on G and H. If F and J are assigned to benches 1 and 2, this would force G and H to be consecutive, and if F and J are assigned to benches 3 and 4, this would also force G and H to be consecutive, so the VFJ super-block must be assigned to benches 2 and 3:

```
Non:  ___    V    ___    ___
```

```
Maj:  G/H    F     J    H/G
       1     2     3     4
```

Consequently answer choice (A) is proven correct.

Should you find yourself having difficulty with this question, it is interesting to note that the hypothetical produced in question #2 (where G and H were not consecutive) can be used to eliminate answer choices (B), (C), and (D), leaving just answer choices (A) and (E) in play. This a great example of how using applicable prior work can get you out of a difficult situation.

Question #4: Local, Could Be True. The correct answer choice is (D)

When H and Y are assigned to bench 1, the VFJ super block has only two options: benches 2 and 3 or benches 3 and 4. Since that much information could be tough to juggle in your mind, why not make two quick hypotheticals showing both possibilities?

Possibility #1: VFJ assigned to benches 2 and 3

```
Non:   Y     V     W     X
                          W̶
```

```
Maj:   H     F     J     G
       1     2     3     4
```

Possibility #2: VFJ assigned to benches 3 and 4

```
Non:   Y     X     V     W
             W̶
```

```
Maj:   H     G     F     J
       1     2     3     4
```

In both possibilities the key to assigning the remaining variables is in the GW not-block. In possibility #1, when G is assigned to bench 4, W cannot be assigned to bench 4 and must instead be assigned to bench 3. In possibility #2, when G is assigned to bench 2, W cannot be assigned to bench 2 and must instead be assigned to bench 4. Possibility #1 proves that answer choice (D) is correct.

Question #5: Local, Could Be True, Except. The correct answer choice is (E)

Since this is an Except question, four of the answer choices Could Be True, and the one correct answer choice Cannot Be True. The question states that G is assigned to bench 4, and X to bench 3. From the global conditions, we know that W cannot be at the same bench as G, so she cannot be at bench 4. From the super-block, we know that V cannot be at bench 4. Since X is at bench 3, he cannot be at bench 4. This leaves Y as the only possible non-major to sit at bench 4, so she must be seated there, and we now know that bench 4 seats only G and Y. Thus, answer choice (E) is correct because J cannot be assigned to the same bench as Y.

If you do not see the inference pattern above, remember that you can make hypotheticals based on the limited positions of the VFJ super-block. In this case, the VFJ super-block has only two possible assignments: benches 1 and 2 or benches 2 and 3:

Possibility #1: VFJ assigned to benches 1 and 2

Non: V   W   X   Y / W̶

Maj: F   J   H   G
       1   2   3   4

Possibility #2: VFJ assigned to benches 2 and 3

Non: W   V   X   Y / W̶

Maj: H   F   J   G
       1   2   3   4

Again, after the VFJ super-block is placed, the application of the GW not-block allows all the variables to be assigned. By comparing each answer choice against the two hypotheticals, you could still determine that answer choice (E) is correct.

Question #6: Local, Must Be True. The correct answer choice is (A)

The question stem sets up the following sequence:

$$W > J$$

Although this rule interrelates the majors and nonmajors, more importantly it ties in the VFJ super-block. If W is assigned to a lower-number bench than J, it follows that W is assigned to a lower-numbered bench than V and F as well:

Consequently, the VFJ super-block is again forced into only two possible positions: benches 2 and 3 or benches 3 and 4. As in the previous two questions, the best attack is to quickly make the two applicable hypotheticals:

Possibility #1: VFJ assigned to benches 2 and 3

Non:	W	V	X/Y	Y/X

Maj:	H	F	J	G
	1	2	3	4

Possibility #2: VFJ assigned to benches 3 and 4

Non:	W/	/W	V	___

Maj:	H/G	G/H	F	J
	1	2	3	4

When the above hypotheticals are applied to the answer choices, it is apparent that answer choice (A) is correct. Answer choices (B), (C), and (E) could be true but do not have to be true. Answer choice (D) can never be true.

Question #7: Global, Could Be True, List. The correct answer choice is (D)

This is an unusual List question because it addresses only two of the four benches, and those benches are not sequential. An application of the VFJ super-block and the WG not-block eliminates only answer choice (C) (V is with J instead of F). That is a frustrating result since in normal List questions the application of the rules knocks off several, if not all, of the incorrect answers. Since the rule application only eliminated one answer choice, the key must be in the two benches that are not listed, benches 1 and 3. And this general way of thinking is a powerful tool in many other games as well: if the variables that you are working with do not seem to solve the problem, consider the other variables yet to be placed, or as in this situation, the other spaces that are unlisted and yet to be considered.

Answer choice (A) can be eliminated because the assignment of the given variables leaves no room for the VFJ super-block. If you are uncertain of this, take a moment to make a hypothetical with G and X assigned to bench 2 and H and Y assigned to bench 4. It immediately becomes apparent that F and J will have to be assigned to benches 1 and 3, a violation of the rules.

Answer choices (B) and (E) can both be eliminated for the same reason: the assignment of the respective variables ultimately forces W and G together on one of the benches, a violation of the rules. For answer choice (B), W and G would be assigned together on bench 1, and for answer choice (E), W and G would be assigned together on bench 3.

Since answer choices (A), (B), (C), and (E) have been eliminated, answer choice (D) must be correct.

Overall, this is a tough question to face at the end of the game. Unless you focus on mentally placing the VFJ block and WG not-block into benches 1 and 3, none of the remaining answers appears incorrect. For many students the only solution is to try each answer choice and work out a hypothetical that proves or disproves the answer. Of course this is very time consuming. If you are having time difficulties with the games section, it might be useful to skip this question once you realize how long it is going to take. You could simply guess among answer choices (A), (B), (D), and (E).

Parts of this game—especially questions #4, #6, and #7—can take a considerable amount of work. But by focusing on the two active and powerful rules, you should be able to do this work at a fairly high rate of speed. Plus, the two rules are so potent that their application consistently yields the placement of other variables, and this tends to give most test takers a high degree of confidence with their answer choices. Even if it takes a little extra time to work with the hypotheticals, knowing you have definitively reached the correct answer is a worthwhile reward.

This is a Basic Linear: Balanced game.

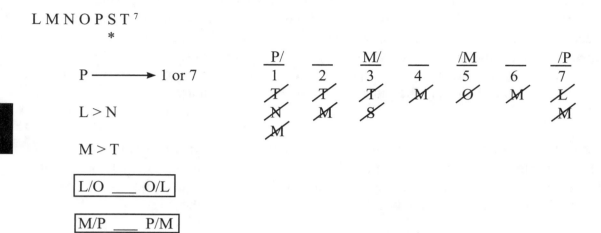

L M N O P S T⁷
　　　*

This game is perfectly Balanced, with 7 variables each filling one of 7 slots. An analysis of the variables reveals that S is a random, and this is indicated by the "*" notation. The first inference that can be made comes from the linkage of M and P. Since P must be delivered first or seventh, and exactly one package is delivered between P and M, it follows that M must be delivered third or fifth. Therefore, M cannot be delivered first, second, fourth, sixth or seventh. Since the earliest M can be delivered is third, that affects the delivery of T, and it can be inferred that T cannot be delivered first, second, or third.

Two other Not Laws also bear further examination. First, S cannot be delivered third because it sets off the following chain: M would be delivered fifth and P would be delivered seventh; in turn L and O have to be delivered second and fourth, with L being delivered second; this causes a problem since there is no room for N, which must be delivered after L. Second, O cannot be delivered fifth because of the problems it causes: M would have to be delivered third and P would have to be delivered first; since O and L must be separated by one package, L would have to be delivered seventh, and that is impossible since L must be delivered ahead of N.

Additionally, since the MP split-block is reduced to exactly two spacing options, one approach to setting up the game involves drawing out the two templates, which are labeled #1 and #2 below:

```
#1:  __   __   __   __   M    T    P
#2:  P    __   M    __   __   __   __
     1    2    3    4    5    6    7
```

In option #1, we can link rules and apply the M > T rule, which yields the inference that T must be sixth when P is seventh and M is fifth. At this point, it should be apparent that you will have to keep an eye on L, N, and O since they are linked together. In general, the variables L, M, and P are the most powerful since each appears in two separate rules.

Question #8: Global, Could Be True, List. The correct answer choice is (C)

This type of question is your best friend when it comes to Games questions. Always make sure to apply the proper List question technique. The best rule to start with is the rule that states that P is delivered either first or seventh. Applying this rule eliminates answer choice (B). Next apply the rule that states that L > N. This eliminates answer choice (D). Now apply the M > T rule, and you can eliminate answer choice (E). Of course, so far we have applied the rules in order, but that also happens to be the preferred order from a visual standpoint. The last two rules are less desirable, because they force you to deal with variables that can switch back and forth, and so they are harder to see within the answer choices. That is why we have held them until the end, not because they are the last two rules. The order in which you apply the rules to a List question should not be determined by the order of the presentation of the rules. Finally, by applying the LO split-block rule, we can eliminate answer choice (A), and it follows that answer choice (C) is correct by process of elimination. This question is very easy and you should have had no trouble with it.

Question #9: Global, Could Be True. The correct answer choice is (E)

This question can easily be attacked by applying the Not Laws deduced in the setup. The Not Laws eliminate answer choices (A), (B), (C), and (D), and thus answer choice (E) is correct.

Question #10: Local, Could Be True. The correct answer choice is (A)

This is a Local question, and thus you should reproduce a mini-setup next to the question. Since this is a Could Be True question, and we have two major templates produced by the MP split-block (one template with P delivered first, and another template with P delivered last), why not reproduce both templates, and show each with N delivered fourth, as follows:

	1	2	3	4	5	6	7
#1:	L/O	S	O/L	N	M	T	P
#2:	~~P~~	~~L~~	~~M~~	~~N~~			

Note that the "#1" and "#2" designations are for our discussion purposes only; during the game you would not want to waste the time writing these designations out. An analysis of the two templates reveals that template #2 can never occur, and thus, that template is crossed out. If N is delivered fourth, then L would have to be delivered second (remember, we are only discussing template #2), but if L is delivered second, then the LO split-block dictates that O must be delivered fourth, and O cannot be delivered fourth in template #2 because N is already delivered there. Thus, in checking the answers, we should only refer to template #1.

In template #1 the only uncertainty involves L and O, and because this is a Could Be True question, you should immediately look at any answer that references L or O. Answer choice (A) references L, and since (A) could be true, it is the correct answer. Answer choice (B) also references L, but (B) cannot be true, and so it is incorrect. Answer choice (D) references O, but (D) cannot be true, and so it is also incorrect. Remember, once you make your mini-diagram in a Could Be True question, attack the answers by ignoring the variables that are placed. Instead, you can gain time by looking only at those answers that contain unplaced or moving variables (such as L and O in this problem).

Question #11: Local, Must Be True. The correct answer choice is (C)

Again, this is a Local question, and we can make a mini-setup in the space next to the question. Start with the condition given in the question stem:

$$\frac{\quad}{1} \quad \frac{\quad}{2} \quad \frac{\quad}{3} \quad \frac{T}{4} \quad \frac{\quad}{5} \quad \frac{\quad}{6} \quad \frac{\quad}{7}$$

Since M > T, we can infer that P must be delivered first, and M must be delivered third:

$$\frac{P}{1} \quad \frac{\quad}{2} \quad \frac{M}{3} \quad \frac{T}{4} \quad \frac{\quad}{5} \quad \frac{\quad}{6} \quad \frac{\quad}{7}$$

And, since L and O are in a split-block, we can continue to add inferences:

$$\frac{P}{1} \quad \frac{\quad}{2} \quad \frac{M}{3} \quad \frac{T}{4} \quad \frac{L/O}{5} \quad \frac{\quad}{6} \quad \frac{O/L}{7}$$

However, since L > N, we can infer that L must be delivered fifth, N must be delivered sixth, and O must be delivered seventh. And since six variables have been placed, it follows that S must be delivered second:

$$\frac{P}{1} \quad \frac{S}{2} \quad \frac{M}{3} \quad \frac{T}{4} \quad \frac{L}{5} \quad \frac{N}{6} \quad \frac{O}{7}$$

Accordingly, the correct answer choice must be (C).

Note how S, the random variable, is the last variable to be placed. Randoms are typically the least powerful variables in a game because they are not involved in any rules and therefore when they are placed they do not affect other variables directly. Randoms do take up space and so they have some power, but a variable such as L or M is much more powerful in this game because each of those variables directly affects two variables. Consider this point a bit more closely by comparing variables S and L:

Variable Placed	Effect
S	1. Takes up the assigned space, thereby prohibiting other variables from occupying that space.
L	1. Takes up the assigned space, thereby prohibiting other variables from occupying that space. 2. Limits the placement of N. 3. Limits the placement of O.

Aside from the fact that L has fewer placement options due to its relationships with other variables, once L is placed it has powerful effects on those variables. S, on the other hand, has no direct effect on other variables. So, when solving a problem, S would not be one of the first variables you should look at. Instead, you should look to the power variables within a game to help you solve the questions. One side effect of the lesser power of randoms is that you often see them placed last within individual solutions. Since they are largely "free," they can often float until the end before they need to be placed.

Question #12: Local, Could Be True, Except. The correct answer choice is (A)

The inclusion of "Except" in the question stem turns the meaning of the question "upside down," and so the four incorrect answer choices have the characteristic of Could Be True, and the one correct answer choice has the characteristic of Cannot Be True. In this way, the question can be analyzed as a simple Cannot Be True question, and in doing so we have negated the confusing effect of the word "except."

By adding the "if" statement in the question stem to our original rules, we arrive at the following chain sequence:

$$O > M > T$$

Once again, this is a Local question and the best approach is to make a mini-diagram next to the question, again accounting for the two basic templates created by the MP split-block:

	1	2	3	4	5	6	7
#1:	(L,	N,	O,	S)	M	T	P
#2:	P	O	M	L	(N,	S,	T)

In the first template, P is delivered last and M is delivered fifth. According to the third rule, T must then be delivered sixth. The remaining four variables—L, N, O, and S—must then be delivered in the first four positions, in accordance with the remaining rules. The parentheses around L, N, O, and S are an efficient notation that indicates the enclosed variables are to be placed in the consecutive spaces in some order.

In the second template, P is delivered first and M is delivered third. According to the condition in the question stem, O must then be delivered second. And, because O is delivered second, L must then be delivered fourth as dictated by the fourth rule. The remaining three variables—N, S, and T—must then be delivered in the final three spaces in some order.

Since the question stem specifically focuses on the fifth package delivered, we can use our mini-diagram to quickly deduce which packages can be delivered fifth and then use that information to eliminate answer choices. From the first template it is proven that package M can be delivered fifth, and thus answer choice (B) can be eliminated. From the second template, it can be determined that packages N, S, and T can be delivered fifth, and this information eliminates answer choices (C), (D), and (E). At this point, the only remaining answer choice is (A), and it follows that response (A) is correct.

An alternate way to use the two templates is to say that the list of variables that could possibly appear fifth includes M from the first template, and N, S, and T from the second template. An examination of the answer choices reveals that only L in answer choice (A) does not appear as a possibility, and thus answer choice (A) must be correct.

This is a Grouping: Defined-Moving, Balanced, Numerical Distribution, Identify the Possibilities game.

The game scenario specifies that five people each participate in one of three activities. From a pure numbers standpoint, then, this game does not appear to be overly difficult at first. But, the multiple negative blocks and shifting setups produced by the two distributions combine to make this game more challenging than it might initially seem.

The information in the game scenario and the second rule combine to produce two Fixed Numerical Distributions:

M	S	R
2	2	1
1	2	2

Visually, these distributions produce two distinct setups:

	M	S	R
	2	2	1

	M	S	R
	1	2	2

Thus, every solution to the game will conform to one of the two setups above.

The first and third rules produce four not-blocks:

N/O   N/P   O/P   T/P

P is severely restricted by the not-blocks, and N and O also are limited significantly. More on these limitations in a moment.

The fourth rule is conditional, and can be diagrammed as:

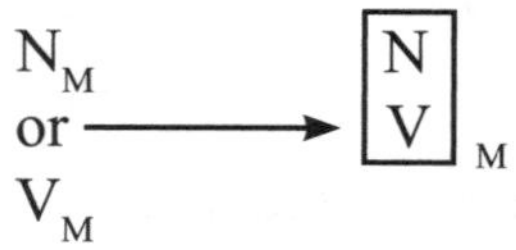

Thus, combining all of the prior information results in the following setup:

NOPTV[5]

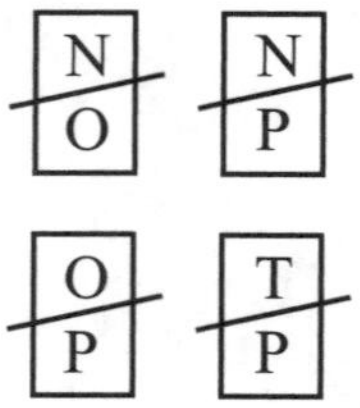

Two Fixed Numerical Distributions:

M	S	R
2	2	1
1	2	2

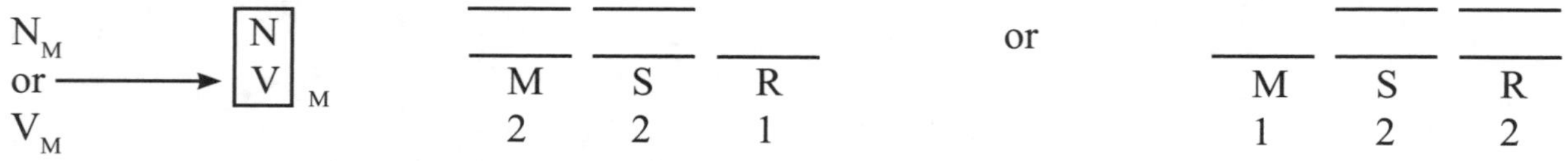

Let's look at the restrictions produced by the not-blocks a bit more closely. P is the most restricted variable, and thus the most important variable in the game. Because P cannot participate in the same activity as N, O, or T, if P participates in a group of 2, P must participate with V. Otherwise, P is alone. This restriction, in combination with the two numerical distributions, leads to the decision to Identify the Possibilities:

#1. P goes to a movie, 1-2-2 distribution:

	T/V	V/T
P	N/O	O/N
M	S	R

#2. P goes to a soccer game, 1-2-2 distribution:

	V	T
O	P	N
M	S	R

#3. P goes to a restaurant, 1-2-2 distribution:

	T	V
O	N	P
M	S	R

#4. P goes to a soccer game, 2-2-1 distribution:

T	V	
O	P	N
M	S	R

#5. P goes to a restaurant, 2-2-1 distribution, N and V go to a movie:

N	O	
V	T	P
M	S	R

#6. P goes to a restaurant, 2-2-1 distribution, N and V go to a soccer game:

O	N	
T	V	P
M	S	R

The last rule has a great impact on the six possibilities. For example, if P goes to a movie, P must go alone (otherwise the NV movie rule will apply because P would be with V). Thus, P can only go to a movie in the 1-2-2 distribution. In addition, in a number of the possibilities, when P and V participate in the same activity, then N cannot go to a movie and must instead go to a soccer game or a restaurant.

Note also that possibility #1 has some further restrictions based on the placement of the two dual-options.

Question #13: Global, Could Be True, List. The correct answer choice is (D)

Answer choice (A) is incorrect because O and P cannot participate in the same activity.

Answer choice (B) is incorrect because P and T cannot participate in the same activity.

Answer choice (C) is incorrect because V goes to a movie, then N must go to a movie.

Answer choice (D) is the correct answer.

Answer choice (E) is incorrect because exactly two persons go to a soccer game, not three.

Question #14: Local, Could Be True, Except. The correct answer choice is (D)

This is a difficult question. Possibilities #1, #2, #4, and #6 all feature the possibility of V going to a soccer game. However, in possibility #1, if V goes to the soccer game, T cannot go to the soccer game, because that would leave N, O, and P to fill the remaining three spaces (in a 1-2 distribution), and because of the negative grouping rules they cannot do that. Thus, if V goes to a soccer game, T can never go to a soccer game, and answer choice (D) is correct.

Question #15: Global, Could Be True. The correct answer choice is (B)

Answer choices (A) and (C) violate the last rule.

Answer choice (B) is the correct answer.

Answer choice (D) violates the first rule.

Answer choice (E) violates the third rule.

Question #16: Global, Could Be True, Except, FTT. The correct answer choice is (B)

As shown in possibilities #5 and #6, P can attend a restaurant alone, and thus answer choice (B) is correct.

Question #17: Local, Could Be True, List. The correct answer choice is (E)

If N goes to a soccer game, then from the last rule V cannot go to a movie, and answer choice (B) and (D) can be eliminated. Possibility #1 shows that when N goes to a soccer game, P can go to a movie, and, as only answer choice (E) contains P, answer choice (E) is correct.

Question #18: Local, Must Be True, Suspension. The correct answer choice is (C)

The question stem specifies a 1-3-1 fixed distribution. As P can only pair with at most one other person (V), P cannot go to a soccer game, and thus P is the correct answer. Answer choice (C) is therefore correct.

This is a Grouping: Defined-Fixed, Unbalanced: Overloaded, Identify the Possibilities game.

The initial scenario establishes that two lawmakers and two scientists will form a four-person panel in each of two years:

Law: F G H I ^{4}
Sci: V Y Z ^{3}

The game is complicated by the presence of a chairperson on each panel, in part because the chairperson can come from either group and because there is a relationship between the chairperson of each panel.

The basic representation of the three rules is fairly straightforward:

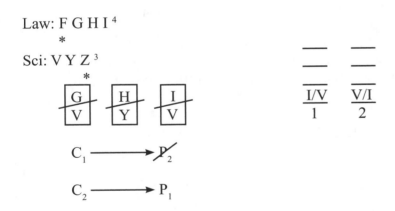

Since V appears in two of the three rules, V is a logical starting point for our analysis. If V serves on a panel, then neither G nor I can serve on that panel. Because exactly two lawmakers must serve on the panel, it follows that if V serves on a panel, then F and H must serve on that panel:

$$V \longrightarrow F, H$$

Of course, if H serves on the panel, then Y cannot serve on that panel:

$$V \longrightarrow F, H \longrightarrow \cancel{Y}$$

Because Y cannot serve on the panel, and there must be two scientists on the panel, Z must serve on the panel:

$$V \longrightarrow F, H \longrightarrow \cancel{Y} \longrightarrow Z$$

This is an extremely important inference because of the rule that states that each year either I or V serves on the panel. When V serves on the panel, the other three members are *always* F, H, and Z. This relationship pattern also reveals an underlying inference of the game: because V and Y can never serve together, we can infer that Z must always serve on the panel. This inference is tested in question #24.

The panel membership is also restricted when I serves on the panel. Because I cannot serve with V, and there must be two scientists, when I serves on the panel we can infer that Y and Z serve on the panel. And, because H and Y cannot serve together, the remaining member is F or G. Thus, when I serves on the panel, the remaining members are *always* Y, Z, and F or G.

Because I or V, but not both, serve on each panel, there are *initially* four possible combinations:

      1. I serves on the panel in the first year, V serves on the panel in the second year.
      2. V serves on the panel in the first year, I serves on the panel in the second year.
      3. I serves on the panel in both years.
      4. V serves on the panel in both years.

However, if V serves on both panels, the rule stating that the chairperson in the first year cannot serve on the panel in the second year is violated. Thus, there are only three combinations of I and V, and the game should be attacked by showing the three templates that Identify the Possibilities:

Template #1			Template #2			Template #3	
Z	H		H	Z		Z	Z
Y	F		F	Y		Y	Y
F/G	Z		Z	F/G		F/G	G/F
I	V		V	I		I	I
1	2		1	2		1	2

The three templates above encompass the only six solutions of the game. The only remaining consideration is the chairperson of each panel. For example, the third template will work only if F or G is the chairperson in the first year. If F is the chairperson in the first year, then G must serve on the panel in the second year, and I, Y, or Z is the chairperson in the second year; If G is the chairperson in the first year, then F must serve on the panel in the second year, and I, Y, or Z is the chairperson in the second year.

Overall, the game is very difficult. The Identify the Possibilities technique makes the game manageable, but it requires some insight in order to apply the technique.

Question #19: Global, Could Be True, List. The correct answer choice is (B)

Answer choice (A) is incorrect because G and V do not serve together.

Answer choice (B) is the correct answer choice.

Answer choice (C) is incorrect because I and V do not serve together.

Answer choice (D) is incorrect because each panel must have exactly two lawmakers and two scientists.

Answer choice (E) is incorrect because H and Y do not serve together.

Question #20: Local, Must Be True. The correct answer choice is (D)

If V serves as the chairperson the first year then I cannot serve that year, and V cannot serve the next year. Since you must always have either V or I, I must serve the second year. Also, since you must have two scientists and V cannot serve the second year, then Y and Z must serve the second year. Hence, answer choice (D) is correct: I and Y must both serve the second year.

Question #21: Local, Could Be True. The correct answer choice is (A)

If H serves the first year as chairperson then H cannot serve the second year. Also, Y cannot serve the first year since Y and H cannot serve together, so the other two scientists—V and Z—must both serve the first year. Since G and I cannot serve with V, then F must be the other lawmaker in year 1. So the people serving in the first year are H (chair), V, Z, and F. That means that only V, Z, or F could be the chairperson the second year, so answer choice (A) is proven correct.

Question #22: Local, Could Be True, Except. The correct answer choice is (A)

If F serves in a given year then you can only have one more lawmaker. If G is the other lawmaker then V cannot serve that year, and since you must have either I or V, then I would have to serve. However that would result in three lawmakers—F, G, and I—which violates the conditions of the scenario. Thus, G cannot serve in the same year as F, and answer choice (A) is correct.

Question #23: Local, Could Be True. The correct answer choice is (A)

The chairperson in the second year must be someone who can serve in the second year and someone who had to serve in the first year, so to answer this question think about who must serve in year 1 and who could still serve in year 2. If I serves as the chairperson in the first year, then I cannot serve in the second year. Further, since V cannot serve with I, then V cannot serve the first year and thus cannot be the chairperson in the second year (eliminating answer choice (D)). However V must serve the second year since I is absent, so G cannot serve in the second year (eliminating answer choice (B)). If Z is absent in the first year then the other two scientists—Y and Z—must be present, meaning that H cannot serve the first year (eliminating answer choice (C)). Finally, since G and I both cannot serve in the second year, then the other two lawmakers—F and H—must both serve in year 2, meaning that Y cannot serve in the second year (eliminating answer choice (E)). That leaves only answer choice (A), the correct answer choice.

Question #24: Global, Must Be True. The correct answer choice is (E)

From the templates you can see that the only answer choice that is consistent for each template is that Z must serve in the second year: answer choice (E).

POWERSCORE®

PrepTest

27

DECEMBER 1998 LOGIC GAMES SETUPS

This is a Basic Linear: Balanced game.

Initially, this game looks promising, as exactly seven investors view a building site on seven consecutive days, creating a Basic Linear scenario:

F G H J K L M ^{7}

1	2	3	4	5	6	7

The first rule creates an F split-option on days 3 and 5:

F G H J K L M ^{7}

		F/		/F		
1	2	3	4	5	6	7

Although F cannot then view the site on any other day, we will not show those Not Laws as that information is redundant.

The second rule creates L Not Laws on days 4 and 6:

F G H J K L M ^{7}

		F/		/F		
1	2	3	4	5	6	7
			Ł		Ł	

The third and fourth rules are conditional:

Rule 3: $J_1 \longrightarrow H_2$

Rule 4: $K_4 \longrightarrow L_5$

More on these rules later in the discussion.

The final rule creates an HG block:

$$\boxed{\text{H G}}$$

From this rule we can infer that G never views the site on day 1, and H never views the site on day 7:

F G H J K L M ^{7}

$$\boxed{\text{H G}}$$

		F/		/F		
—	—	—	—	—	—	—
1	2	3	4	5	6	7
G̸			J̸		J̸	H̸

At this point, the rules have been represented, so the next step is to check for any linkage between rules.

One link occurs between the third and the fifth rules, which are connected by H. When J views the site on day 1, then from the third rule H must view the site on day 2, and from the fifth rule G must view the site on day 3:

$$J_1 \longrightarrow H_2 G_3$$

However, when G views the site on day 3, this affects the first rule, forcing F to view the site on day 5:

$$J_1 \longrightarrow H_2 G_3 \longrightarrow F_5$$

At this point, four variables have been placed, and only three days remain available for viewing the site—day 4, day 6, and day 7. Because L cannot view the site on day 4 or day 6 from the second rule, L must then view the site on day 7. At this point, only two variables remain unplaced—K and M—and only two days are open—day 4 and day 6. The placement of L in turn affects K. Via the contrapositive of the fourth rule, when L does not view the site on day 5, K cannot view the site on day 4. Thus, K cannot view the site on day 4, and must view the site on day 6. M, the random, is the last remaining unplaced investor, and M must view the site on day 4. Therefore, when J views the site on day 1, only one solution to the game exists:

$$J_1 \longrightarrow \text{Only one possibility: J-H-G-M-F-K-L}$$

Another link occurs between the second and fourth rules, which are connected by L. However, as the fourth rule places L, no further inference can be drawn from that relationship. The fourth rule also links to the first rule through day 5. When K views the site on day 4, then L must view the site on day 5. Via the first rule, this affects F, who must then view the site on day 3:

$$K_4 \longrightarrow \begin{array}{c} L_5 \\ + \\ F_3 \end{array}$$

The placement of F on day 3 further affects the third rule. If F views the site on day 3, then J cannot view the site on day 1 because there would not be sufficient room to allow H to view the site on day 2 and then G to view the site on day 3. Hence, when F views the site on day 3, J cannot view the site on day 1:

$$K_4 \longrightarrow \begin{array}{c} L_5 \\ + \\ F_3 \longrightarrow \cancel{J_1} \end{array}$$

When all of the information is combined, including the fact that M is a random, the following diagram results:

F G H J K L M^7
          *

| HG |

$K_4 \longrightarrow \begin{array}{c} L_5 \\ + \\ F_3 \longrightarrow \cancel{J_1} \end{array}$

		F/		/F		
1	2	3	4	5	6	7
$\cancel{G}$			$\cancel{L}$		$\cancel{L}$	$\cancel{H}$

$J_1 \longrightarrow$ Only one possibility: J-H-G-M-F-K-L

Question #1: Global, Could Be True, List. The correct answer choice is (E)

Answer choice (A) is incorrect because from the second rule L cannot view the site on day 6.

Answer choice (B) is incorrect because from the first rule F must view the site on day 3 or day 5, and thus cannot view the site on day 4.

Answer choice (C) is incorrect because from the last rule G must view the site on the day after H views the site.

Answer choice (D) is incorrect because from the fourth rule, when K views the site on day 4, L must view the site on day 5.

Answer choice (E) is the correct answer.

Question #2: Local, Must Be True. The correct answer choice is (E)

If J views the site on day 1, then as discussed during the setup the following diagram results:

$$
\frac{J}{1} \quad \frac{H}{2} \quad \frac{G}{3} \quad \frac{M}{4} \quad \frac{F}{5} \quad \frac{K}{6} \quad \frac{L}{7}
$$

Accordingly, answer choice (E) is correct. Note that M was our last variable placed in our discussion, and not surprisingly, it is the correct answer here.

Question #3: Local, Must Be True. The correct answer choice is (C)

The question stem indicates that K views the site on day 4, and that a JM block is in effect. If K views the site on day 4, then from the fourth rule L views the site on day 5:

$$
\frac{}{1} \quad \frac{}{2} \quad \frac{}{3} \quad \frac{K}{4} \quad \frac{L}{5} \quad \frac{}{6} \quad \frac{}{7}
$$

Because L views the site on day 5, from the first rule F views the site on day 3:

$$
\frac{}{1} \quad \frac{}{2} \quad \frac{F}{3} \quad \frac{K}{4} \quad \frac{L}{5} \quad \frac{}{6} \quad \frac{}{7}
$$

At this point, the JM block is still unplaced, as is the HG block from the fifth rule. However, the JM block cannot be placed on days 1 and 2 because that would violate the third rule. Thus, the JM block must be placed on days 6 and 7, leaving the HG block on days 1 and 2:

$$
\frac{H}{1} \quad \frac{G}{2} \quad \frac{F}{3} \quad \frac{K}{4} \quad \frac{L}{5} \quad \frac{J}{6} \quad \frac{M}{7}
$$

Accordingly, answer choice (C) is correct.

Question #4: Local, Could Be True, List. The correct answer choice is (C)

If H views the site on day 2, then from the final rule G must view the site on day 3, and from the first rule F must view the site on day 5:

	H	G		F		
1	2	3	4	5	6	7

From the contrapositive of the fourth rule, if L does not view the site on day 5, then K cannot view the site on day 4. This information eliminates answer choices (A), (D), and (E).

Only answer choices (B) and (C) remain in contention, and the difference between the two is J. As J can view the site on day 4, answer choice (C) is correct.

Question #5: Local, Must Be True. The correct answer choice is (D)

The question stem creates two blocks: a KHG block and a LF block. Because of the actions of the first and second rules, the LF block must be placed on days 2 and 3:

	L	F				
1	2	3	4	5	6	7

The KHG block must then be placed on days 4-5-6 or 5-6-7. But, the fourth rule prohibits K from being placed on day 4, and so the KHG block must be placed on days 5, 6, and 7:

	L	F		K	H	G
1	2	3	4	5	6	7

Due to the third rule, J cannot view the site on day 1, and must view the site on day 4, leaving M to view the site on day 1:

M	L	F	J	K	H	G
1	2	3	4	5	6	7

Accordingly, answer choice (D) is correct.

Question #6: Local, Could Be True. The correct answer choice is (B)

The conditions imposed by the question stem produce the following sequence:

$$\boxed{HG}$$
$$\text{- - - > F}$$
$$L$$

Because there are three investors ahead of F, and therefore the earliest day F could view the site is day 4, from the first rule we can infer that F must view the site on day 5.

Because H, G, and L must all view the site before F, an inference can made that either H, G, or L *must* view the site on day 3. If H, G, and L do not view the site on day 3, then H and G view the site on day 1 and 2, respectively, and the only remaining day for L to view the site is day 4, a violation of the second rule. Among the answer choices, only answer choice (B) lists one of the three investors H, G, or L, and therefore answer choice (B) is correct.

This is a Grouping/Linear Combination, Numerical Distribution, Identify the Templates game.

This is the most difficult game on this test. While the five numbered habitats are fairly innocuous, the game quickly ramps up the difficulty by overloading the habitats with seven reptiles divided into two types, and then adding a male/female component to each reptile. Simply put, there is a lot of information to track in this game.

The initial scenario for the game appears as follows:

S S S S ^{4}
L L L ^{3}

F F F F F ^{5}
M M ^{2}

$$\underline{\quad}\ \underline{\quad}\ \underline{\quad}\ \underline{\quad}\ \underline{\quad}$$
$$\ \ 1\quad 2\quad 3\quad 4\quad 5$$

Normally, when variables such as the lizards and snakes have an additional characteristic—in this case, the male/female designation—this would be shown with an extra stack for the additional characteristic. This game presents problems, however, because of the Overloaded aspect: there are seven reptiles for the five habitats, meaning some habitats will house more than one reptile, and it is also possible that a habitat may house no reptiles. Thus, instead of separating the reptiles and their corresponding sexes into different stacks, we will combine them. For example, a male lizard will be designated as ML, and a female snake will be designated as FS.

In further examining the relationship between the snakes and lizards, and the males and females, the Overlap Principle comes into play:

Because there are only two males, the maximum number of male snakes (MS) is two. Yet, there are four snakes total, so, at a minimum, there must be at least two female snakes (FS).

The same reasoning can be applied to the relationship of the males and the lizards. Because there are only two males, the maximum number of male lizards (ML) is two. Yet, there are three lizards total, so, at a minimum, there must be at least one female lizard (FL).

The inference that there are at least two FS and at least one FL can be used to identify the three possible male/female and snake/lizard combinations for the seven reptiles:

Possibility #1:   FS, FS, FL   FS, FS, ML, ML

Possibility #2:   FS, FS, FL   FL, FL, MS, MS

Possibility #3:   FS, FS, FL   FS, FL, MS, ML

When the first rule is considered, along with the fact that no minimum number of reptiles for each habitat is established in the game, two possible Numerical Distributions of reptiles-to-habitats result:

Distribution #1:   2-2-1-1-1

Distribution #2:   2-2-2-1-0

More on these distributions in a moment.

The second rule establishes that snakes and lizards cannot be housed in the same habitat:

This rule can be combined with the distributions to determine how the reptiles are distributed in the habitats (this does not account for the sex of the reptiles):

2-2-1-1-1 Distribution, Possibility #1:

Under this scenario, the two habitats housing two reptiles contain two snakes each:

2	2	1	1	1
S	S	L	L	L
S	S			

2-2-1-1-1 Distribution, Possibility #2:

Under this scenario, the two habitats housing two reptiles contain two snakes and two lizards:

2	2	1	1	1
S	L	S	S	L
S	L			

2-2-2-1-0 Distribution:

There is only one distribution of reptiles under this scenario:

2	2	2	1	0
S	S	L	L	
S	S	L		

The astonishing thing is that we've reached this level of inference-making from just two rules.

The third and final rule establishes that a female snake cannot be housed next to a male lizard:

$$\boxed{FS \,/\, ML}$$

$$\boxed{ML \,/\, FS}$$

Combined, the information results in the following diagram:

S S S S ^{4}
L L L ^{3}

	1	2	3	4	5

F F F F F ^{5}
M M ^{2} Numerical Distributions

At Lst 2 FS   #1:   2   2   1   1   1
At Lst 1 FL   S   S   L   L   L
                                  S   S

$\boxed{\dfrac{L}{S}\!\!\!/}$

                     #2:   or

$\boxed{FS \,/\, ML}$ S   L   S   S   L
                                           S   L

$\boxed{ML \,/\, FS}$

                     #3:   2   2   2   1   0
                                  S   S   L   L
                                  S   S   L

Male/Female Reptile Possibility #1:   FS, FS, FL   FS, FS, ML, ML

Male/Female Reptile Possibility #2:   FS, FS, FL   FL, FL, MS, MS

Male/Female Reptile Possibility #3:   FS, FS, FL   FS, FL, MS, ML

Even with all of the information above (and perhaps because of it), this remains a very difficult game.

Question #7: Global, Could Be True, List. The correct answer choice is (B)

Answer choice (A) is incorrect, because habitat 4 cannot house both a snake and a lizard, according to the second rule.

Answer choice (B) is correct answer choice.

Answer choice (C) is incorrect because it violates the third rule.

Answer choice (D) is incorrect because it violates the first rule (habitat 5 houses three reptiles).

Answer choice (E) is incorrect because it violates the third rule.

Question #8: Local, Could Be True. The correct answer choice is (E)

The new condition provided by this question stem creates the following diagram:

With the two males placed and one female placed, there are four females remaining to be placed, exactly one of which is a lizard:

Remaining to be placed: FL, FS, FS, FS

Answer choice (A) cannot be true because two reptiles housed in habitat 3 would have to include at least one female snake, who is prohibited from being housed near the male lizards in habitat 4 due to the third rule.

Answer choice (B) is incorrect for the same reason answer choice (A) is incorrect. Housing two reptiles in habitat 5 would mean at least one female snake would have to be housed in habitat 5, which cannot occur due to the third rule.

Answer choice (C) is incorrect because if habitat 1 were to house a female lizard, that would leave only habitats 3 and 5 for the female snakes, both of which have to avoid being next to habitat 4 in accordance with the third rule.

Answer choice (D) is prohibited by the second rule of the game.

Answer choice (E) is the correct answer choice.

Question #9: Global, Must Be True. The correct answer choice is (C)

In this game there are an odd number of lizards, and none of them can be housed with a snake. Since no more than two lizards can be housed together, at least one lizard must be alone in a habitat, and so choice (C) is the correct answer choice.

Question #10: Global, Cannot Be True, List. The correct answer choice is (D)

Answer choice (D) is the correct answer choice. This scenario would leave three lizards and three snakes unplaced. Because lizards and snakes cannot live together, there is no allowable placement for these reptiles in habitats 3, 4, and 5.

The remaining four answer choices could be true and are thus incorrect.

Question #11: Local, Not Necessarily True, FTT. The correct answer choice is (A)

Because this question asks for the answer choice which could be false (i.e., is not necessarily true), the answer choices which must be true can be ruled out.

The initial condition in the question stem produces the following setup:

$$\underline{} \quad \underline{} \quad \overset{\text{E}}{\underline{}} \quad \underline{} \quad \underline{}$$
$$\quad 1 \qquad 2 \qquad 3 \qquad 4 \qquad 5$$

This condition leaves only habitats 1, 2, 4, and 5, available for the remaining reptiles. the second condition in the question stem establishes that no snake is housed in a habitat next to another snake. Because there are four snakes, and the maximum number of reptiles housed in a habitat is two, we can infer that two of the snakes are housed in habitat 1 or 2, and the other two snakes are housed in habitat 4 or 5:

$$\overset{\text{S}/}{\underset{\text{S}/}{\underline{}}} \quad \underline{} \quad \overset{\text{E}}{\underline{}} \quad \overset{\text{S}/}{\underset{\text{S}/}{\underline{}}} \quad \underline{}$$
$$\quad 1 \qquad 2 \qquad 3 \qquad 4 \qquad 5$$

Answer choice (A) is the correct answer choice because none of the rules would preclude the placement of snakes in one or both remaining odd numbered habitats.

Answer choice (B) is incorrect, because it must be true that there are no male lizards—if there were any, they would be forced to be next to female snakes, which is not allowed.

Answer choices (C) and (E) must be true based on the numerical distributions in this game. There are four snakes and three lizards, with only four habitats to hold them. Since lizards and snakes cannot be housed together, the distribution must be as follows: two habitats with two snakes each, one with two lizards, and one with one lizard.

Answer choice (D) is incorrect, because if the snakes must be separated, each snake habitat must be next to a lizard habitat. Therefore it must be the case that the lizard habitats are not next to one another. Since it must be true, answer choice (D) is incorrect.

Question #12: Local, Cannot Be True. The correct answer choice is (C)

If there are four female snakes, remaining are the three lizards, two of which must be male (the other of which must obviously be female). Because each of the three lizards has a habitat to itself, the distribution must be 2-2-1-1-1:

2	2	1	1	1
FS	FS	FL	ML	ML
FS	FS			

If each lizard is housed in its own habitat, then two of the habitats must house male lizards. Since all of the female snakes must be separated from the male lizards, the setup must push the male lizards to one side of the five habitats or the other—that is, they must be housed in either 1 and 2 respectively, or 4 and 5 respectively with the female lizard in 3 to act as a separator, and the snakes on the other side of the female lizard (any other setup would place female snakes next to male lizards, which is prohibited). Since there must be a female lizard in habitat 3, answer choice (C) is correct.

Note that in this question, if you were guessing, you still should choose answer choice (C). Why? Because the game itself and this question stem do not assign reptiles to any specific habitat, all of the cages are roughly "equal" in terms of their initial value. Answer choices (A) and (E) both refer to habitats at the ends of the line, making them roughly the same type of answer. According to the Uniqueness Theory of Answer choices, then, these two answers must be incorrect. The same analysis can be applied to answer choices (B) and (D), eliminating both of those answers. The one answer choice that has truly unique characteristics—habitat 3—is thus the correct answer.

This a Grouping: Defined-Moving, Balanced, Numerical Distribution, Identify the Possibilities game.

The information in the game scenario establishes that there are seven film buffs attending a showing of three movies. Each film buff sees exactly one film. The first rule establishes two fixed distributions:

	Fellini	Hitchcock	Kurosawa
Fixed Distribution #1:	1	2	4
Fixed Distribution #2:	2	4	1

Although virtually all games contain a Numerical Distribution, the distribution becomes a significant element if there are multiple distributions, or if the single distribution is unusual. This game is one of the former.

The two fixed distributions create two distinctly different scenarios. And since each scenario requires a different analysis, the best strategy is to create two templates, one for the 1-2-4 distribution, and another for the 2-4-1 distribution:

The rules can now be considered:

G I L M R V Y [7]

Of course, the rules impact each template:

Let us analyze the two diagrams. The fifth rule states that L sees the Hitchcock film. In the 1-2-4 this leaves one open space at Fellini, one open space at Hitchcock, and four open spaces at Kurosawa. But the third rule states that V and Y see the same film as each other, so in the 1-2-4 it can be inferred that V and Y see the Kurosawa film. In the 2-4-1 we can infer that V and Y see either the Fellini film or the Hitchcock film, but at the moment it is uncertain which one. G cannot see the Hitchcock film, and so Not Laws are drawn on both templates, and G split-options are placed on Fellini and Kurosawa.

The two negative grouping rules help fill in both templates. In the 1-2-4, there are four remaining spaces for G, R, I, and M: one space at Fellini, one space at Hitchcock, and two spaces at Kurosawa. Since G and R, as well as I and M, cannot see the same film, it can be inferred that one of G and R must see the Kurosawa film, and one of I and M must see the Kurosawa film.

In the 2-4-1 there are still six open spaces: two at Fellini, three at Hitchcock, and one at Kurosawa. Of the six remaining variables, two—V and Y—must see the same film. If V and Y see the Fellini film, then there would be three open spaces at Hitchcock and one open space at Kurosawa. Since G and R cannot see the same film, one must see Hitchcock and the other must see Kurosawa. That leaves two spaces at Hitchcock for I and M. But wait, I and M cannot see the same film, and so this scenario causes a violation of the rules. Essentially, when V and Y see the Fellini film, there are not enough remaining spaces to properly separate G, R, I, and M. It can therefore be inferred that in the 2-4-1 distribution V and Y see the Hitchcock film.

In both templates there are still several possible solutions, and in the next section we will discuss Identifying the Templates further. For now, it is important to be aware of G, R, I, and M since they are the only variables still in play.

Question #13: Global, Could Be True, List. The correct answer choice is (D)

Answer choice (A) is incorrect because G cannot see the Hitchcock film. Answer choices (B) and (C) are incorrect because V can never see the Fellini film. Answer choice (E) is incorrect because M and R could never see the Hitchcock film at the same time. Answer choice (D) is therefore correct. Overall a much more difficult List question than usual, but easy if you have used the distributions to identify the two templates!

Question #14: Global, Could Be True. The correct answer choice is (A)

Remember, convert false into true when you analyze the question stem. Answer choices (D) and (E) are eliminated by applying the distributions. Answer choice (C) is eliminated by applying the templates, and answer choice (B) is eliminated by the fifth rule that states that L sees the Hitchcock film. Answer choice (A) is correct.

Question #15: Global, Could Be True, List. The correct answer choice is (C)

The first step is to apply the VY block rule because, if one does not see Hitchcock, it is certain the other will not see Hitchcock either. Answer choice (D) contains Y, but not V, and is incorrect.

The second step is to consider the Numerical Distributions. In the 1-2-4 distribution, two film buffs see the Hitchcock film, and five film buffs do not see the Hitchcock film. In the 2-4-1 distribution, four film buffs see the Hitchcock film, and three film buffs do not see the Hitchcock film. Thus, since this question stem asks for a complete and accurate list of the film buffs who do NOT see the Hitchcock film, the correct answer choice must contain either three or five film buffs. Since answer choices (A) and (B) contain only two film buffs, they can both be rejected without further analysis.

Since answer choices (C), (D), and (E) each contain three film buffs, it is apparent that they are each generated by the 2-4-1 distribution. In the 2-4-1 distribution we have already ascertained that L, V, and Y each see the Hitchcock film, and so any answer choice that contains L, V, or Y will be incorrect. This again eliminates answer choice (D) and also eliminates answer choice (E). Answer choice (C) is therefore correct.

Question #16: Local, Must Be True. The correct answer choice is (A)

According to the information in the question stem, the film buffs are in the 2-4-1 fixed distribution. Accordingly, answer choice (A) is correct. Again, note the usefulness of the distributions and templates.

Question #17: Global, Must Be True. The correct answer choice is (E)

This question can be solved by either referring to the templates or by using the rules.

If the rules are used, the final two rules indicate that G and L must see different films. Consequently, answer choice (E) is proven correct.

If the templates are used, nothing in either template suggests that answer choice (A), (B), or (C) is correct. In answer choice (D), I, L, and V could all see the Hitchcock film under the 2-4-1. The templates ultimately show that answer choice (E) must be true.

Question #18: Local, Could Be True. The correct answer choice is (B)

V and G can only see the same film under the 1-2-4 template:

```
         1      2      4

                      I/M
                      ___
                       G
                      ___
                       Y
                      ___
                L      V
         ___   ___    ___
          F     H      K
```

The final two spaces are filled by R and the remainder of I/M. Accordingly, answer choice (B) is correct.

Question #19: Global, Cannot Be True, List. The correct answer choice is (E)

Since each answer choice contains two film buffs, the 2-4-1 fixed distribution applies. Under that distribution we have already inferred that L, V, and Y each see the Hitchcock film, and so any answer choice that contains L, V, or Y would be correct (remember, this is an Except question). Answer choice (E) contains V and Y and is therefore correct.

This game provides an excellent example of how the test makers use Numerical Distributions. Many of the questions force you to examine the templates created by each distribution and then attack the answer choices. The distributions are central to understanding this game: if you do not identify the distributions, the questions in this game cannot be answered correctly.

This is a Basic Linear: Balanced, Identify the Possibilities game.

The initial scenario for the game is relatively simple:

G G O O P P [6]

1	2	3	4	5	6

The first rule establishes that no car can be the same color as the car next to it:

The C designation in the not-block above stands for "color." The CC not-block is a shorthand notation that indicates that no two cars of similar color can be adjacent, as required by the first rule. This representation saves the time of writing out PP, GG, and OO not-blocks. Note that in a game with only six spaces, and only three colors, this is a significantly more inhibiting rule than might at first be suspected.

The second rule is relatively easy to represent:

G G O O P P [6]

1	2	3	4	P/ 5	/P 6

The third and fourth rules are represented as Not Laws under the diagram. Of course, since there are only three colors, removing one color from the options leaves only two color possibilities for that car:

G G O O P P [6]

G/P 1	2	3	O/P 4	P/ 5	/P 6

The rule that states that car 1 cannot be orange leads to the important Not Law that car 2 cannot be green. Let's examine why this is the case, using the two scenarios for car 1:

1. <u>Car 1 is green</u>. If car 1 is green, then car 2 cannot be green.

2. <u>Car 1 is purple</u>. When car 1 is purple, then car 5 or 6 is also purple, and we can deduce that car 4 is orange. When car 4 is orange, then car 3 cannot be orange (from the rule that no two adjacent cars can be of the same color) and car 3 cannot be purple (because the two purple cars are either 1-5 or 1-6). Consequently, car 3 must be green. And, when car 3 is green, car 2 cannot be green.

Thus, regardless of whether Car 1 is purple or green, Car 2 can never be green:

27

G G O O P P [6]

G/P			O/P	P/	/P
1	2	3	4	5	6
∅	∅		∅		

An analysis of the diagram above reveals that the placement of the two P cars is restricted. Combining that with the first rule, the best approach is to attack the game by Identifying the Possibilities:

Three possibilities with P in 6:

#1:	G	O	G	P	O	P
#2:	P	O	G	O	G	P
#3:	G	O	P	O	G	P

Three possibilities with P in 5:

#4:	G	P	G	O	P	O
#5:	P	O	G	O	P	G
#6:	G	O	P	O	P	G

Thus, there are only six solutions to the game. With these solutions in hand, the questions are easy to attack.

Question #20: Global, Cannot Be True. The correct answer choice is (A)

An examination of the six solutions reveals that cars 1 and 4 can never be the same color. Thus, answer choice (A) is correct.

Question #21: Local, Must Be True. The correct answer choice is (B)

If car 2 and car 4 are the same color, then only possibilities #2, #3, #5, or #6 apply. In each of those scenarios, car 2 is orange, and so answer choice (B) is correct.

Question #22: Local, Must Be True. The correct answer choice is (E)

If car 4 is purple, then only possibility #1 applies. In possibility #1, car 6 is purple, and so answer choice (E) is correct.

Question #23: Global, Cannot Be True, FTT. The correct answer choice is (A)

As discussed in the game setup, car 2 can never be green, and thus answer choice (A) is correct.

Question #24: Global, Must Be True, List, Suspension. The correct answer choice is (D)

This suspension question forces you to re-create your setup to the game. The substitution of another green car for one of the orange cars allows for only three solutions to the game:

Possibility #1:	G	P	G	O	P	G
Possibility #2:	G	P	G	O	G	P
Possibility #3:	G	O	G	P	G	P
	1	2	3	4	5	6

As cars 1 and 3 must be green, answer choice (D) is correct.

POWERSCORE®

PREPTEST
28

JUNE 1999 LOGIC GAMES SETUPS

This is a Basic Linear: Balanced, Identify the Templates game.

This is a nearly ideal game to start any LSAT. The scenario assigns six racehorses to six positions, creating a Basic Linear setup:

K L M N O P⁶

$$\underline{\hspace{1cm}} \quad \underline{\hspace{1cm}} \quad \underline{\hspace{1cm}} \quad \underline{\hspace{1cm}} \quad \underline{\hspace{1cm}} \quad \underline{\hspace{1cm}}$$
$$\;\;1 \qquad 2 \qquad 3 \qquad 4 \qquad 5 \qquad 6$$

The first rule creates a KL split-block:

$$\boxed{\text{K/L} \;\underline{\hspace{1cm}}\; \text{L/K}}$$

Because this block rotates, no Not Laws can be drawn initially.

The second rule establishes a KN not-block:

$$\boxed{\begin{array}{c}\text{K}\!\!\!\not{}\text{N}\\ \text{N}\!\!\!\not{}\text{K}\end{array}}$$

While this block could be written out in K/N N/K not-block form, writing both prohibited blocks is easier to see visually. This explains the difference in the representations between the first rule and the second rule (not taking into account the negative in the second rule, of course). Again, no Not Laws can be drawn from this rule because it rotates.

The third rule establishes a basic sequence:

$$M > N$$

This produces two Not Laws:

K L M N O P⁶

$$\underline{\hspace{1cm}} \quad \underline{\hspace{1cm}} \quad \underline{\hspace{1cm}} \quad \underline{\hspace{1cm}} \quad \underline{\hspace{1cm}} \quad \underline{\hspace{1cm}}$$
$$\;\;1 \qquad 2 \qquad 3 \qquad 4 \qquad 5 \qquad 6$$
$$\;\;\not{N} \qquad\qquad\qquad\qquad\qquad\qquad \not{M}$$

The final rules places P:

K L M N O P ^{6}

		P			
1	2	3	4	5	6
N̸					M̸

Because P is assigned to position 3, the KL split-block must be assigned to positions 2 and 4, or positions 4 and 6. Thus, L and K can never be assigned to position 1, and L and K can never be assigned to position 5. Additionally, K or L must always be assigned to position 4:

K L M N O P ^{6}

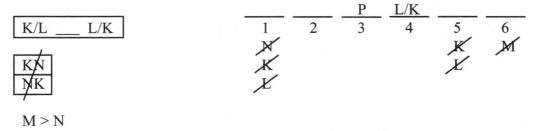

		P	L/K		
1	2	3	4	5	6
N̸				K̸	M̸
K̸				L̸	
L̸					

M > N

In examining the diagram, two other positions are also somewhat restricted. Position 1 cannot be N, K, or L, or P (who is assigned to position 3), so position 1 must be M or O. Position 5 cannot be K, L, or P, so position 5 must be M, N, or O. Adding in that O is a random results in the final diagram:

K L M N O P ^{6}

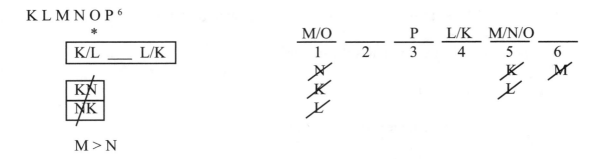

M/O		P	L/K	M/N/O	
1	2	3	4	5	6
N̸				K̸	M̸
K̸				L̸	
L̸					

M > N

The K and L split-block is clearly the most restricted element in the game. This restriction, in combination with the remaining rules and limitations, suggests Identifying the Templates:

Template #1:	M	N	P	K/L	O	L/K
Template #2:	M/O	K/L	P	L/K	(O/M, N)	
	1	2	3	4	5	6

If the two templates are confusing, another option would be to Identify the Possibilities:

L in 4, K in 6:

Possibility #1:	M	N	P	L	O	K		(1 solution)
	1	2	3	4	5	6		

K in 4, L in 6:

Possibility #2:	M	N	P	K	O	L		(1 solution)
	1	2	3	4	5	6		

K in 2, L in 4:

Possibility #3:	M/O	K	P	L	O/M	N		(2 solutions)
Possibility #4:	M	K	P	L	N	O		(1 solution)
	1	2	3	4	5	6		

L in 2, K in 4:

Possibility #5:	M/O	L	P	K	O/M	N		(2 solutions)
	1	2	3	4	5	6		

There are seven total possibilities. By using either the Templates or Possibilities approach, the game becomes relatively easy.

Question #1: Global, Could Be True, List. The correct answer choice is (B)

Answer choice (A) is incorrect because it violates the first rule.

Answer choice (B) is the correct answer choice.

Answer choice (C) is incorrect because it violates the fourth rule.

Answer choice (D) is incorrect because it violates the third rule.

Answer choice (E) is incorrect because it violates the second rule.

Question #2: Global, Could Be True, List. The correct answer choice is (E)

As shown in the two templates, K can be assigned to positions 2, 4, or 6. Hence, answer choice (E) is the correct answer.

Question #3: Global, Cannot Be True. The correct answer choice is (E)

As shown in the templates, O can never be assigned to position 2, and thus answer choice (E) is correct.

This inference is extremely difficult to deduce, in part because O is a random. However, this is one of the benefits of the Templates/Possibilities approach: even if you miss an inference in your initial diagram, the Templates/Possibilities will show all the solutions, and so missing the inference becomes a non-issue.

Question #4: Global, Must Be True. The correct answer choice is (B)

As discussed during the setup, either K or L must be assigned to position 4, and so answer choice (B) is correct.

Question #5: Global, Cannot Be True. The correct answer choice is (C)

As shown in the templates, M and O can never be assigned to adjacent positions, and thus answer choice (C) is correct.

Note that answer choices (A) and (B) can both be eliminated by applying the hypothetical created by question #1.

Interestingly, all five questions in this game are Global. Normally, when that occurs, that is a sign that the game can be solved (or should be solved) with Templates or Possibilities.

This is a Grouping: Defined-Fixed, Unbalanced: Underfunded game.

The size of each group is fixed, and thus the game is Defined-Fixed. And, there are fewer variables (four researchers) than spaces available (eight language slots) and so the game can be classified as Unbalanced: Underfunded. The complete classification is Defined-Fixed, Unbalanced: Underfunded.

When you create the setup, it is critical that the correct base be selected. There are two choices: the four researchers or the four languages. Since the researchers can learn one to three languages but it is uncertain exactly how many languages each researcher learns, the researchers seem a poor choice for the base. On the other hand, the number of researchers learning each language is clearly specified in the rules and as such the languages are the best choice for the base:

$$\begin{array}{cccc} & & & \underline{\quad} \\ & \underline{\quad} & \underline{\quad} & \underline{\quad} \\ \underline{\quad} & \underline{\quad} & \underline{\quad} & \underline{\quad} \\ R & S & T & Y \end{array}$$

The distribution of researchers to languages is thus fixed at 1-2-2-3, and since there are only four researchers, it is clear that at least two researchers will have to learn more than one language (in fact, at least two researchers and at most three researchers will learn more than one language). Using the above base, we can set up the game as follows:

G H L P [4]

$$3 \geq R \geq 1$$

From the rules it is clear that G is a power variable, since G appears in both the non-numerical rules. The key inference involving G comes with Yoruba. Because Yoruba must be learned by exactly three researchers, and G cannot be selected with either L or P, it can be inferred that G cannot learn Yoruba, and the other three researchers must learn Yoruba. Additionally, since when G is selected H must also be selected, it is not possible for G to learn Rundi, as there is no room for H to be selected. Consequently, since G must learn at least one language, G (in the form of a GH block) must learn either Swahili or Tigrinya or both. From this inference it follows that neither L nor P can learn *both* Swahili and Tigrinya.

Question #6: Global, Could Be True. The correct answer choice is (D)

Since it has already been established that H, L, and P must each learn Yoruba, answer choices (A), (C), and (E) can be eliminated. Since we have established that G must at a minimum learn either Swahili or Tigrinya, and it is therefore known that neither L or P can learn *both* Swahili and

Tigrinya, answer choice (B) (as well as answer choices (A) and (E)) can be eliminated. Thus, answer choice (D) is proven correct by process of elimination.

Question #7: Local, Must Be True. The correct answer choice is (B)

Keeping in mind the inference that L cannot learn both Swahili and Tigrinya, when L learns three languages, we can Hurdle the Uncertainty to determine those languages must be Yoruba, Rundi, and either Swahili or Tigrinya. Consequently, answer choice (B) is correct.

Question #8: Global, Cannot Be True. The correct answer choice is (C)

Since G cannot learn Rundi, it can automatically be deduced that either H, L, or P must learn Rundi. Since H, L, and P each learn Yoruba, it must be the case that the researcher who learns Rundi also learns Yoruba. It follows that answer choice (C) cannot occur and is therefore correct.

Question #9: Global, Cannot Be True, List. The correct answer choice is (B)

In a question requiring a complete list of researchers who cannot learn both Swahili and Yoruba, the first researcher to check is G, because G cannot learn Yoruba. Unfortunately, G does not appear in any answer choice. The next step is to consider the implications of learning both Swahili and Yoruba. Since H, L, and P each learn Yoruba, it seems likely that any combination of two of those three researchers could learn Swahili. Since answer choice (C), (D), and (E) each list two of H, L, or P, it seems unlikely that any of those answer choices are correct. Thus, let us focus on answer choices (A) and (B). Answer choice (A) lists just H, but under the following hypothetical H can be the only researcher who learns both Swahili and Yoruba:

$$
\begin{array}{cccc}
 & \dfrac{H}{G} & & \dfrac{\dfrac{P}{L}}{H} \\
\overline{R} & \overline{S} & \overline{T} & \overline{Y}
\end{array}
$$

Let us check answer choice (B):

$$
\begin{array}{cccc}
 & & & \dfrac{\dfrac{P}{L}}{H} \\
 & \overline{P} & & \\
\overline{R} & \overline{S} & \overline{T} & \overline{Y}
\end{array}
$$

In this instance the second researcher who learns Swahili cannot be H or L since neither is listed in the answer choice. G also cannot learn Swahili since there is no room for H. Thus P cannot be the only person who learns both Swahili and Yoruba and answer choice (B) is correct.

With answer choice (B), when P is the sole researcher learning both Swahili and Yoruba, a problem arises because a second researcher is needed to learn Swahili, but according to the conditions of the question it must be one who does not also learn Yoruba. In this situation, who could you choose? You cannot choose L or H because they already learn Yoruba. That leaves only G, but if you select G for the second researcher slot in Swahili, you immediately violate the last rule because there is no room for H (and H could not be chosen anyway because that would be a violation as H learns Yoruba already). Hence, answer choice (B) cannot be a complete and accurate list of researchers who learn both Swahili and Yoruba.

When you are trying to figure out a situation such as the one above, always remember to try to work out the solution by creating hypotheticals. In this instance you can create viable hypotheticals for (A), (C), (D), and (E), but you cannot create one for (B).

Question #10: Local, Could Be True. The correct answer choice is (A)

If G learns exactly two languages, those languages must be Swahili and Tigrinya:

Since H will then learn Swahili, Tigrinya, and Yoruba, due to the rule that limits a researcher to learning at most three languages, it follows that H cannot learn Rundi, and only P or L can learn Rundi. Answer choice (A) is thus correct.

Question #11: Global, Must Be True. The correct answer choice is (B)

The correct answer choice, answer choice (B), partially tests your understanding of the conditional relationship between G and H. According to the rule, every time G learns a language then H must also learn that same language. Consequently, H must learn at least as many languages as G. And since H also learns Yoruba and G cannot learn Yoruba, it must be that G learns fewer languages than H. The hypothetical from question #10 can be used to disprove answer choices (A), (C), and (D).

Question #12: Local, Must Be True. The correct answer choice is (D)

Since it has already been established that H learns Yoruba, the second language that H learns must come in conjunction with G, since G must learn at least one language. Since G must learn either Swahili or Tigrinya, it follows that H cannot learn Rundi and thus answer choice (D) is correct.

Like game #1, one possible approach to this game is to create three basic templates based on the position of G: G learning Swahili only, G learning Tigrinya only, and G learning both Swahili and Tigrinya. As with the first game, we believe this approach is less efficient than using the diagram and inferences described earlier, in part because the templates still leave a large number of possibilities unrealized.

This is an Advanced Linear: Balanced game.

The initial scenario establishes that six buildings will be inspected over three days, one each morning and one each afternoon. This creates an Advanced Linear setup:

H: G J L ³
R: S V Z ³

PM: ___   ___   ___

AM: ___   ___   ___
      M   Tu   W

As always, you can place the morning row on the top or bottom of your diagram—the decision is entirely up to your personal preference.

The first rule establishes that no hotels are inspected on Wednesday, creating G, J, and L Not Laws on each Wednesday time period:

H: G J L ³
R: S V Z ³

PM: ___   ___   ___
                        G̸
                        J̸
                        L̸

AM: ___   ___   ___
      M   Tu   W
                        G̸
                        J̸
                        L̸

The first rule, which states that hotels are not inspected on Wednesday, leads to an interesting set of inferences. First, the three hotels—G, J, and L—must be inspected on Monday and Tuesday, and thus only S, V, and Z are available for inspection on Wednesday. Therefore, exactly two of S, V, and Z are inspected on Wednesday, and G, J, L and the remainder of S, V, and Z are inspected on Monday and Tuesday:

H: G J L ^{3}
R: S V Z ^{3}

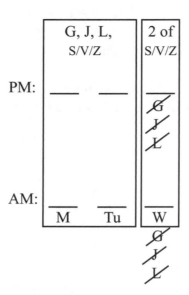

The second rule establishes a sequence, namely that G > J. As with all Advanced Linear games, this does not preclude the variables from being inspected on the same day; G must only be inspected at an earlier time than J. This leads to two Not Laws, one for J on Monday morning, and one for G on Tuesday afternoon (because neither G nor J can be inspected on Wednesday):

H: G J L ^{3}
R: S V Z ^{3}

G > J

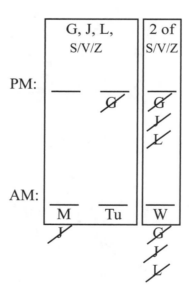

Because G, J, and L must be inspected on Monday and Tuesday, further inferences can be drawn about the relationship of G and J. Because G must be inspected at some time before J, G cannot be inspected on Tuesday afternoon, and if G is inspected on Tuesday morning, then J must be inspected on Tuesday afternoon. Conversely, if J is inspected on Monday afternoon, G must be inspected on Monday morning. These relationships are tested repeatedly in the game.

The third rule establishes a vertical, rotating not-block:

The fourth and final rule establishes that if Z is inspected in the morning, then L is inspected in the morning:

$$Z_{AM} \longrightarrow L_{AM}$$

Because every building must be inspected in the morning or afternoon, this game contains a two-value system. When a two-value system is present, *always* consider the contrapositive of any conditional rule. In this case, when L is not inspected in the morning, it must be inspected in the afternoon, and when Z is not inspected in the morning, it must be inspected in the afternoon, resulting in the following translated contrapositive:

$$L_{PM} \longrightarrow Z_{PM}$$

Note that Z and L are not always in the same time slot: L can be inspected in the morning while Z can be inspected in the afternoon.

Adding in that V is a random, we arrive at the final diagram for the game:

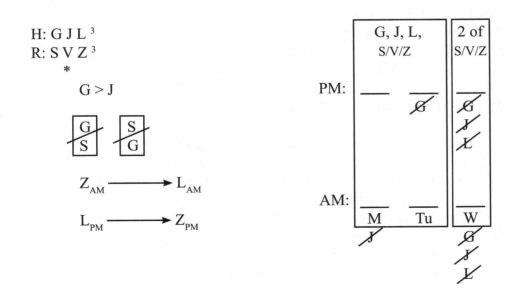

Question #13: Global, Could Be True, List. The correct answer choice is (D)

Answer choice (A) is incorrect because it violates the third rule.

Answer choice (B) is incorrect because it violates the first rule.

Answer choice (C) is incorrect because it violates the second rule.

Answer choice (D) is the correct answer.

Answer choice (E) is incorrect because it violates the fourth rule.

Question #14: Global, Could Be True, List. The correct answer choice is (C)

This is a very difficult List question.

Answer choice (A) is incorrect because it violates the fourth rule.

Answer choice (B) is incorrect because it would violate the second rule: as discussed during the setup, because of that rule, J can never be inspected on Monday morning.

Answer choice (C) is the correct answer. This is not a violation of the fourth rule: as discussed during the setup, L can be inspected in the morning and Z can be inspected in the afternoon.

Answer choice (D) is incorrect because it cause a violation of the third rule: when J is inspected on Tuesday morning, then from the second rule G must be inspected on Monday, but with S already inspected on Monday, a violation ensues.

Answer choice (E) is incorrect because it ultimately causes a violation of the third rule. With S, L, and Z as the morning inspections, only V remains to be inspected on Wednesday afternoon. At that point, 4 of the 6 buildings have been inspected, leaving only G and J. Due to the second rule, G must then be inspected on Monday afternoon, and J on Tuesday afternoon. But, that results in G and S both being inspected on Monday, a violation of the third rule.

Question #15: Global, Must Be True. The correct answer choice is (B)

The question asks for a pair of buildings that can be inspected together only on Monday. G is a natural building choice for analysis since G is so restricted: G cannot be inspected on Wednesday, and if G is inspected on Tuesday, it would have to be inspected on Tuesday morning, forcing J to be inspected on Tuesday afternoon. Thus, on Tuesday, G must be inspected with J. Of course, at this point, you may be asking, "Why are we talking about Tuesday? Isn't this question about Monday?" Yes, it is, but consider G's situation at this juncture: it cannot be inspected on Wednesday, and on Tuesday it must be paired with J. Thus, if G is to be paired with any other variable besides J, that pairing *must* occur on Monday. Therefore, any answer choice pairing G and L, V, or Z would be correct. Only answer choice (B) makes such a pairing.

Note that the hypothetical created in question #13 answer choice (D) can be used to eliminate answer choice (A) from contention.

Question #16. Local, Could Be True, List. The correct answer choice is (B)

If G is inspected on Tuesday, then G must be inspected on Tuesday morning and J must be inspected on Tuesday afternoon.

```
PM  ___    J    ___
AM  ___    G    ___
     M     Tu    W
```

Accordingly, answer choices (C) and (D) can immediately be eliminated because neither reflects the fact that J must be inspected on Tuesday afternoon.

Answer choice (A) can be eliminated because, from the contrapositive of the fourth rule, if L is inspected in the afternoon, then Z must also be inspected in the afternoon.

Answer choice (E) can be eliminated for two reasons: first, from the first rule L cannot be inspected on Wednesday, and, second, from the contrapositive of the fourth rule, if L is inspected in the afternoon, then Z must also be inspected in the afternoon.

Thus, answer choice (B) is the correct answer.

Question #17: Local, Must Be True. The correct answer choice is (D)

If S is inspected on Monday morning, G cannot be inspected on Monday afternoon. Because G cannot be inspected on Wednesday due to the first rule, G must then be inspected on Tuesday. From the second rule, G cannot be inspected on Tuesday afternoon, and thus G must be inspected on Tuesday morning, and J must be inspected on Tuesday afternoon:

```
PM  ___    J    ___
AM   S     G    ___
     M     Tu    W
```

Only L, V, and Z remain to be placed, and as L cannot be inspected on Wednesday due to the first rule, L must be inspected on Monday afternoon:

```
PM   L     J    ___
AM   S     G    ___
     M     Tu    W
```

From the contrapositive of the fourth rule, Z must then be inspected on Wednesday afternoon, leaving V to be inspected on Wednesday morning:

$$
\begin{array}{c c c c}
\text{PM} & \underline{L} & \underline{J} & \underline{Z} \\
\text{AM} & \underline{S} & \underline{G} & \underline{V} \\
& M & Tu & W
\end{array}
$$

Accordingly, answer choice (D) is correct. Note that the correct answer trades on V, which is the very last variable placed.

Question #18: Local, Must Be True. The correct answer choice is (D)

If G is inspected on Monday morning and Z is inspected on Wednesday morning, then from the fourth rule L must be inspected on Tuesday morning:

$$
\begin{array}{c c c c}
\text{PM} & \underline{} & \underline{} & \underline{} \\
\text{AM} & \underline{G} & \underline{L} & \underline{Z} \\
& M & Tu & W
\end{array}
$$

From the third rule, S cannot be inspected on Monday afternoon, and so S must be inspected on Tuesday afternoon or Wednesday afternoon:

$$
\begin{array}{c c c c}
\text{PM} & \underline{} & \underline{S/} & \underline{/S} \\
\text{AM} & \underline{G} & \underline{L} & \underline{Z} \\
& M & Tu & W
\end{array}
$$

Accordingly, answer choice (D) is correct.

Overall, this is a very tough game, and most students felt it was the most difficult game on this exam.

This is an Advanced Linear: Balanced, Identify the Possibilities game.

This game features four variables sets: the three bills, R, S, and T; the three votes of Fu; the three votes of Gianola; and the three votes of Herstein. Notably, either the three bills or the three voters could be chosen as the base. Operationally they will produce no difference. We have chosen to use the three bills as the base and create stacks for Fu, Gianola, and Herstein:

H:	__	__	__
G:	__	__	__
F:	__	__	__
	R	S	T

The choice of voting for (F) or against (A) will fill each space. Applying the rules creates the following basic diagram:

H:	__	__	A	(at lst 1F)
G:	A	__	__	(at lst 1F)
F:	F	A	__	
	R	S	T	
	(2F,	(1F,	(1F,	
	1A)	2A)	2A)	

The rules provide a considerable amount of specific information: the number of "for" and "against" votes each bill receives; the minimum "for" and "against" votes by Fu, Gianola, and Herstein; and certain votes each voter casts. From the supplied information several inferences can be made. First, since there are two votes for the Recreation bill and one vote against the Recreation bill, and it has already been established that Fu votes for the bill and Gianola votes against the bill, it can be inferred that Herstein votes for the Recreation bill:

H:	F	__	A
G:	A		__
F:	F	A	__
	R	S	T

Furthermore, since only two voting options exist (F or A), dual-options can be placed on the remaining open spaces:

H:	F	F/A	A
G:	A	F/A	F/A
F:	F	A	F/A
	R	S	T

Of course, further information about some of the dual-options would affect the choices in other dual-options. Regardless, examining the diagram makes it apparent that the voting possibilities are limited. Since there are only four uncertain spaces and even those have restrictions, why not try to show every possibility? Although there are several ways to identify each possibility, the first step we will take is to look at the votes for the school bill. If Gianola votes against the school bill and Herstein votes for the school bill, only one solution exists:

$$
\begin{array}{cccc}
\text{H:} & \dfrac{F}{} & \dfrac{F}{} & \dfrac{A}{} \\[4pt]
\text{G:} & \dfrac{A}{} & \dfrac{A}{} & \dfrac{F}{} \\[4pt]
\text{F:} & \dfrac{F}{R} & \dfrac{A}{S} & \dfrac{A}{T}
\end{array}
$$

Possibility #1

In the diagram above, Gianola must vote for the tax bill since each council member votes for at least one bill; since there must be two votes against the tax bill, it can then be inferred that Fu votes against the tax bill.

The other scenario with the school bill switches the votes of Gianola and Herstein:

$$
\begin{array}{cccc}
\text{H:} & \dfrac{F}{} & \dfrac{A}{} & \dfrac{A}{} \\[4pt]
\text{G:} & \dfrac{A}{} & \dfrac{F}{} & \dfrac{F/A}{} \\[4pt]
\text{F:} & \dfrac{F}{R} & \dfrac{A}{S} & \dfrac{F/A}{T}
\end{array}
$$

Unfortunately, this information does not completely determine the votes of Fu and Gianola on the tax bill. One must vote for the bill and the other must vote against. Since this produces only two scenarios, show each one:

$$
\begin{array}{cccc}
\text{H:} & \dfrac{F}{} & \dfrac{A}{} & \dfrac{A}{} \\[4pt]
\text{G:} & \dfrac{A}{} & \dfrac{F}{} & \dfrac{A}{} \\[4pt]
\text{F:} & \dfrac{F}{R} & \dfrac{A}{S} & \dfrac{F}{T}
\end{array}
\qquad
\begin{array}{cccc}
\text{H:} & \dfrac{F}{} & \dfrac{A}{} & \dfrac{A}{} \\[4pt]
\text{G:} & \dfrac{A}{} & \dfrac{F}{} & \dfrac{F}{} \\[4pt]
\text{F:} & \dfrac{F}{R} & \dfrac{A}{S} & \dfrac{A}{T}
\end{array}
$$

Possibility #2   Possibility #3

Thus, since all the options for the school bill have been explored, it follows that all the options for the entire voting record have been explored. These three solutions comprise the final setup to the game:

$$
\begin{array}{cccc}
\text{H:} & \dfrac{F}{} & \dfrac{F}{} & \dfrac{A}{} \\[4pt]
\text{G:} & \dfrac{A}{} & \dfrac{A}{} & \dfrac{F}{} \\[4pt]
\text{F:} & \dfrac{F}{R} & \dfrac{A}{S} & \dfrac{A}{T}
\end{array}
\qquad
\begin{array}{cccc}
\text{H:} & \dfrac{F}{} & \dfrac{A}{} & \dfrac{A}{} \\[4pt]
\text{G:} & \dfrac{A}{} & \dfrac{F}{} & \dfrac{A}{} \\[4pt]
\text{F:} & \dfrac{F}{R} & \dfrac{A}{S} & \dfrac{F}{T}
\end{array}
\qquad
\begin{array}{cccc}
\text{H:} & \dfrac{F}{} & \dfrac{A}{} & \dfrac{A}{} \\[4pt]
\text{G:} & \dfrac{A}{} & \dfrac{F}{} & \dfrac{F}{} \\[4pt]
\text{F:} & \dfrac{F}{R} & \dfrac{A}{S} & \dfrac{A}{T}
\end{array}
$$

Possibility #1   Possibility #2   Possibility #3

With all of the possibilities fully realized, the questions can be destroyed at light speed.

Question #19: Global, Could Be True. The correct answer choice is (D)

Possibility #3 proves that answer choice (D) could be true and is therefore correct.

Question #20: Local, Must Be True. The correct answer choice is (E)

Only Possibility #3 meets the criteria in the question stem. Possibility #3 confirms that answer choice (E) is correct.

Question #21: Local, Could Be True. The correct answer choice is (A)

Possibilities #1 and #3 meet the condition established in the question stem. Possibility #2 does not meet the condition and is not considered while attacking the question. Possibility #1 proves that answer choice (A) could be true and is therefore correct.

Question #22: Local, Must Be True. The correct answer choice is (C)

Only possibility #3 meets the condition in the question stem. Consequently, it can be determined that answer choice (C) is true.

Question #23: Local, Must Be True. The correct answer choice is (E)

As with question #22, only possibility #3 meets the condition in the question stem. Consequently, it can be determined that answer choice (E) is true.

The test makers build the game around the two-value system of the votes and then provide a considerable amount of information about the game. Since there are only four undetermined votes and each vote has only two options, it follows that there cannot be a large number of possibilities. This inherently restricted situation leads to the decision to Identify the Possibilities.

POWERSCORE®

29

PREPTEST

OCTOBER 1999 LOGIC GAMES SETUPS

This is a Grouping: Defined-Moving, Balanced game.

Even though the bills appear to have a numerical order, it quickly becomes apparent that they can be paid in any order or configuration. More important are the groups of bills paid on the two days, and the key to the game is the Numerical Distribution of the bills to the days. There are seven bills that must be paid on Wednesday or Thursday, and the first rule establishes that three or four will be paid each day. This leads to two fixed distributions:

	Wednesday	Thursday
Fixed Numerical	3	4
Distributions	4	3

These two fixed distributions suggest Identifying the Templates. We will initially set the game up that way and then discuss the decision to Identify the Possibilities. Let us begin by creating a basic diagram:

1 2 3 4 5 6 7

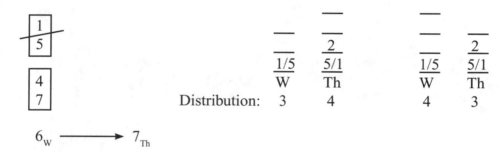

This game also contains a two-value system: all bills must be paid on Wednesday or Thursday. Since bill 1 and bill 5 cannot be paid on the same day, they must be paid on different days. But it is uncertain on which day each is paid, and so a 1/5 dual-option is placed on each day.

The two-value system also affects the last rule. The contrapositive of the last rule is:

$$\cancel{7}_{Th} \longrightarrow \cancel{6}_{W}$$

Of course, if bill 7 is not paid on Thursday it must be paid on Wednesday, and if bill 6 is not paid on Wednesday, it must be paid on Thursday:

$$7_{W} \longrightarrow 6_{Th}$$

An examination of the final two rules suggests that the number of solutions is limited. Both rules contain bill 7, and especially important is the power of the 4-7 block. When the 4-7 block is applied to the 4-3 distribution, it has only one placement option; when the 4-7 is applied to the 3-4 distribution, it has only two placement options. On the basis of this limitation, a decision should be made to show all the possibilities of those three options. Each appears as follows:

Possibilities #1 and #2:   Possibilities #3 and #4:   Possibilities #5 and #6:

```
          3                                 7                           3
  7       6                         3       4                   7       6
  4       2                         6       2                   4       2
 1/5     5/1                       1/5     5/1                  1/5     5/1
 ───     ───                       ───     ───                  ───     ───
  W       Th                        W       Th                   W       Th
  3       4                         3       4                    4       3
 (4-7 on Wed.)                     (4-7 on Thu.)                (4-7 on Wed.)
```

Each of the three templates includes two possibilities, each dependent on the placement of bill 1 and bill 5. Overall the game has only six solutions. Let us examine each of the three templates in more detail:

> Possibilities #1 and #2: 3-4 Numerical Distribution. When the 4-7 block is placed on Wednesday, no other bills can be paid on Wednesday, and they must all be paid on Thursday. The only remaining uncertainty involves bill 1 and bill 5. Since there are only two options for bill 1 and bill 5, this template contains two solutions.

> Possibilities #3 and #4: 3-4 Numerical Distribution. When the 4-7 block is placed on Thursday, no other bills can be paid on Thursday, and they must all be paid on Wednesday. The only remaining uncertainty involves bill 1 and bill 5. Since there are only two options for bill 1 and bill 5, this template contains two solutions.

> Possibilities #5 and #6: 4-3 Numerical Distribution. The 4-7 block must be placed on Wednesday since there is only one open space on Thursday. When 7 is paid on Wednesday, it can be inferred from the contrapositive of the last rule that bill 6 is paid on Thursday. Since three bills are now paid on Thursday, bill 3 must be paid on Wednesday. The only remaining uncertainty involves bill 1 and bill 5. Because there are only two options for bill 1 and bill 5, this template contains two solutions.

Note that the use of templates to show two possibilities reduces the amount of setup time required. The templates compactly display the uncertainty about bill 1 and bill 5, and there is no need to draw each of the six solutions out individually.

Question #1: Local, Could Be True, List. The correct answer choice is (D)

Possibility template #5 and #6 proves answer choice (D) correct. Using the templates for this question is actually somewhat difficult since the bills are listed in numerical order. Glancing at the 4-3 template, it is apparent that bills 3, 4, and 7 must be paid on Wednesday. Thus, any answer choice that does not contain bills 3, 4, and 7 can be eliminated. That leaves only answer choices (D) and (E). Since answer choice (D) contains bill 5, it is correct. Another approach is to realize that any answer choice that contains bill 2 or 6 must be incorrect. That eliminates every answer choice except answer choice (D).

Question #2: Global, Could Be True, List. The correct answer choice is (C)

The question requests a complete list of the bills that could ever be paid on Wednesday. From possibility template #1 and #2 it can be determined that bills 1, 4, 5, and 7 can be paid on Wednesday. Furthermore, from possibility template #3 and #4 it can be determined that bills 3 and 6 can be paid on Wednesday. Possibility template #5 and #6 does not add any insight. Thus, bills 1, 3, 4, 5, 6, and 7 can be paid on Wednesday and answer choice (C) is correct.

Question #3: Local, Must Be True. The correct answer choice is (A)

Only possibility template #3 and #4 meets the condition in the question stem. Accordingly answer choice (A) is correct. Answer choices (C) and (E) could be true, but they do not *have* to be true.

Question #4: Local, Must Be True. The correct answer choice is (B)

Only possibility template #3 and #4 meets the condition in the question stem. Accordingly answer choice (B) is correct. Answer choices (A) and (E) could be true, but they do not *have* to be true.

Question #5: Local, Could Be True. The correct answer choice is (B)

For the third question in a row, only possibility template #3 and #4 meets the condition in the question stem. Accordingly answer choice (B) is correct. Answer choice (A) could never occur since bill 1 and bill 5 cannot be paid on the same day.

Question #6: Global, Must Be True. The correct answer choice is (C)

This question requires checking all of the possibility templates. Answer choice (A) can be eliminated by possibility template #1 and #2. Answer choice (B) can be eliminated by possibility template #3 and #4. Answer choice (C) is proven correct since only possibility template #3 and #4 pays bill 4 on Thursday, and it is also the case that bill 3 is paid on Wednesday. Answer choice (D) can be eliminated by possibility template #5 and #6. Answer choice (E) can be eliminated by possibility template #1 and #2 and possibility template #5 and #6.

This game is a perfect display of the limiting power of Numerical Distributions. The two fixed distributions in combination with the grouping rules lead to the decision to Identify the Possibilities. And since this is the first game on the October 1999 LSAT, getting off to a good start is critical. Identifying the Possibilities in this game not only allows the smart test taker to answer the questions correctly, but, equally important, also allows the questions to be answered quickly.

This is a Grouping: Defined-Fixed, Unbalanced: Overloaded, Identify the Templates game.

This game is widely regarded as the most difficult game on the October 1999 LSAT. The initial scenario and the fourth rule establish the basic setup for the game:

Hat: N R Y [3]
Jacket: N R Y [3]
Skirt: N R Y [3]
Tie: R [1]

	1	2
Tie:	R	
Skirt:	___	___
Jacket:	___	___
Hat:	___	___

The first rule establishes that neither mannequin wears all three colors:

Of course, because mannequin 1 already wears the red tie, the rest of mannequin 1's outfit will be red and navy, or red and yellow. More on this later.

The second rule indicates that each individual mannequin wears a different colored hat and jacket:

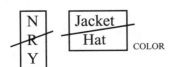

The third rule indicates that mannequin 2 wears a navy skirt:

Hat: N R Y [3]
Jacket: N R Y [3]
Skirt: N R Y [3]
Tie: R [1]

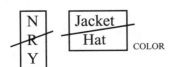

	1	2
Tie:	R	
Skirt:	___	N
Jacket:	___	___
Hat:	___	___

A logical starting point for our inference analysis is the skirt of mannequin 1. Because mannequin 2's skirt is navy (and there is only one navy skirt, so mannequin 1 cannot wear a navy skirt), the skirt of mannequin 1 must be red or yellow:

Hat: N R Y [3]
Jacket: N R Y [3]
Skirt: N R Y [3]
Tie: R [1]

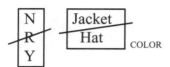

Tie:	R	
Skirt:	R/Y	N
Jacket:	___	___
Hat:	___	___
	1	2

This inference, when combined with the first two rules, results in a situation where:

1. If the skirt of mannequin 1 is yellow, then either the jacket of mannequin 1 is red and the hat of mannequin 1 must be yellow, or the jacket of mannequin 1 is yellow and the hat of mannequin 1 must be red;

2. If the skirt of mannequin 1 is red, then the jacket and hat of mannequin 1 is some combination of red and yellow or of red and navy.

Because the options for the jacket and hat of mannequin 1 are restricted according to the color of the skirt of mannequin 1, one approach is to Identify the Templates:

When mannequin 1's skirt is yellow:

Template #1:

Tie:	R	
Skirt:	Y	N
Jacket:	R	N/Y
Hat:	Y	R/N
	1	2

Template #2:

	R	
	Y	N
	Y	R/N
	R	N/Y
	1	2

Under both scenarios, the jacket and hat on mannequin 2 are locked into a dual-option, which is represented by the two blocks and the slash. For example, in Template #1 if the jacket of mannequin 2 is navy, then the hat of mannequin 2 is red.

Of course, mannequin 1's skirt does not have to be yellow, and could be red instead:

When mannequin 1's skirt is red:

Template #3:

Tie:	R	
Skirt:	R	N
Jacket:	R	N/Y
Hat:	N/Y	
	1	2

Template #4:

Tie:	R	
Skirt:	R	N
Jacket:	N/Y	
Hat:	R	N/Y
	1	2

This second set of templates is very open, but still quite useful. If you feel that those two templates are insufficient, you could instead show the four basic possibilities when the skirt of Mannequin 1 is red. We'll show those possibilities for demonstration purposes:

Template #3 Possibilities—Mannequin 1's skirt is red, and the jacket and hat are red and navy, or red and yellow:

Tie:	R	
Skirt:	R	N
Jacket:	R	N
Hat:	N	R/Y
	1	2

Template #4 Possibilities—Mannequin 1's skirt is red, and the jacket and hat are navy and red, or yellow and red:

Tie:	R	
Skirt:	R	N
Jacket:	N	R/Y
Hat:	R	N
	1	2

Tie:	R	
Skirt:	R	N
Jacket:	R	N / Y
Hat:	Y	R / N
	1	2

Tie:	R	
Skirt:	R	N
Jacket:	Y	N / R
Hat:	R	Y / N
	1	2

While we have shown these last four possibilities under Templates #3 and #4, it is not essential that you do so, because it can be a bit too time-consuming (not to mention that space is limited in this game because the seven questions take up so much room). The basic template approach is sufficient.

Question #7: Global, Could Be True, List. The correct answer choice is (D)

Answer choice (A) is incorrect because mannequin 1 violates the first rule.

Answer choice (B) is incorrect because mannequin 1 violates the second rule.

Answer choice (C) is incorrect because mannequin 2 violates the third rule.

Answer choice (D) is the correct answer.

Answer choice (E) is incorrect because mannequin 1 does not wear the red tie and thus violates the fourth rule.

Question #8: Global, Could Be True. The correct answer choice is (E)

As shown clearly in Templates #1 and #2 (and less clearly in Templates #3 and #4), mannequin 2 does not have to wear any red articles of clothing, and thus answer choice (E) is correct.

Question #9: Local, Could Be True. The correct answer choice is (E)

Mannequin 1 can wear the navy jacket only under Template #4:

Template #4:

Tie:	R	
Skirt:	R	N
Jacket:	N/Y	
Hat:	R	N/Y
	1	2

This template quickly eliminates answer choices (A), (B), and (C). Answer choice (D) can be eliminated because when mannequin 1 wears the navy jacket, mannequin 2 must wear a navy or yellow hat, and ultimately, from the first and second rules mannequin 2 must wear a navy hat. Thus, answer choice (E) is correct.

Question #10: Local, Must Be True. The correct answer choice is (E)

If all four red articles of clothing are included, then Template #3 or #4 must be in effect:

Template #3:

Tie:	R	
Skirt:	R	N
Jacket:	R	N/Y
Hat:	N/Y	
	1	2

Template #4:

Tie:	R	
Skirt:	R	N
Jacket:	N/Y	
Hat:	R	N/Y
	1	2

Of course, when the fourth red article is added to each Template, the possibilities narrow further:

Template #3:

	1	2
Tie:	R	
Skirt:	R	N
Jacket:	R	N
Hat:	N/Y	R

Template #4:

	1	2
Tie:	R	
Skirt:	R	N
Jacket:	N/Y	R
Hat:	R	N

Accordingly, answer choice (E) is correct.

Question #11: Local, Must Be True. The correct answer choice is (B)

If mannequin 2 wears the red jacket, then only Templates #2 and #4 apply. In each, mannequin 1 wears the red hat, and thus answer choice (B) is correct.

Question #12: Local, Could Be True. The correct answer choice is (B)

If all three yellow articles of clothing are included, then Template #1 or #2 must be in effect:

Template #1:

	1	2
Tie:	R	
Skirt:	Y	N
Jacket:	R	N / Y
Hat:	Y	R / N

Template #2:

	1	2
Tie:	R	
Skirt:	Y	N
Jacket:	Y	R / N
Hat:	R	N / Y

Of course, when the third yellow article is added to each Template, the possibilities narrow further:

Template #1:

	1	2
Tie:	R	
Skirt:	Y	N
Jacket:	R	Y
Hat:	Y	N

Template #2:

	1	2
Tie:	R	
Skirt:	Y	N
Jacket:	Y	N
Hat:	R	Y

Accordingly, answer choice (B) is correct.

Question #13: Local, Must Be True. The correct answer choice is (C)

If mannequin 1's skirt is the same color as mannequin 2's jacket, only Templates #1 and #4 can apply. The two Templates appear as follows, after the condition in the question stem is added:

Template #1:

Tie:	R	
Skirt:	Y	N
Jacket:	R	Y
Hat:	Y	N
	1	2

Template #4:

Tie:	R	
Skirt:	R	N
Jacket:	N/Y	R
Hat:	R	N
	1	2

In both templates mannequin 2 wears a navy hat, and thus answer choice (C) is correct.

Note that answer choices (A), (B), and (E) could be true but do not have to be true, and answer choice (D) cannot be true.

This is a Basic Linear: Balanced game.

On the heels of the hardest game on this test comes the easiest game on the test. The initial scenario is fairly simple, and involves presenting seven awards in order, leading to the following initial setup:

F G H J K L S⁷

$$\overline{}_{1} \quad \overline{}_{2} \quad \overline{}_{3} \quad \overline{}_{4} \quad \overline{}_{5} \quad \overline{}_{6} \quad \overline{}_{7}$$

The first rule establishes a G Not Law on the first presentation:

F G H J K L S⁷

$$\overline{}_{1} \quad \overline{}_{2} \quad \overline{}_{3} \quad \overline{}_{4} \quad \overline{}_{5} \quad \overline{}_{6} \quad \overline{}_{7}$$
$$\cancel{G}$$

The second and third rules each create basic sequences:

H > K

L > J

Each sequence creates two Not Laws:

F G H J K L S⁷

$$\overline{}_{1} \quad \overline{}_{2} \quad \overline{}_{3} \quad \overline{}_{4} \quad \overline{}_{5} \quad \overline{}_{6} \quad \overline{}_{7}$$
$$\cancel{G} \cancel{H}$$
$$\cancel{K} \cancel{L}$$
$$\cancel{J}$$

The fourth and fifth rules each create rotating blocks:

$$\boxed{\text{F H}}$$
$$\text{or}$$
$$\boxed{\text{H F}}$$

$$\boxed{\text{K L}}$$
$$\text{or}$$
$$\boxed{\text{L K}}$$

These blocks conveniently connect to the sequences created in the second and third rules:

$$\boxed{\text{F H}}$$
$$\text{or} \quad > \text{K}$$
$$\boxed{\text{H F}}$$

$$\boxed{\text{K L}}$$
$$\text{or} \quad > \text{J}$$
$$\boxed{\text{L K}}$$

These two block-sequences can also be connected to create the following chain:

$$\boxed{\text{F H}} \quad \boxed{\text{K L}}$$
$$> \qquad > \text{J}$$
$$\boxed{\text{H F}} \quad \boxed{\text{L K}}$$

This chain is the key to the game, and creates a number of additional Not Laws:

F G H J K L S [7]

1	2	3	4	5	6	7
G̶	K̶	J̶	J̶	F̶	F̶	H̶
K̶	L̶			H̶	H̶	L̶
J̶	J̶					F̶
L̶						K̶

29

An analysis of the most restricted spaces reveals that only F, H, or S can be presented first, and only G, J, or S can be presented seventh. This information, when combined with the fact that S is a random, leads to the final setup for the game:

F G H J K L S^7
      *

F/H/S						G/J/S
1	2	3	4	5	6	7
G̶	J̶	J̶	J̶	F̶	F̶	K̶
J̶	L̶			H̶	H̶	L̶
L̶	K̶					F̶
K̶						H̶

$$\boxed{FH} \quad \boxed{KL}$$
$$\quad > \quad \quad > J$$
$$\boxed{HF} \quad \boxed{LK}$$

As mentioned previously, the super-sequence is the key to the game and should be tracked constantly throughout the questions. It incorporates the second, third, fourth, and fifth rules, meaning that the sequence and the first rule are the only two elements you must consider in each question.

Question #14: Global, Must Be True. The correct answer choice is (A)

As shown by the super-sequence, F must always be presented before J, and so answer choice (A) is correct.

Question #15: Local, Must Be True. The correct answer choice is (E)

The condition in the question stem establishes that H is presented fourth. When considered alone, the fourth rule indicates that F must be presented third or fifth. However, the presence of the super-sequence makes it impossible for F to be presented fifth because there would not be sufficient room for K, L, and J to be presented later. Thus, F must be presented third, and K, L, and J after:

		F	H	K/L	L/K	J
1	2	3	4	5	6	7

Because G cannot be presented first, G must be presented second, leaving S to be presented first:

S	G	F	H	K/L	L/K	J
1	2	3	4	5	6	7

Accordingly, answer choice (E) is correct. Note how the very last variable placed (S, a random) is the variable that produces the correct answer.

Question #16: Local, Could Be True. The correct answer choice is (C)

If G is presented third, the possible positions for the sequence are immediately affected. Specifically, F and H cannot be presented after G because then there would not be enough room to present K, L, and J. Hence, F and H must be presented first and second:

F/H	H/F	G				
1	2	3	4	5	6	7

Thus, K, L, and J must be presented after G, with J unable to be presented fourth or fifth:

F/H	H/F	G			J/	S/J
1	2	3	4̸	5̸	6	7

Accordingly, answer choice (C) is correct.

Answer choice (E) is incorrect because there would be no viable placement option for the KL block.

Question #17: Global, Must Be True, Minimum. The correct answer choice is (C)

As shown during the setup, J cannot be presented in any of the first four spaces due to the two blocks that must be presented before J. However, J can be presented fifth, and so answer choice (C) is correct.

Question #18: Local, Could Be True, Except. The correct answer choice is (A)

If J is presented ahead of S (J > S), then S cannot be presented first, leaving only F or H to be presented first:

F/H	H/F					
1	2	3	4	5	6	7

S̸

This information immediately indicates that answer choice (A) is correct. F is either presented first, or presented second immediately after H, and so G can never be presented immediately before F. Thus, answer choice (A) cannot be true and is the correct answer.

Question #19: Global, Justify. The correct answer choice is (D)

In this Justify question you must find the answer that produces just a single solution to the game. This is what you should seek in the correct answer:

- As both the blocks in the game rotate, they must be addressed within the correct answer, and so you should expect to see answers that address F or H or both, and K or L or both.

- J must also be addressed because it is sequentially linked to the KL block, and while that limits its range of placement, it does not determine where it is placed.

- Because the super-sequence has multiple placement options within the game, the correct answer must directly anchor at least part of the sequence. The easiest way for this to occur is by removing variables from the triple-options that start and finish the game.

- One last tip: answers that include fewer variables are less likely to be correct.

Answer choice (A) is incorrect because while this answer orders the variables in each block, it does not limit the placement of those blocks in any way.

Answer choice (B) is incorrect because while it produces a FHKL block, it does not limit the placement of that block. This answer also addresses only three variables, the fewest of any answer.

Answer choice (C) is incorrect because while it produces a HFLKJ block, it does not limit the placement of that block, and the block has no impact on G and S.

Answer choice (D) is the correct answer. This answer starts by forming a GFH block, which from the triple-option on the first space means that only S remains to be presented first. The remainder of the answer produces a KLJ block. The GFH block must then be presented second, third, and fourth, and the KLJ block must be presented fifth, sixth, and seventh. This results in a single solution:

$$\frac{S}{1} \quad \frac{G}{2} \quad \frac{F}{3} \quad \frac{H}{4} \quad \frac{K}{5} \quad \frac{L}{6} \quad \frac{J}{7}$$

Answer choice (E) produces two blocks—HF and GKL—but it does not limit J or S in any manner.

This is a Basic Linear: Unbalanced: Overloaded, Numerical Distribution game.

The game scenario indicates that nine students will attend a total of six classes, creating an Overloaded Linear situation:

F: G H I K⁴

M: L N O P S⁵

$\underline{\quad}\ \ \underline{\quad}\ \ \underline{\quad}\ \ \underline{\quad}\ \ \underline{\quad}\ \ \underline{\quad}$
  1   2   3   4   5   6

The scenario further states that some classes will have multiple students and that four will have exactly one student. This creates a classic Numerical Distribution, and we will consider the distributions after analyzing the rules.

The first rule establishes that I and L form a single class:

This affects the distribution by establishing that one of the multiple-person classes is made up of two people, I and L.

The second rule indicates that the other multi-person class consists of P and two other students:

This creates a box with a blank line over P_M.

When combined with the game scenario, the first two rules establish that there is a single unfixed Numerical Distribution:

3 - 2 - 1 - 1 - 1 - 1

Of course, I, L, and P can be assigned to certain groups:

$$3 - 2 - 1 - 1 - 1 - 1$$
$$\text{P} \quad \text{L}$$
$$\quad \text{I}$$

We will revisit the distribution after considering the remaining rules.

The third rule indicates that K is the first female—but not the first student—to attend a class:

$$K_F \longrightarrow \text{1st F}$$

Because K is not the first student to attend a class, K cannot attend the first class. Because K must be the first female to attend a class, we can infer that G, H, and I (the other three females) cannot attend the first class (and thus K > IL block, G, and H). And, since K cannot attend the first class, the earliest class that K can attend is the second, we can infer that G, H, and I cannot attend the second class. In addition, because I and L form a block, we can infer that L cannot attend the first or second class, leading to the following:

F: G H I K [4]

M: L N O P S [5]

1	2	3	4	5	6
K̶	G̶				
G̶	H̶				
H̶	I̶				
I̶	L̶				
L̶					

$$\boxed{\begin{array}{c}I_F\\L_M\end{array}} \quad \boxed{\begin{array}{c}-\\P_M\end{array}}$$

$$K_F \longrightarrow \text{1st F}$$

$$3 - 2 - 1 - 1 - 1 - 1$$
$$\text{P} \quad \text{L}$$
$$\quad \text{I}$$

The fourth and fifth rules can be combined with the first and third rules to produce a powerful chain sequence:

$$K_F > \boxed{\begin{array}{c}I_M\\L_F\end{array}} > G_F > \begin{array}{c}P_M\\------\\O_M\end{array}$$

Note: O and P could attend the same class.

Without consideration of the other requirements of the game, the sequence indicates that O and P cannot be in the first, second, or third class, that I and L cannot be in the fifth or sixth class, and that G cannot be in the sixth class. Consequently, seven of the nine students are eliminated from attending the first class, and therefore only N or S—but not both—can attend the first class. The N/S inference is one of the keys to the game.

When the chain sequence is considered in conjunction with the other rules of the game and the numerical distribution, a number of additional inferences can be made:

> Either H or O or both must be in the group of three.
> Either N or S or both must be alone.
> Because K's class is ahead of P's class, K must attend class alone.
> Because G's class is ahead of P's class, G must attend class alone.
> The group of three must attend either the fifth or sixth class.
> The group of two must attend either the third or fourth class.
> The sole attendee at the first class is male.

All of this information culminates in the final setup to the game:

F: G H I K⁴
M: L N O P S⁵

				P/	/P
				O/	/O
N/S	K/	/K	G/	/G	
1	2	3	4	5	6
K̶	G̶	G̶	K	K̶	K̶
G̶	H̶	O̶		I̶	I̶
H̶	I̶	P̶		L̶	L̶
I̶	L̶				G̶
L̶	O̶				
O̶	P̶				
P̶					

K_F ——→ 1st F

K_F > [I_F / L_M] > G_F > ----- P_M / O_M

3 - 2 - 1 - 1 - 1 - 1
P   L   K   G N/S
H/O I

Overall, this is a very complicated sequence of inferences, and a tremendous amount of information to juggle during a setup.

Question #20: Global, Could Be True. The correct answer choice is (E)

As established during the latter part of the setup discussion, N or S must attend the first class, and thus answer choice (E) is correct.

Question #21: Global, Must Be True, List. The correct answer choice is (A)

The Not Laws show that G cannot attend the first, second, third, or sixth classes. Thus, G is shown as a dual-option on the fourth and fifth classes, and answer choice (A) is correct.

Question #22: Global, Could Be True. The correct answer choice is (B)

Our analysis of the distribution shows that I, L, K, and G cannot attend class with P. This information eliminates answer choices (A), (C), and (D) from further consideration.

Because one of N or S must attend the first class alone, answer choice (E) can be eliminated.

Thus, answer choice (B) is correct.

Question #23: Local, Could Be True. The correct answer choice is (D)

If O and P do not attend the same class, then P attends the class with H and either N or S. And, based on our prior analysis, P must attend the fifth or sixth class.

Answer choice (A) is incorrect because if G attends the fifth class, then P, H, and N or S attend the sixth class. This results in no possible class for O to attend.

Answer choice (B) is incorrect because, as mentioned above, H must attend the fifth or sixth class with P.

Answer choice (C) is incorrect because if I attends the fourth class, then from the sequence G would have to attend the fifth class, which was shown impossible in answer choice (A).

Answer choice (D) is the correct answer.

Answer choice (E) is incorrect because if S attends the second class, then N must attend the first class, resulting in P not being able to attend the fifth or sixth class with two other students.

Question #24: Local, Must Be True, Suspension. The correct answer choice is (E)

The new condition in the question stem results in the following sequence:

$$K_F > \boxed{\begin{array}{c} I_F \\ L_M \end{array}} \;-----\; > G_F > P_M$$
$$O_M$$

Because K still cannot attend the first class, this sequence forces a number of students into certain classes. Here is the scenario, with distribution information:

F: G H I K ^{4}

M: L N O P S ^{5}

	1	1	2/1	1/2	1	3
		K	$\boxed{\begin{array}{c}I\\L\end{array}}$ /	O	G	P
1		2	3	4	5	6

Only H, N, and S are not accounted for on the above diagram. Because either N or S must still attend the first class (remember, H is a female and from the third rule cannot attend the first class), we can infer that H and the N/S remainder attend the sixth class. Accordingly, answer choice (E) is correct.

29

POWERSCORE®

30 PREPTEST

DECEMBER 1999 LOGIC GAMES SETUPS

30

This is a Grouping: Defined-Fixed, Unbalanced: Underfunded game.

The game scenario indicates that a bakery delivers exactly six loaves of bread, each with two characteristics: kind of bread (O, R, W) and sliced/unsliced (S, U). Because the loaves are not ordered, this is a Grouping game. The basic scenario appears as follows:

Kind: O R W ³
Sliced: S U ²   S U: ___ ___ ___ ___ ___ ___
                       O R W: ___ ___ ___ ___ ___ ___
                                          6 Loaves

Although the sliced/unsliced option could be shown as S and ~~S~~, in this instance we have chosen S and U so as to avoid any possible confusion over a missed slash. If you represented it otherwise, there is no problem with that.

The first rule establishes that there are at least two kinds of loaves. Thus, all six loaves cannot be of a single kind:

Min 2 kinds

The second rule establishes that there are a maximum of three rye loaves:

Max 3 R

or

The third rule states that no unsliced wheat loaf exists:

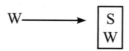

Correspondingly, because all loaves are sliced or unsliced, this means that every wheat loaf is sliced:

W ⟶ [S / W]

Because every wheat loaf is sliced, if a loaf is unsliced, it must be oatmeal or rye:

$$U \longrightarrow \boxed{\begin{array}{c} U \\ O \end{array}} \text{ or } \boxed{\begin{array}{c} U \\ R \end{array}}$$

The fourth rule indicates that there is at least one unsliced oatmeal loaf:

Kind: O R W ^{3}
Sliced: S U ^{2}

S U: U __ __ __ __ __
O R W: O __ __ __ __ __
                 6 Loaves

Of course, from the first rule there must be at least two kinds of loaves, and since there is an oatmeal loaf, we can infer that at least one other loaf is rye or wheat, a fact that can be shown on our diagram with a dual-option:

Kind: O R W ^{3}
Sliced: S U ^{2}

S U: U __   __ __ __ __
O R W: O R/W __ __ __ __
                 6 Loaves

The fifth rule is very specific, and states that if two or more loaves are unsliced, then at least one is rye:

$$2U \longrightarrow \boxed{\begin{array}{c} \text{at lst 1} \\ U \\ R \end{array}}$$

The information from all of the rules can be combined to form the final diagram:

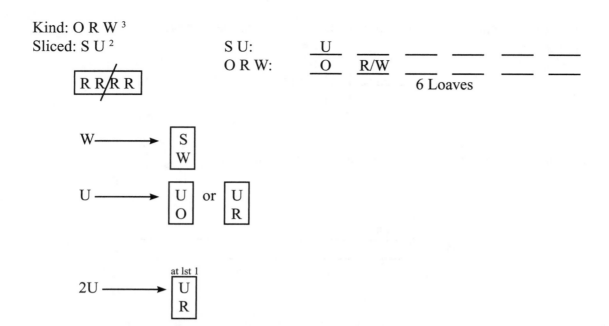

Kind: O R W [3]
Sliced: S U [2]

S U: U ___ ___ ___ ___ ___
O R W: O   R/W ___ ___ ___ ___
                    6 Loaves

W ⟶ S / W

U ⟶ U/O or U/R

2U ⟶ (at lst 1) U/R

Question #1: Global, Could Be True, List. The correct answer choice is (D)

Answer choice (A) is incorrect because according to the first rule there must be at least two kinds of loaves.

Answer choice (B) is incorrect because from the fifth rule when there are two or more unsliced loaves, at least one must be rye.

Answer choice (C) is incorrect because the third rule states that there are no unsliced wheat loaves. Further, from the fifth rule when there are two or more unsliced loaves, at least one must be rye.

Answer choice (D) is the correct answer.

Answer choice (E) is incorrect because from the fifth rule when there are two or more unsliced loaves, at least one must be rye.

Question #2: Global, Could Be True, Except, List. The correct answer choice is (A)

The question stem specifies that the lists are of unsliced loaves. From our discussion of the rules, the third, fourth, and fifth rules address unsliced loaves, and thus you should look to one of those rules to produce the correct answer in this Could Be True Except question (which is identical to Cannot Be True).

Answer choice (A) cannot occur because from the fifth rule when there are two or more unsliced loaves, at least one must be rye. Thus, answer choice (A) is correct.

Question #3: Global, Cannot Be True. The correct answer choice is (C)

Answer choice (C) cannot be true because the fourth rule establishes that there is at least one unsliced oatmeal loaf. Thus, answer choice (C) is correct.

Question #4: Global, Must Be True. The correct answer choice is (D)

From our analysis of the rules, none of the statements in answer choices (A), (B), or (C) appear to have to be true. Thus, you should focus on answer choices (D) and (E) as the most likely candidates in this question.

Answer choice (D) must be true because if there are more than four sliced oatmeal loaves, then there would be five sliced oatmeal loaves, and from the fourth rule the sixth loaf would be an unsliced oatmeal loaf. That would result in a delivery of six oatmeal loaves, a violation of the first rule. Thus, there cannot be more than four sliced oatmeal loaves, and answer choice (D) is correct.

Question #5: Local, Could Be True. The correct answer choice is (B)

The condition in the question stem adds exactly four wheat loaves, each of which must be sliced according to the third rule:

Kind: O R W ^{3}
Sliced?: S U ^{2}

S U:	U	S	S	S	S	
O R W:	O	W	W	W	W	O/R

6 Loaves

The other two loaves that are delivered must be an unsliced oatmeal loaf (from the fourth rule), and then an oatmeal or rye loaf. Answer choices (A), (C), and (E) can be eliminated because none of them contains an unsliced oatmeal loaf.

Answer choice (D) can be eliminated because if the bakery delivers two unsliced oatmeal loaves, then the entire delivery is two unsliced oatmeal loaves and four sliced wheat loaves. This violates the fifth rule, which states that if two or more of the loaves are unsliced, at least one of the unsliced loaves must be rye.

Consequently, answer choice (B) is correct.

Although this game seems hard at first because the rules are a bit random, in hindsight the game is actually quite reasonable.

30

This is a Grouping/Linear Combination, Numerical Distribution game.

At first glance, this game appears to be a simple Basic Linear game:

F G H L P T ^{6}

$$\overline{}\ \overline{}\ \overline{}\ \overline{}\ \overline{}\ \overline{}$$
$$\ \ 1\quad\ 2\quad\ 3\quad\ 4\quad\ 5\quad\ 6$$

However, the first and second rules indicate that this game is not Balanced, opening up a host of numerical possibilities. These possibilities ultimately make the game much more difficult.

<u>Unfixed Numerical Distributions: Messages to people</u>

Distribution #1:   1-1-1-1-1-1

Each person leaves exactly one message.

Distribution #2:   2-1-1-1-1-0

One person leaves two messages, four people leave one message, and one person does not leave a message.

Distribution #3:   3-1-1-1-0-0

One person leaves three messages (ex-boyfriend or girlfriend, maybe?), three people leave one message, and two people do not leave a message.

We will reconsider these distributions once the remaining rules have been analyzed.

The third rule establishes a basic conditional relationship:

$$H_1 \longrightarrow P_6$$

The fourth rule is also conditional, and it indicates that when G leaves a message, so do F and P:

$$G \longrightarrow \begin{array}{c} F \\ + \\ P \end{array}$$

The fifth and sixth rules are similar. Both are conditional, and include sequential information:

$$F \longrightarrow P > T$$

$$P \longrightarrow H > L$$

One of the critical inferences of the game is initiated by the combination of the fourth, fifth, and sixth rules:

$$G \longrightarrow \begin{array}{c} F \\ + \\ P > T \\ + \\ H > L \end{array}$$

The diagram above indicates that if G leaves a message, then every other variable must also leave a message. Thus, since the first two rules create several Unfixed Numerical Distributions, the composition of the people leaving messages under each distribution can be determined:

Unfixed Distribution #1:

1	1	1	1	1	1
F	G	H	L	P	T

All must leave messages, with P > T and H > L. H cannot be first.

Unfixed Distribution #2:

2	1	1	1	1	0
					G

F, P, T, H, and L each leave a message, with P > T and H > L. H cannot be first.

Unfixed Distribution #3:

3	1	1	1	0	0
				F	G

H, L, P, and T each leave a message, with H > L

30

Other inferences: If F leaves a message, then P > T and P cannot leave the sixth message. Via the contrapositive of the third rule, H cannot leave the first message: F ──→ H̶₁. If H does leave the first message, then F cannot leave a message and the 3-1-1-1-0-0 distribution is in effect: H₁ ──→ 3-1-1-1-0-0

H, L, P, and T always leave messages. Because P must always leave a message, and thus H > L, L can never leave the first message and H can never leave the sixth message.

This is the final diagram for the game:

F G H L P T ^{6}

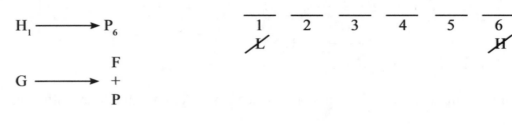

H_1 ──────→ P_6

G ──────→ F + P

F ──────→ P > T

P ──────→ H > L

G ──────→ F + P > T + H > L

$\overline{1}$ $\overline{2}$ $\overline{3}$ $\overline{4}$ $\overline{5}$ $\overline{6}$

Under 1: L̶   Under 6: H̶

Underlined **Unfixed Distribution #1:**

1	1	1	1	1	1
F	G	H	L	P	T

All must leave a message, with P > T and H > L. H cannot be first.

**Unfixed Distribution #2:**

2	1	1	1	1	0
					G

F, P, T, H, and L each leave a message, with P > T and H > L. H cannot be first.

**Unfixed Distribution #3:**

3	1	1	1	0	0
				F	G

H, L, P, and T each leave a message, with H > L

Question #6: Global, Could Be True, List. The correct answer choice is (D)

Answer choice (A) is incorrect because it violates the fifth rule: F leaves a message, but all of P's messages do not precede T's message.

Answer choice (B) is incorrect because it violates the fourth rule: G leaves a message but F does not leave a message.

Answer choice (C) is incorrect because it violates the third rule: H leaves the first message but P does not leave the last message.

Answer choice (D) is the correct answer.

Answer choice (E) is incorrect because it violates the first rule in that two people leave exactly two messages.

Question #7: Global, Could Be True. The correct answer choice is (A)

The question stem in this problem is a bit odd, and most people read it at least twice before getting a clear picture of what is being asked. The question asks for who could leave the first and sixth messages, and have those two messages be their only two messages. So, a caller such as H is immediately eliminated because the third rule stipulates that if H makes the first call, P makes the last call. This removes answer choice (B) from consideration.

The fact that a caller leaves exactly two messages means that the 2-1-1-1-1-0 distribution is in effect:

Unfixed Distribution #2:   2   1   1   1   1   0
                                                          G

          F, P, T, H, and L each leave a message, with P > T and H > L. H cannot be first.

Accordingly, L and T can also be eliminated as they can never leave the first message, removing answer choices (C) and (E) from consideration. P can also be eliminated as P > T, and therefore P can never leave the last message. This removes answer choice (D) from consideration.

Hence, answer choice (A) is correct.

Question #8: Local, Cannot Be True. The correct answer choice is (A)

This is the first Local question of the game. If G leaves the fifth message, then the 1-1-1-1-1-1 distribution is in effect:

Unfixed Distribution #1:   1   1   1   1   1   1
                           F   G   H   L   P   T

          All must leave a message, with P > T and H > L. H cannot be first.

Accordingly, the setup for this question appears as:

F G H L P T [6]

$$\frac{}{1} \quad \frac{}{2} \quad \frac{}{3} \quad \frac{}{4} \quad \frac{G}{5} \quad \frac{}{6}$$

L̸   H̸
T̸   P̸
H̸

Accordingly, T cannot leave the first message, and answer choice (A) is correct.

Question #9: Global, Must Be True, Except. The correct answer choice is (D)

As shown by the three distributions, it does not have to be true that exactly one person left two messages, and thus answer choice (D) is not necessarily true and is correct.

Question #10: Local, Could Be True. The correct answer choice is (C)

If P leaves exactly one message, then any of the three distributions are still possible. If P's message is the fifth, then from the contrapositive of the third rule H cannot leave the first message. This information eliminates answer choice (A).

From the sixth rule, when P leaves a message, then H and L also leave messages, with H > L. Because H cannot leave the first message, the earliest message H could leave is the second, and thus the earliest message that L could leave is the third. Thus, answer choice (D) can be eliminated.

The remaining three answers all concern individuals leaving two messages.

Answer choice (B): if T leaves exactly two messages, under the 2-1-1-1-1-0 distribution, F, P, T, H, and L each leave a message, with P > T and H > L. But, with P leaving the fifth message, and the fifth rule stipulating that all of P's messages precede all of T's messages, there is not sufficient room to accommodate both of T's messages and still conform to the fifth rule. Thus, this answer choice is incorrect.

Answer choice (E): if F leaves the third and fourth messages, under the 2-1-1-1-1-0 distribution, F, P, T, H, and L each leave a message, with P > T and H > L. But, with P leaving the fifth message, T must leave the last message, forcing H to leave the first message and L to leave the second message. Because this violates the third rule, this answer cannot be correct.

Thus, answer choice (C) is correct. L could leave the third and fourth messages.

PrepTest 30. December 1999 Game #3: *11. B 12. A 13. B 14. E 15. B 16. A*

This is an Advanced Linear: Balanced, Identify the Templates game.

The game scenario creates a setup where five cars are washed in order, with each car belonging to a certain individual and each car receiving a particular type of wash. Because each position has both a car owner and a wash type, this is an Advanced Linear game, and the basic scenario appears as follows:

R S P ³
F M O T V ⁵   Wash: ___ ___ ___ ___ ___   R S P

                Car: ___ ___ ___ ___ ___   F M O T V

                        1   2   3   4   5

The first rule establishes that the first car does not receive a super wash, although at least one car does. This means that the first car receives a regular or premium wash:

R S P ³
F M O T V ⁵   Wash: R/P ___ ___ ___ ___   R S P

                Car: ___ ___ ___ ___ ___   F M O T V

    At Lst 1 S   1   2   3   4   5

The second rule establishes that exactly one car receives a premium wash:

           Exactly 1 P

The third rule indicates that the second and third cars receive the same wash, which cannot be a premium wash according to the second rule. Thus, the second and third washes are either regular or super:

R S P ³
F M O T V ⁵   Wash: R/P | R/S R/S | ___ ___   R S P
                          P̸   P̸

                Car: ___ ___ ___ ___ ___   F M O T V

                        1   2   3   4   5

    At least 1 S

    Exactly 1 P

The fourth and fifth rules create a super-sequence of the individuals:

$$O > M > F$$
$$V > -------------$$
$$T$$

This sequence controls the game and creates four possible orders of the cars:

1.	V	O	M	F	T
2.	V	O	M	T	F
3.	V	O	T	M	F
4.	V	T	O	M	F

Given that there are also four rules about the washes, after we consider the final rule we will examine those possibilities above in connection with the washes.

The final rule indicates that M and the car immediately before M receive regular washes:

$$\boxed{\underline{\quad\quad}_R \quad M_R}$$

Linking the four rules about wash types to the four possible car orders above yields four basic templates:

Template #1:

R/P	R	R	S/	/S
V	O	M	F	T
1	2	3	4	5

Template #2:

R/P	R	R	S/	/S
V	O	M	T	F
1	2	3	4	5

Template #3:

P	R	R	R	S
V	O	T	M	F
1	2	3	4	5

Template #4:

P	R	R	R	S
V	T	O	M	F
1	2	3	4	5

Templates #3 and #4 contain exactly one possibility each. With the templates, the game is relatively easy and certain inferences such as O is always regular, and the second wash is always regular, are made clear.

Note: if you do not wish to make this a multi-stacked game, you can use subscripts for the type of wash each car receives, e.g. M_R.

Question #11: Global, Could Be True, List. The correct answer choice is (B)

Answer choice (A) is incorrect because it violates the fourth rule.

Answer choice (B) is the correct answer.

Answer choice (C) is incorrect because it violates the fifth rule.

Answer choice (D) is incorrect because it violates the first rule.

Answer choice (E) is incorrect because it violates the first rule: no car has received a super wash.

Question #12: Local, Must Be True. The correct answer choice is (A)

V does not have to receive a premium wash under Templates #1 and #2. In each Template, then, V would receive a regular wash. Accordingly, answer choice (A) is correct because O always receives a regular wash.

Question #13: Local, Could Be True. The correct answer choice is (B)

The last two cars can receive the same kind of wash in Templates #1 and #2. In Template #1 T's car is washed fifth, and so answer choice (B) is correct.

Question #14: Global, Must Be True. The correct answer choice is (E)

In all four Templates the second car receives a regular wash, and so answer choice (E) is correct.

Question #15: Global, Must Be True. The correct answer choice is (B)

A scan of all four Templates reveals that only M and O must receive regular washes, and so answer choice (B) is correct.

Question #16: Local, Cannot Be True. The correct answer choice is (A)

Perhaps because the four Templates make the first five questions so easy to solve, the test makers finish this game by adding an entirely new variable to the game. This variable is added without suspending any of the rules, so all of the previous conditions still hold. But, the addition of a new, unfettered variable (a random, actually) opens up the game to more than four basic orders.

Because there were previously four basic orders, the addition of a new variable creates six additional options for each basic order (one when J is first, another when J is second, and so on). Thus, the introduction of the new variable means there are now 24 possible orders of the cars instead of 4. Thus, the answer to this question is unlikely to be found through re-diagramming the game. Instead, search the answers for a more universal statement that can never be true.

Answer choice (A) is the correct answer. If O is second or third, then O can never receive a premium wash because the second and third cars receive the same type of wash, and there is only one premium wash. If O is fourth—the only other position for O based on the super-sequence—then O will be in front of M and receive a regular wash per the sixth rule. Thus, O can never receive a premium wash, and this answer choice cannot be true and is thus correct.

Answer choices (B) through (E) all could be true, and are therefore incorrect.

This is a Basic Linear: Balanced game.

The initial scenario establishes that seven toy-truck models will be assembled on seven numbered lines, creating a Basic Linear setup:

F G H J K M S ⁷

```
  1   2   3   4   5   6   7
```

The first rule establishes that F is assembled on a lower-numbered line than J:

$$F > J$$

Remember, the "greater than" sign we use does not refer to numerical value; it refers to which variable is to the left of the other. This rule creates two Not Laws:

F G H J K M S ⁷

F > J

```
  1   2   3   4   5   6   7
  J                       F
```

The second rule creates a block:

$$\boxed{M\,G}$$

The block also produces two Not Laws:

F G H J K M S ⁷

F > J

$\boxed{M\,G}$

```
  1   2   3   4   5   6   7
  J                       F
  G                       M
```

The third rule creates a split-option for H, and the fourth rule assigns S to line 4, resulting in the final diagram (with K notated as a random):

F G H J K M S [7]
   *

F > J

MG

H/			S			/H
1	2	3	4	5	6	7

One of the keys to this game is to realize that the MG block is limited in placement, and that when it is before S then M or G must be in 2, and when it is after S then M or G must be in 6. You could create four basic templates to reflect the four positions of the MG block (1-2, 2-3, 5-6, 6-7), but the game appears so simple this is probably unnecessary.

Question #17: Global, Could Be True, List. The correct answer choice is (B)

Answer choice (A) is incorrect because it violates the third rule.

Answer choice (B) is the correct answer.

Answer choice (C) is incorrect because it violates the second rule.

Answer choice (D) is incorrect because it violates the fourth rule.

Answer choice (E) is incorrect because it violates the first rule.

Question #18: Global, Must Be True. The correct answer choice is (C)

The Not Laws produced by the first rule show that J can never be assembled on line 1, and thus the lowest-numbered line that J can be assembled on is line 2. Hence, answer choice (C) is correct.

Question #19: Local, Could Be True. The correct answer choice is (C)

If K is assembled on line 5, the following scenario results:

F G H J K M S [7]

F > J

MG

H/			S	K		/H
1	2	3	4	5	6	7

When considering which variables can and cannot be consecutive, you should immediately hone in on the MG block because it naturally has limitations in its placement, and, because M and G are consecutive, they buffer each other from certain positions. Not surprisingly, each of the four incorrect answers contains one of the two members of the MG block.

Answer choice (C) can occur under the following hypothetical:

H	F	J	S	K	M	G
1	2	3	4	5	6	7

Accordingly, answer choice (C) is correct.

Question #20: Global, Must Be True, Maximum. The correct answer choice is (D)

The question asks for the maximum number of lines that can separate F and J, so you must select the answer choice that contains the maximum number of lines *between* F and J. Because there are seven total lines in this game, the initial maximum number would be five. But, because of the third rule, that can only occur when H is one of the toy-trucks involved. So, the most promising answer is four, which could occur when F and J are assembled on lines 1 and 6 or lines 2 and 7. But, you should check to make sure that at least one of those two possibilities can occur. The following hypothetical shows that F and J can be successfully assembled on lines 2 and 7:

H	F	K	S	M	G	J
1	2	3	4	5	6	7

Accordingly, answer choice (D) is correct.

Question #21: Local, Must Be True. The correct answer choice is (A)

If K is assembled on line 2, then the MG block is assembled after S, and two basic templates result, based on the position of H:

	H	K	F	S	(M G , J)		
Template #1:	H	K	F	S	(M G ,	J	)
Template #2:	F	K	J	S	M	G	H
	1	2	3	4	5	6	7

In each Template, F is assembled on a lower-numbered line than S, and so answer choice (A) is correct.

Question #22: Local, Must Be True. The correct answer choice is (A)

The condition in the question stem creates an MGF block. Initially, it would appear that this block has two placement options: lines 1-2-3 or lines 5-6-7. But, placing the block on lines 5-6-7 would force F to be assembled on line 7, and that would create a violation of the first rule. Thus, the block must be assembled on lines 1-2-3:

M	G	F	S	J/K	K/J	H
1	2	3	4	5	6	7

Accordingly, answer choice (A) is correct.

Question #23: Local, Could Be True. The correct answer choice is (D)

If you produced a hypothetical for question #22, then you can use that hypothetical to attempt to choose an answer in this question because the hypothetical from #22 meets the condition in this question stem. However, the hypothetical above does not ultimately prove any answer choice is correct. Still, checking that hypothetical was worth the time because if it had worked, then the time savings would have been tremendous.

If M is assembled on line 1, the following setup results:

M	G		S			H
1	2	3	4	5	6	7

F, J, and K remain to be assigned, with the F > J rule still in effect. Thus, the following Not Laws are also in play:

M	G		S			H
1	2	3	4	5	6	7
		J̶			F̶	

Accordingly, answer choice (D) is correct.

Most students found this to be the easiest game of the December 1999 LSAT.

POWERSCORE®

PrepTest 31

JUNE 2000 LOGIC GAMES SETUPS

This is an Advanced Linear: Unbalanced: Overloaded game.

The game scenario indicates that boys and girls will be assigned to numbered lockers, creating a Linear scenario where some lockers must be assigned more than one child, although which lockers will be assigned more than one child is unknown:

Boys: F J M P [4]
Girls: N R T [3]

$$\frac{\quad}{1} \quad \frac{\quad}{2} \quad \frac{\quad}{3} \quad \frac{\quad}{4} \quad \frac{\quad}{5}$$

While the game scenario indicates that a Numerical Distribution will be in effect in this game, the first rule lends structure to the Distribution. With each locker assigned to exactly one or two children, the result is a single Unfixed Numerical Distribution of the seven children to the five lockers:

7 ———→ 5

Unfixed Distribution: 2   2   1   1   1

The second rule establishes that each of the two shared lockers are comprised of one boy and one girl. As this removes two boys and two girls from the pool, the remaining three single lockers must be assigned to two boys and one girl:

7 ———→ 5

Unfixed Distribution: 2   2   1   1   1
                            boy   boy   girl   boy   boy
                            girl   girl

The third rule further refines the children assigned to each locker. Because J must share a locker, and R cannot share a locker, J must share a locker with N or T. The remainder of N and T must share the other shared locker, with R assigned to an unshared locker. These inferences can be applied to the distribution:

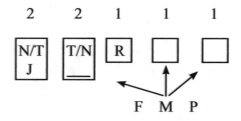

As indicated in the diagram, F, M, and P can never share a locker, and exactly one of F, M, and P is assigned to a shared locker. This inference is critical to dominating the game.

The final two rules apply to the linear ordering of the variables. The fourth rule creates a rotating NT not-block, and the fifth rule assigns F to the third locker. Adding in the fact that M and P are randoms results in the final diagram for the game:

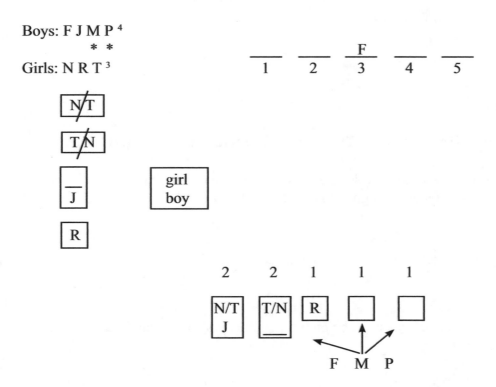

Also, because N and T cannot be consecutive, the two shared lockers cannot be consecutive.

Question #1: Global, Could Be True, List. The correct answer choice is (E)

As indicated above, J, N, and T must all be assigned to a shared locker. Thus, answer choice (E) is correct.

Question #2: Local, Must Be True. The correct answer choice is (B)

If T is assigned to locker 3, and M alone is assigned to locker 1, the following base setup results:

$$
\begin{array}{c c c c c}
 & & \text{T} & & \\
\text{M} & & \text{F} & & \\
\overline{} & \overline{} & \overline{} & \overline{} & \overline{} \\
1 & 2 & 3 & 4 & 5 \\
 & \cancel{N} & & \cancel{N} & \\
\end{array}
$$

Because T and F share locker three, N must share a locker with J in order to meet the conditions in the second and third rules. Further, because N cannot be assigned a locker adjacent to T, N (and J) cannot be assigned to locker 2 or 4. N also cannot be assigned to locker 1 (M is alone), and so N must be assigned to locker 5:

$$
\begin{array}{ccccc}
 & & \dfrac{\text{T}}{\dfrac{\text{F}}{}} & & \dfrac{\text{J}}{\dfrac{\text{N}}{}} \\
\dfrac{\text{M}}{1} & \dfrac{}{2} & \dfrac{}{3} & \dfrac{}{4} & \dfrac{}{5} \\
 & \cancel{} & & \cancel{} &
\end{array}
$$

Accordingly, answer choice (B) is correct.

Question #3: Local, Cannot Be True, List. The correct answer choice is (D)

With J assigned to locker 5, for the boys to be assigned to consecutively numbered lockers they must be assigned to lockers 2-3-4-5. R, a female assigned to a single locker, must then be assigned to locker 1:

$$
\begin{array}{ccccc}
\dfrac{\text{R}}{1} & \dfrac{}{2} & \dfrac{\text{F}}{3} & \dfrac{}{4} & \dfrac{\text{J}}{5}
\end{array}
$$

As locker 1 must be a single locker, locker 1 must be on our list and thus answer choices (A), (B), and (E) can be eliminated.

Of course, because J is assigned to locker 5, locker 5 must be a shared locker. Because N and T are assigned to the shared lockers and N and T cannot be consecutive, locker 4 cannot be a shared locker. Thus, lockers 1 and 4 cannot be shared, and answer choice (D) is correct.

Question #4: Local, Must Be True, Maximum. The correct answer choice is (C)

J must be assigned to a locker with N or T. Thus, J cannot be assigned to a locker with R or F. Because R and F must be assigned separate lockers, that means that two lockers must be reserved for R and F, leaving three lockers that J could be assigned. Hence, answer choice (C) is correct.

Question #5: Local, Must Be True. The correct answer choice is (A)

If the first three lockers are assigned to girls, then because N and T cannot be assigned to adjacent lockers they must be assigned to lockers 1 and 3, not necessarily in that order. R must then be assigned to locker 2. And, because F is already assigned to locker 3, J must then be assigned to locker 1, leading to the following scenario:

$$
\begin{array}{ccccc}
\dfrac{\text{N/T}}{\dfrac{\text{J}}{1}} & \dfrac{\text{R}}{2} & \dfrac{\text{T/N}}{\dfrac{\text{F}}{3}} & \dfrac{}{4} & \dfrac{}{5}
\end{array}
$$

Accordingly, answer choice (A) is correct.

Question #6: Local, Must Be True. The correct answer choice is (C)

If you understood the principle at work in question #5, this question should feel relatively comfortable.

If lockers 1 and 2 are unshared lockers assigned to boys, they must be assigned to M and P, not necessarily in that order. The shared lockers must then be assigned to lockers 3, 4, or 5. Because N and T are assigned shared lockers that cannot be adjacent lockers, they must be assigned to lockers 3 and 5, not necessarily in that order. R must then be assigned to locker 4. And, because F is already assigned to locker 3, J must then be assigned to locker 5, leading to the following scenario:

		N/T		T/N
M/P	P/M	F	R	J
1	2	3	4	5

Accordingly, answer choice (C) is correct.

This is a Grouping: Undefined game.

This is an extremely challenging game. The difficulty arises because the store carries ten CDs, but the number of CDs for sale is Undefined. As discussed in our courses and the *Logic Games Bible*, Undefined Grouping games can at times present a severe challenge. Increasing the complexity of the game, four of the rules involve a double conditional. The variables can be listed as follows:

$$NJ \quad N\!\!\!/O \quad NP \quad NR \quad NS \;^{10}$$
$$UJ \quad UO \quad \boxed{UP} \quad UR \quad US$$
$$ *$$

One critical inference involves identifying UO as a random. Because NO is not on sale, and none of the rules involve UO, answers to questions about the CDs that must or cannot be on sale are *not* likely to involve O. For example, #8 (C), #10 (A), (B), and (C), and #12 (B) each focus on O in a Must Be True or Cannot Be True question. Because we know nothing about the actions of UO, these answers are likely to be incorrect. A similar line of reasoning can be used to attack question #11. Question #11 asks for what Must Be True EXCEPT. Thus, each incorrect answer Must Be True, and the correct answer is Not Necessarily True. At first glance, answer choice (A), which addresses UO, is very likely to be correct because we know nothing about the actions of UO and thus almost anything is possible, the opposite of Must Be True. Note that, in question #13, the restrictions in the question stem are so severe as to ultimately affect UO.

The diagramming of the rules presents some choices. The second, third, fourth, and fifth rules contain multiple sufficient and necessary conditions. For example, the third rule can be diagrammed as follows:

$$\begin{array}{ccc} NJ & & N\!\!\!/R \\ + & \longrightarrow & + \\ UJ & & U\!\!\!/R \end{array}$$

Some students, however, may find this notation cumbersome. An alternate representation would be to diagram the rule as follows:

$$J \longrightarrow \cancel{R}$$

While this representation is easier to digest, because the rules vary between "and" and "or" conditions, some consideration must be given to the impact of those differences. For example, the conditions involving "all," "both," or "neither" could appear with an NU (new and used) designator:

$$J_{NU} \longrightarrow \cancel{R}_{NU}$$

Rules involving "either," or contrapositives involving "or" could be diagrammed without designators, thus indicating that the presence of either the new or used type of music would enact the rule.

Ultimately, either representation presents drawbacks: showing each type of music separately is cluttered, whereas using subscripts could be confusing. On the next page we will show both types of diagrams.

Separate music type representation:

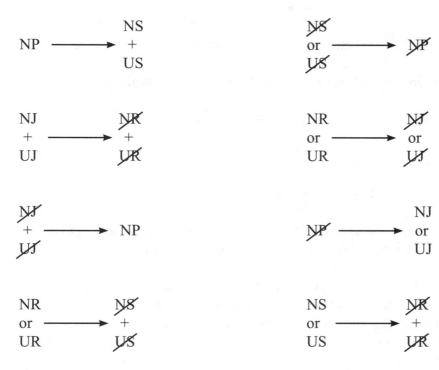

Please note that the second and fourth rules in the game are modified above to reflect the fact that UP must be on sale.

Subscript music type designator representation:

In attacking the game, we choose to use the second set of representations, but if you feel more comfortable with the first set of representations, you can certainly use those instead.

The relationships above lead to several inferences. For example, the second and fourth rules of the game can be combined:

$$\not{J}_{NU} \longrightarrow P \longrightarrow S_{NU}$$

This combination leads to the following inference:

$$\cancel{J}_{NU} \longrightarrow S_{NU}$$

This inference answers question #10, and eliminates answer choices (D) and (E) in question #11.

The last rule and the extended contrapositive of the second rule can be combined:

$$R \longrightarrow \cancel{S}_{NU} \longrightarrow \cancel{P}_{N}$$

This combination reduces to:

$$R \longrightarrow \cancel{P}_{N}$$

On some of the questions, a simple application of the contrapositive can be sufficient to answer them. For example, question #8 can be answered by applying the contrapositive of the second rule.

Largely, solving this game requires a simple application of the rules. However, because there are so many variables and the rules are complex in nature, that application process takes time. In addition, the lack of definition makes the game more difficult. Students would have been best served by recognizing that this is an Undefined game with a large number of variables and then pushing this game to last on this test on that basis.

Question #7: Global, Could Be True, List. The correct answer choice is (E)

Answer choice (A) is incorrect because, from the third rule, when both types of jazz are on sale, then no rap is on sale.

Answer choice (B) is incorrect because, from the last rule, when either type of rap is on sale, then no soul is on sale.

Answer choice (C) is incorrect because, from the fourth rule, when neither type of jazz is on sale, then new pop is on sale.

Answer choice (D) is incorrect because, from the second rule, when both types of pop are on sale, then all soul is on sale.

Answer choice (E) is the correct answer.

Question #8: Local, Must Be True. The correct answer choice is (E)

The condition in the question stem establishes that new soul is not on sale. As discussed in the setup, the contrapositive of the second rule then indicates both types of pop are not on sale (which functionally means that new pop is not on sale). This inference corresponds with the statement in answer choice (E), which is the correct answer.

31

Question #9: Local, Must Be True, Minimum. The correct answer choice is (A)

If both types of jazz are on sale, then the third rule applies, and no types of rap are on sale. As neither piece of information is sufficient to force anything else to occur, the only new type of music that must be on sale is jazz, and the correct answer is one.

Question #10: Global, Cannot Be True. The correct answer choice is (D)

As discussed in the setup, the second and fourth rules of the game can be combined to produce the following inference:

$$\cancel{J}_{NU} \longrightarrow S_{NU}$$

Thus, it cannot be true that neither type of jazz and neither type of soul is on sale, and answer choice (D) is correct.

Also as noted in the setup, answer choices (A), (B), and (C) are likely to be possible because they involve O.

Question #11: Local, Must Be True, Except. The correct answer choice is (A)

The inference discussed in question #10 leads to the elimination of answer choices (D) and (E) in this question (if neither type of jazz is on sale, then all soul is on sale). Of course, if both types of soul are on sale, then from the contrapositive of the last rule neither type of rap can be on sale, and answer choices (B) and (C) can be eliminated. Thus, answer choice (A) is proven correct by process of elimination.

Question #12: Local, Cannot Be True. The correct answer choice is (A)

If new soul is the *only* type of new CD on sale, then all other new types of CDs are not on sale. From the contrapositive of the fourth rule, then, if new pop is not on sale, then at least one type of jazz must be on sale. Since new jazz cannot be on sale, used jazz must be on sale. Therefore, answer choice (A) cannot be true and is correct.

Question #13: Local, Could Be True. The correct answer choice is (C)

The question stem defines the size of the group: four CDs are for sale, each of them used. As used pop is on sale from the first rule, the question setup appears as follows:

$$\underset{\text{Four CDs}}{\underline{P_U \quad \underline{} \quad \underline{} \quad \underline{}}}$$

Thus, used jazz, used opera, used rap, and used soul are the four contenders for the three remaining spaces. As only one of these four can be removed from the pool, we can eliminate answer choice (E) immediately because it attempts to remove two of the remaining types of used CDs.

The best approach at this point is to consider what happens when certain used CDs are eliminated:

If used jazz is not on sale, then neither type of jazz is on sale, and the fourth rule is enacted. Consequently, new pop would have to be on sale, which is impossible given the constraints of the question stem. Thus, used jazz must be on sale:

$$\underline{\quad P_U \quad} \quad \underline{\quad J_U \quad} \quad \underline{} \quad \underline{}$$
$$\text{Four CDs}$$

Answer choices (A) and (D)—both of which indicate that used jazz is not on sale—can thus be eliminated.

If used opera is not on sale, a problem arises because of the rules involving the other CDs. When used opera is not on sale, both used rap and used soul must be on sale. But, this creates a problem because according to the last rule, if either type of rap is on sale, then no soul is on sale. Thus, used opera must be on sale, and answer choice (B) can be eliminated.

Hence, by process of elimination, answer choice (C) is proven correct.

This is a Basic Linear: Defined, Unbalanced: Underfunded, Identify the Templates game.

The game is Underfunded because three division tours—O, P, and S—must be toured five times (3 into 5). The Underfunded aspect leads to a Numerical Distribution:

> Because S is toured exactly twice and each division is toured at least once, the five tours are distributed among the three divisions in a 2-2-1 partially fixed distribution. The distribution is partially fixed since S is toured twice, but the remaining three tours are assigned to P or O in a 2-1 unfixed distribution:

Partially		2	2	1
Fixed		S	O/P	P/O
Distribution				

> One of the challenges of the game is to keep track of the distribution of O and P.

Initially, most students diagram the game as follows:

O P S [3]

Because S is toured twice and the tours are consecutive, the placement options of the SS block are limited to four positions: Monday-Tuesday, Tuesday-Wednesday, Wednesday-Thursday, and Thursday-Friday. These four options split the game in four directions and are the basis for Identifying the Templates:

	M	Tu	W	Th	F
1. SS on Mon-Tue:	S	S	O	O/P	O/P
2. SS on Tue-Wed:	P	S	S	O/P	P/O
3. SS on Wed-Thu:	P	O/P	S	S	O/P
4. SS on Thu-Fri:	P	O/P	O	S	S

Although it is not necessary to number each template during the game, we do so here for purposes of the discussion to follow. Let us examine each template in greater detail:

1. SS on Mon-Tue: Since P cannot be toured on Wednesday, and the two tours of S are already scheduled, it can be inferred that O is toured on Wednesday. The only uncertain days are Thursday and Friday. Since neither can be S, O/P options have been placed on each. Note, however, that there are several possibilities for Thursday and Friday, such as O-P, P-O, and P-P. O-O is impossible because of the last rule.

2. SS on Tue-Wed: Since O cannot be toured on Monday, and the two tours of S are already scheduled, it can be inferred that P is toured on Monday. The only uncertain days are Thursday and Friday. Since neither can be S, dual O/P options have been placed on each. There are only two possibilities for Thursday and Friday, O-P and P-O. O-O is impossible because of the last rule, and P-P is impossible since O must be toured at least once during the five days.

3. SS on Wed-Thu: Since O cannot be toured on Monday, and the two tours of S are already scheduled, it can be inferred that P is toured on Monday. The only uncertain days are Tuesday and Friday. Since neither can be S, O/P options have been placed on each. There are three possibilities for Tuesday and Friday, O-P, P-O, and O-O. P-P is impossible since O must be toured at least once during the five days.

4. SS on Thu-Fri: Since O cannot be toured on Monday, and the two tours of S are already scheduled, it can be inferred that P is toured on Monday. Since P cannot be toured on Wednesday, it can be inferred that O is toured on Wednesday. The only uncertain day is Tuesday, which has either tour O or P.

This setup highlights the difference between Identify the Templates and Identify the Possibilities: The templates capture the four major directions of the game but do not map out every single possibility. With the templates in hand, there is sufficient information to attack the questions effectively.

When using the templates, you simply need to scan each to find the correct information. The questions will naturally direct you towards using some templates and away from using others.

Question #14: Global, Cannot Be True. The correct answer choice is (C)

Template #1 eliminates answer choice (A). Template #2 or #3 can be used to eliminate answer choice (B). Checking all four templates proves that answer choice (C) is correct. Template #1 eliminates answer choice (D). Template #4 (and less resoundingly, Template #2) eliminates answer choice (E).

Question #15: Local, Could Be True. The correct answer choice is (B)

The conditions in the question stem eliminate Template #2 from consideration. Since there are still three templates in consideration and thus a considerable number of possibilities, it is best to consider each answer choice against all remaining templates. For answer choice (A) only Templates #3 and #4 have P toured on Monday; but neither have O on Thursday, and so answer choice (A) is incorrect. For answer choice (B) only Templates #3 and #4 could have P toured on Tuesday, and Template #3 allows S to be toured on Wednesday, so answer choice (B) is correct. For answer choice (C) only Templates #3 and #4 have O toured on Tuesday. Template #4 does not have P toured on Friday, and so it does not apply; Template #3 could have P toured on Friday, but to do so would violate the condition in the question stem requiring one other division beside S to be toured on two consecutive days. Consequently, answer choice (C) is incorrect. For answer choice (D), only Template #1 applies, and if O were toured on Friday again, the condition in the question stem requiring one other division beside S to be toured consecutively would be violated. So answer choice (D) is incorrect. Finally, for answer choice (E) only Template #3 applies, but if P were toured on Friday, the condition in the question stem requiring one other division beside S to be toured consecutively would be violated. So answer choices (C), (D), and (E) each can be eliminated by the condition in the questions stem. In this question it is easier to find the correct answer than it is to eliminate the incorrect answers.

Question #16: Local, Must Be True. The correct answer choice is (A)

Only Template #3 allows the tours on Tuesday and Friday to be identical (O on both days). Therefore answer choice (A) is correct.

Question #17: Local, Could Be True. The correct answer choice is (E)

Template #1 is eliminated from consideration by the condition in the question stem, and for Templates #3 and #4 to apply, O must be toured on Tuesday. If necessary, write out the three templates in consideration:

2. SS on Tue-Wed:	P	S	S	O/P	P/O
3. SS on Wed-Thu:	P	O	S	S	O/P
4. SS on Thu-Fri:	P	O	O	S	S

The first four answer choices can each be rejected by scanning the three remaining templates. Template #4 proves answer choice (E) correct.

Question #18: Local, Must Be True. The correct answer choice is (A)

Only Templates #2 and #4 meet the condition in the question stem. Consequently answer choice (A) is correct.

The decision to diagram the four templates results in large part from the SS block, but it is also important to consider the impact of the O, S, and P trio. When the LSAT supplies only three options for a space the situation is inherently limited. If just one of the options is removed, then a dual-option would result automatically, making the situation easier to handle.

In this game the benefit of Identifying the Templates is obvious. And spending a bit more time during the setup simplifies the process of answering the questions.

This is a Grouping/Linear Combination, Numerical Distribution game.

Because the five tasks (F, W, T, S, and P) must be done in order, you must use the tasks as the base of the game, and show the seven workers (G, H, I, K, L, M, and O) available above each task. According to the information in the rules, only the following people could complete each of the listed tasks:

I/K	L/O	G/L	H/K/M	H/I/O
F	W	T	S	P

While the above diagram lends a Basic Linear aspect to the game, the number of days it takes to complete the partition adds a Grouping element. The game scenario and second rule establish that the workers must install the partition in either two or three days. Accordingly, the rules allow for several different Numerical Distributions of tasks-to-days:

1-2-2	Unfixed
1-3-1	Fixed
3-1-1	Fixed
3-2	Fixed
4-1	Fixed

A 1-1-3 or a 1-4 fixed distribution is impossible since T and P are done on different days. A 3-2 distribution is possible since the five tasks must be done in *at most three days*. Even though the first rule states that "At least one task is done each day," this allows for a situation wherein the partition completion takes two days and three tasks are done the first day and two tasks are done the second day. As further support, note question #22, which begins, "*If* the installation takes three days…" The first rule about at least one task per each rules out a distribution such as 3-0-2.

Thus, with the above information we have enough information to attack the questions, but note that this is clearly an unconventional game.

Question #19. Global, Could Be True, List. The correct answer choice is (B)

The diagram of workers-to-tasks at the top of the page makes this List question easy to solve. For example, only I or K can do the framing, and therefore either I or K must be on the list. Answer choice (E) contains neither I nor K, and thus answer choice (E) can be eliminated. The same process can be applied to each of the other answer choices:

Answer choice (A) is incorrect because L or O must do the wallboarding.

Answer choice (B) is the correct answer.

Answer choice (C) is incorrect because G or L must do the taping.

Answer choice (D) is incorrect because G or L must do the taping.

Question #20. Local, Could Be True. The correct answer choice is (D)

The conditions in the question stem create a 2-1-2 fixed numerical distribution, with the tasks apportioned as follows:

$$
\begin{array}{ccc}
\textcircled{2} & \textcircled{1} & \textcircled{2} \\[1em]
\underline{W} & & \underline{P} \\
\underline{F} & \underline{T} & \underline{S} \\
\text{day 1} & \text{day 2} & \text{day 3}
\end{array}
$$

The question asks you to identify a pair of crew members who could work on both the first and third days. According to our workers-to-tasks diagram, only I or K, and L or O could work on the first day, and H or K or M, and H or O or I could work on the third day. Immediately, several variables can be eliminated from contention. For example, L could work on day 1, but couldn't work on day 3. H and M could work on day 3 but not day 1. Ultimately, only I, K, and O are common to both days, and thus the correct answer must include two members of that group *and* be a pair who can cover all four tasks. Only K and O meet the criteria. Therefore, (D) is the correct answer choice.

Question #21. Global, Could Be True, List, Except. The correct answer choice is (A)

To attack this question, we must find the crew list that cannot complete all of the tasks listed. It is important to note that each of these lists represents a complete crew (not four out of five members). Thus it is valuable to focus on the abilities of the crew members listed. The correct answer is answer choice (A), because between H, I, K, and M, the crew has no one to do the taping or the wallboarding, so this could not be an acceptable crew.

Question #22. Local, Could Be True, List. The correct answer choice is (E)

Because the second sentence of the game scenario requires that the tasks be completed in the prescribed order, we know that for this question, where S is done on the third day, P must also be done on the third day as well.

As we know from the introductory discussion, there is no numerical distribution which allows for more than two tasks to be done on Wednesday, so we know that S and P must be the only tasks completed that day. Since at least one task must be completed on each, we know that the first task, F, must be completed on the first day, and that the third task, T, must be done on the second day. The only question which then remains is whether W is done on the first or the second day:

W/	/W	P
F	T	S
Day 1	Day 2	Day 3

With T established as being done on the second day, the correct answer must include G or L. That inference eliminates answer choices (A), (B), and (C).

As answer choices (D) and (E) each contain two names, the distribution in this question must be fixed at 1-2-2, with taping and wallboarding completed on the second day. Thus, the correct answer must include G or L for the taping (both answers do so), and a person capable of completing wallboarding. Only L or O can complete wallboarding, and answer choice (E) must therefore be correct.

Question #23. Local, Could Be True. The correct answer choice is (D)

This is a potentially confusing question. The question stem requires that the two workers each complete two tasks, and that they work on the same days as each other. Thus, we need a pair of workers that must meet the following criteria:

1. Each worker must be able to complete two tasks. This immediately eliminates answer choice (A), which includes both G and M, workers who can each complete just one task each.

2. The workers must also be able to jointly complete four separate tasks (two different tasks for each worker). This fact eliminates answer choices (B) and (E). Answer choice (B) is eliminated because H and K can only complete three total tasks (sanding, priming, and framing), and answer choice (E) is eliminated because L and O can only complete three total tasks (wallboarding, taping, and priming).

3. Finally, the workers must also be able to complete the first two tasks on the same day as each other, and the other two tasks on the same day as each other. This eliminates answer choice (C) because while I and L can complete two tasks together on the first day (framing and wallboarding), they cannot complete the other two tasks on the same day as each other because the two tasks would have to taping and priming, and those two tasks must be completed on different days according to the second rule.

Answer choice (D) is the correct answer choice, because K and L are the only pair listed which can meet the new criteria: If the first two tasks are completed on Day 1 (by K and L, respectively), and the next two tasks are completed on Day 2 (by L and K, respectively), then this is a pair that can work on the same two days, and each can complete two tasks. Day 3 would be priming, and would be completed by H, I, or O.

POWERSCORE®

32
PREPTEST

OCTOBER 2000 LOGIC GAMES SETUPS

32

This is a Grouping/Linear Combination game.

This game bears a striking resemblance to the third game of the December 1994 LSAT. The only difference is that the December 1994 game contained an extra not-block rule.

This Grouping/Linear Combination game features eight reports filling six spaces, and the six spaces are spread over three days, in morning and afternoon slots:

GHIKLNOR⁸

```
        PM   ___   ___   ___
        AM   ___   ___   ___
              M     Tu    W
```

As always, the choice of putting the morning row on the top or bottom is yours; each presentation is functionally identical.

The first rule indicates that if G gives a report, then it must be on Tuesday. Thus, G cannot give a report on Monday or Wednesday:

GHIKLNOR⁸

```
        PM   ___   ___   ___
        AM   ___   ___   ___
              M     Tu    W
              Ǥ           Ǥ
```

The second rule eliminates O and R from giving afternoon reports, which can be shown with side Not Laws:

GHIKLNOR⁸

```
        PM   ___   ___   ___      Ø Ɍ
        AM   ___   ___   ___
              M     Tu    W
              Ǥ           Ǥ
```

The third rule is an unusual one, and it indicates that if Nina gives a report on Monday or Tuesday, then H and I must give reports the following day:

$$N_{M/Tu} \longrightarrow \boxed{\begin{array}{c} H/I \\ I/H \end{array}}_{Tu/W}$$

The previous information can be compiled to produce the final setup for the game:

GHIKLNOR[8]
     * *

$$N_{M/Tu} \longrightarrow \boxed{\begin{array}{c} H/I \\ I/H \end{array}}_{Tu/W}$$

	M	Tu	W	
PM	___	___	___	Ø̷ K̷
AM	___	___	___	
	Ø̷		Ø̷	

Because this game features eight reports filling six spaces, any time two students are eliminated from the scheduling, the remaining six students must be scheduled. Question #2 is a prime example of the application of this inference. Because neither K nor L is scheduled, therefore G, H, I, N, O, and R must be scheduled. Because O and R cannot give an afternoon report, they must be scheduled for the morning. Only answer choice (D) contains both O and R, and thus answer choice (D) is correct.

A second application of the above inference is found in question #6. The question stem in #6 indicates that H, K, and L occupy the morning spaces, leaving only the afternoon spaces open. From the second rule, we can determine that neither O nor R can give an afternoon report. Thus, the afternoon spaces must be occupied by G, I, and N in some order. The rules and question stem indicate that G must give a report on Tuesday afternoon, and therefore N cannot give a report on Monday afternoon from the contrapositive of the third rule. Instead, N must give her report on Wednesday afternoon and I is forced to give his report on Monday afternoon. Answer choice (B) is therefore correct.

Question #1: Global, Could Be True, List. The correct answer choice is (C)

The second rule prohibits afternoon reports by either R or O. This restriction rules out answer choices (A) and (B).

Answer choice (D) is not an acceptable schedule because if N reports on Monday, H and I must report on Tuesday. And since George can only report on Tuesday, answer choice (E) is ruled out as well.

This leaves only choice (C), which is the correct answer choice.

Question #2: Local, Could Be True, List. The correct answer choice is (D)

As discussed during the setup, answer choice (D) is correct.

Question #3: Global, Must Be True. The correct answer choice is (B)

This is a very unique question, and we must determine which of the answer choices contains a pair of students that, if they give reports on the same day, can only do so on Wednesday. If we consider the rules that apply to Wednesday, the first rule tells us that G cannot report on Wednesday, and this fact rules out answer choice (A).

The third rule tells us that if N does not report on Wednesday, she must be followed by H and I on the day after N's report. Since we know that there is a rule dealing with N and Wednesday, we should next consider the answer choices that include N. Answer choice (B) is the correct answer choice: N and H can never report together on any other day besides Wednesday—if N reports on Monday or Tuesday, H must report on the following day. Therefore, if N and H are to report together, they have no choice but to report on Wednesday.

Question #4: Local, Could Be True. The correct answer choice is (A)

Given the stipulations, we can determine that G must give a report on Tuesday. Thus, according to the contrapositive of the third rule, N cannot give a report on Monday, and since R, G, and N give reports on different days, N must therefore give a report on Wednesday. Consequently, R must give a report on Monday, in the morning per the second rule. This information is sufficient to immediately eliminate answer choices (B), (C), and (E).

Answer choice (D) can be eliminated since if O were to give a report on Monday, she would have to do so in the afternoon, a violation of the second rule. Therefore, answer choice (A) is correct.

Question #5: Local, Could Be True, List. The correct answer choice is (D)

According to the question stem, K and H give afternoon reports on Tuesday and Wednesday, respectively. This leaves Monday afternoon as the most restricted space: O and R cannot give reports on Monday afternoon, G cannot give a report on Monday, and N cannot give a report on Monday since K gives a report on Tuesday. Thus, either I or L must give a report on Monday afternoon:

$$
\begin{array}{cccc}
\text{PM} & \underline{\text{I/L}} & \underline{\text{K}} & \underline{\text{H}} \\
\text{AM} & \underline{\quad} & \underline{\quad} & \underline{\quad} \\
& \text{M} & \text{Tu} & \text{W}
\end{array}
$$

Each of the four incorrect answers contains both I and L as students giving morning reports. Answer choice (D) is thus correct.

Question #6: Local, Must Be True. The correct answer choice is (B)

As discussed in the setup, answer choice (B) is correct.

This is a Grouping: Partially Defined, Numerical Distribution game.

The first sentence of the scenario establishes that either 5 or 6 works will be selected:

Because the game is Partially Defined at five or six works selected, the diagram above shows that at least five works must be selected; the bar between the fifth and sixth work indicates that a sixth works can possibly be selected.

The second sentence establishes that the group of nine works is composed of French and Russian novels and plays. As each work has two characteristics, one method is to show them in a vertical format:

F	F	F		R	R	R		F	F		R
N	N	N		N	N	N		P	P		P

Thus, our diagram should also have two rows, one for the nationality and one for the type of work:

F/R: ___ ___ ___ ___ ___ | ___

N/P: ___ ___ ___ ___ ___ | ___

The first three rules each address a numerical aspect of the game. The first rule indicates that at most four French works are selected, meaning that at least one Russian work is selected. The combination of the second and third rules creates four basic Numerical Distributions for FN and RN:

FN	≥	RN
2		1
2		2
3		1
3		0

Other seemingly possible numerical combinations of FN and RN, such as 3-2 or 3-3, are impossible because the maximum number of novels is 4. Combinations such as 1-0, 1-1, and 2-0 are impossible because they would cause fewer than five total works to be selected.

These four distributions indicate that at least two FNs must always be selected. Also, since the maximum number of novels is four, *at least one* P must always be selected. The two FNs can easily be shown on the diagram, and then the choice is yours as to show the minimum one P or the minimum one R. Here is the diagram with both FNs, the minimum of three Ns, and one P:

F/R: F   F   ___   ___   ___ | ___
N/P: N   N   N   P   ___ | ___

The four FN/RN distributions have a powerful effect on the questions. For example, on question #8, the distributions show that answer choice (A) could be true and is therefore correct. On question #10, the distributions prove that answer choice (D) is correct. The distribution even has an impact on question #11 as it shows that answer choice (A) is impossible: if no RNs are selected, the maximum number of FN's selected is three, and three FNs plus exactly one P equals four total works, one less than the required minimum.

The last rule of the game states that if both FPs are selected, then no RP is selected. But, because at least one R work must be selected, if both FPs are selected then at least one RN is selected:

```
F
P
 +  ──────────▶  R̸  ──────────▶   R
F                P̸                 N
P
```

Consequently, at most two plays can be selected, which corresponds to the second rule that at least three novels are always selected.

Overall, the rules in the game are not precise, and thus they are not easy to display conventionally. This situation gives the game a piecemeal or random feel. However, if you can focus on the rules involving numbers and thereby create the FN/RN distribution, this game is not difficult. Here is the final diagram for this game:

```
F/R:   F      F    ___   ___   ___   | ___
N/P:   N      N     N     P    ___   | ___
```

Max 4 F = Min 1 R

N ———→ 3/4

FN	≥	RN
2		1
2		2
3		1
3		0

```
F
P
 + ———→  R̸ ———→  R
F        P̸       N
P
```

Question #7: Global, Could Be True, List. The correct answer choice is (C)

As always, in List questions apply the rules to the answer choices—this normally allows you to solve the questions quickly and easily.

Answer choice (A) is incorrect because from the third rule at least as many French novels as Russian novels are selected.

Answer choice (B) is incorrect because from the fourth rule when both French plays are selected, the Russian play is not selected.

Answer choice (C) is the correct answer.

Answer choice (D) is incorrect because from the first rule at most four French works are selected.

Answer choice (E) is incorrect because from the second rule no more than four novels can be selected.

Question #8: Global, Could Be True. The correct answer choice is (A)

As discussed during the setup, one of the novel distributions allows for three French novels and no Russian novels to be selected. Hence, answer choice (A) is correct.

Answer choice (B) is incorrect because selecting only one French novel would result in fewer than five works being selected, a violation of the condition in the game scenario.

Answer choice (C) is incorrect because the fourth rule disallows all three plays from being selected.

Answer choice (D) is incorrect because from the third rule all three French novels would have to be selected, which would result in a violation of the second rule that a maximum of four novels are selected.

Answer choice (E) is incorrect because this selection would violate the first rule, which limits the number of French works to four.

Question #9: Local, Could Be True, List. The correct answer choice is (C)

The question stem establishes that three French novels are selected:

F/R: F F F
N/P: N N N P

Thus, there must be at least two remaining works in order to meet the minimum of five works. This fact eliminates answer choice (A), which would create a group of only four works.

Applying the first rule, the two remaining works can include at most one French work. This fact eliminates answer choices (B) and (D).

Because three novels have already been selected, from the second rule at most one additional novel can be selected. This eliminates answer choice (E).

Consequently, answer choice (C) is correct.

Question #10: Global, Must Be True. The correct answer choice is (D)

As established during the setup, at least two French novels must always be selected. Hence, answer choice (D) is correct.

Question #11: Global, Could Be True, Except. The correct answer choice is (A)

Answer choice (A) cannot occur, and thus is the correct answer. Under answer choice (A), there would only be a total of four works available to be selected, a violation of the condition in the game scenario that requires at least five works to be selected.

The remaining answer choices all could be true. Note that answer choice (D) is proven possible by the hypothetical produced in question #7.

This is a Basic Linear: Balanced game.

The initial scenario for the game places eight compositions in order, creating a Basic Linear game:

F H L O P R S T [8]

$$\underline{\quad}_1 \quad \underline{\quad}_2 \quad \underline{\quad}_3 \quad \underline{\quad}_4 \quad \underline{\quad}_5 \quad \underline{\quad}_6 \quad \underline{\quad}_7 \quad \underline{\quad}_8$$

The first rule creates an unusual block that places T ahead of F or behind R:

or
$$\boxed{TF}$$
$$\boxed{RT}$$

This block could also be diagrammed as:

$$\boxed{R/ \quad T \quad /F}$$

Note that this rule is unusual in that it links T to two separate variables, and those two variables are independent of each other. Because of the uncertain nature of this block, no Not Laws can be drawn.

The second rule creates a rotating RF split-block, with at least two compositions between R and F:

min
$$\boxed{F/R \quad \underline{\quad} \quad \underline{\quad} \quad R/F}$$

Jumping ahead, the sixth rule is similar to the second rule:

min
$$\boxed{O/S \quad \underline{\quad} \quad S/O}$$

The presence of the words "at least" at the start of the second and sixth rules make this game a bit more difficult than would otherwise be expected. The split-blocks diagrammed above have the "min" designation in order to indicate that the designated split is the *minimum* required by the rule. For example, R and F must be separated by *at least* two spaces, but they could be separated by three or more spaces. Because of the uncertainty in these two rules, a large number of the questions are Local.

According to the third rule, O is first or fifth, and according to the fourth rule H or L is performed eighth:

F H L O P R S T ⁸

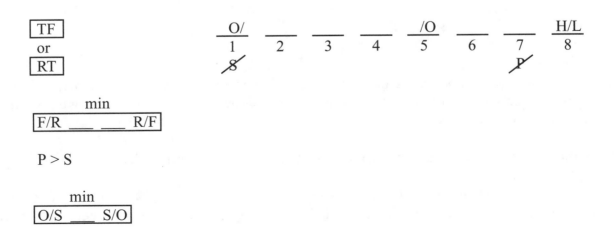

Finally, the fifth rule states that P is performed at some time before S, creating a basic sequence:

$$P > S$$

Accordingly, S cannot be performed first, and P cannot be performed seventh (the last available open spot), leading to the final diagram for the game:

F H L O P R S T ⁸

Note that O is also linked to S through the last rule. If O is fifth, then S must be second (and P must be first), or S must be third, or S must be seventh (it cannot be eighth due to the fourth rule).

The key to the game is to fit all of the blocks together. You must constantly be on the watch for scenarios where not all the blocks can fit together.

Question #12: Global, Could Be True, List. The correct answer choice is (A)

Answer choice (A) is the correct answer.

Answer choice (B) is incorrect because it violates the first rule.

Answer choice (C) is incorrect because O must be performed first or fifth.

Answer choice (D) is incorrect because there is not at least one composition between S and O, a violation of the last rule.

Answer choice (E) is incorrect because R and F are not separated by at least two compositions, a violation of the second rule.

Question #13: Global, Cannot Be True. The correct answer choice is (E)

The fifth rule stipulates that P must be performed before S, and the fourth rule states that the eighth composition is L or H. Thus, if P were performed seventh, then S would have to be performed eighth, which would violate the fourth rule. Thus, answer choice (E) is correct.

Question #14: Local, Must Be True. The correct answer choice is (A)

If T is performed fifth, then from the third rule O must be performed first. If F is performed sixth, then from the second rule R must be performed second or third. S cannot be performed second due to the last rule. S also cannot be performed third because if S were third, then P would be second, and there would be no place for R. This information leads to the following setup:

O	R/	/R		T	F		H/L
1	2	3	4	5	6	7	8
	S̶	S̶					

Remember, because R must be second or third, and P must be performed at some time before S, S cannot be performed second or third. Hence, the only options available to S are fourth and seventh, and answer choice (A) is correct.

Question #15: Local, Must Be True. The correct answer choice is (E)

If O is performed immediately after T, then O cannot be performed first, and O must be performed fifth. With T in fourth, the first rule comes into play, and we can infer that R must be performed third.

When R is performed third, from the second rule we can infer that F must be performed sixth or seventh, leading to the following setup:

$$\frac{}{1} \quad \frac{}{2} \quad \frac{R}{3} \quad \frac{T}{4} \quad \frac{O}{5} \quad \frac{F/}{6} \quad \frac{/F}{7} \quad \frac{H/L}{8}$$

Accordingly, answer choice (E) is correct.

Question #16: Local, Could Be True, List. The correct answer choice is (C)

If S is performed fourth, then from the last rule O cannot be performed fifth, and we can conclude that O must be performed first. This information eliminates answer choices (A), (B), and (E). Answer choice (D) can be eliminated because if P is second, and T is third, and we already know that S is fourth, then the placement of T violates the first rule. Thus, answer choice (C) is correct.

Question #17: Local, Must Be True. The correct answer choice is (C)

If S is performed sixth, then from the last rule O cannot be performed fifth, and we can conclude that O must be performed first, creating the following setup:

$$\frac{O}{1} \quad \frac{}{2} \quad \frac{P}{3} \quad \frac{}{4} \quad \frac{}{5}_{\cancel{O}} \quad \frac{S}{6} \quad \frac{}{7} \quad \frac{H/L}{8}$$

The first rule creates either an RT or TF block, and the only remaining place for that block to fit on this diagram is in spaces four and five. Hence, the composition performed fifth must be either F or T, and answer choice (C) is correct.

Question #18: Local, Must Be True. The correct answer choice is (D)

The condition in the question stem creates an F __ __ O block. Consequently, O cannot be performed first, and O must be performed fifth (and F must be performed second). From the second rule, we know that at least two compositions must separate R and F, and since F is second, we can conclude that R must be sixth or seventh. This information eliminates answer choices (A), (B), and (C). If R is performed seventh, then from the first rule we can conclude that T is performed first, and from the last rule we can conclude that S is performed third. But, if S is performed third, then there is no room for P to be performed before S, and the fifth rule is violated. Hence, R cannot be performed seventh, and R must be performed sixth. Answer choice (D) is thus correct.

32

This is an Advanced Linear: Unbalanced: Underfunded, Identify the Templates game.

The game scenario establishes that on each of seven consecutive days, a pet shop features one of three breeds of kitten, and one of three breeds of puppy. This creates an Advanced Linear setup:

G N R ³
H M S ³   pup: ___ ___ ___ ___ ___ ___ ___   G N R

                kit: ___ ___ ___ ___ ___ ___ ___   H M S
                      1   2   3   4   5   6   7

The first rule places G on day 1, and the second rule eliminates G from day 2. Thus, day 2 must be N or R. The third rule eliminates G from day 7, leaving day 7 as N or R:

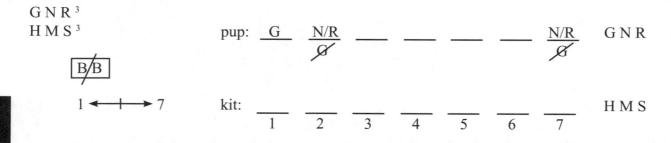

The second rule is represented above as a BB not-block, which indicates that no breed can be featured on consecutive days. This is a more concise representation than drawing all six not-blocks. The third rule is represented with a double-not arrow between 1 and 7.

The fourth rule establishes that exactly three Hs are featured, but that no H is featured on day 1. Thus, M or S must be featured as the kitten on day 1. The fifth rule indicates that R is not featured on day 7. This fact, when combined with the inference that G cannot be featured on day 7, results in the inference that N must be featured on day 7. If day 7 must be N, then from the second rule day 6 cannot be N, and must therefore be G or R.

The fifth rule also establishes that R cannot be featured on the same day as H, which results in a vertical not-block:

Combining the above information results in the following setup:

GNR³
HMS³

pup: ___G___ __N/R__ ___ ___ ___ __G/R__ __N__   GNR
              Ø̸   X̸   R̸
                                           Ø̸

B̸/B

1 ◄──┼──► 7   kit: __M/S__ ___ ___ ___ ___ ___ ___   HMS
                      1   2   3   4   5   6   7

3 Hs   H̸

R̸
H̸

While the above setup is the final setup for many students, the interaction of the second and fourth rules restricts the placement of the three Hs to just four possibilities:

Template #1: ___ ___ _H_ ___ _H_ ___ _H_
Template #2: ___ _H_ ___ ___ _H_ ___ _H_
Template #3: ___ _H_ ___ _H_ ___ ___ _H_
Template #4: ___ _H_ ___ _H_ ___ _H_ ___
               1   2   3   4   5   6   7

These four possibilities can be (but do not have to be) used to Identify the Templates:

Template #1:   ___G___ __N/R__ __G/N__   ___   __N/G__ __G/R__ __N__
               __M/S__ __S/M__ ___H___ _M/S_ ___H___ __M/S__ __H__
                  1   2   3   4   5   6   7

Template #2:   ___G___ __N__   __G/R__   ___   __N/G__ __G/R__ __N__
               __M/S__ __H__   __M/S__ _S/M_ ___H___ __M/S__ __H__
                  1   2   3   4   5   6   7

Template #3:   ___G___ __N__   __G/R__ __N/G__   ___   __G/R__ __N__
               __M/S__ __H__   __M/S__ ___H___ _M/S_ __S/M__ __H__
                  1   2   3   4   5   6   7

Template #4:   ___G___ __N__   __G/R__ __N/G__ __R/N__ __G__   __N__
               __M/S__ __H__   __M/S__ ___H___ __M/S__ __H__ __S/M__
                  1   2   3   4   5   6   7

The only drawback to showing the four templates is that the process can be somewhat time-consuming, and overall the questions can still be done without the templates, albeit less efficiently.

Question #19: Global, Could Be True, List. The correct answer choice is (E)

Answer choice (A) is incorrect because from the fourth rule H cannot be featured on day 1.

Answer choice (B) is incorrect because it violates the third rule about the same breed not being featured on day 1 and day 7.

Answer choice (C) is incorrect because H is only featured twice, a violation of the fourth rule.

Answer choice (D) is incorrect because S is featured on consecutive days, a violation of the second rule.

Answer choice (E) is the correct answer.

Question #20: Local, Could Be True. The correct answer choice is (B)

If H is not featured on day 2, only Template #1 applies:

Template #1:	G	N/R	G/N		N/G	G/R	N
	M/S	S/M	H	M/S	H	M/S	H
	1	2	3	4	5	6	7

Accordingly, answer choice (B) is correct.

Question #21: Global, Could Be True. The correct answer choice is (D)

This question can be easily solved using the Templates, or by applying the rules.

From the discussion of the first three rules, answer choices (A) and (B) can be eliminated.

Answer choice (C) can be eliminated by applying the fifth rule.

Answer choice (D) is the correct answer.

Answer choice (E) can be eliminated because N is featured on day 7, and from the second rule N cannot then be featured on day 6.

Question #22: Local, Cannot Be True. The correct answer choice is (B)

If H is not featured on day 7, then only Template #4 applies:

Template #4:	G	N	G/R	N/G	R/N	G	N
	M/S	H	M/S	H	M/S	H	S/M
	1	2	3	4	5	6	7

32

As days 2 and 6 have established pairs of puppies and kittens that are different, answer choice (B) is the correct answer.

Question #23: Global, Could Be True. The correct answer choice is (A)

Answer choice (A) is the correct answer. Here's one hypothetical where this could occur:

Template #3:	$\frac{G}{S}$	$\frac{N}{H}$	$\frac{G}{S}$	$\frac{N}{H}$	$\frac{R}{M}$	$\frac{G}{S}$	$\frac{N}{H}$
	1	2	3	4	5	6	7

Answer choice (B) reflects a conditional relationship:

$$H \longrightarrow G$$

H must always be featured on day 2 and/or day 7. When H is featured on day 2, G cannot be featured on day 2, and when H is featured on day 7, N is already featured on day 7. Thus, while H and G can sometimes be featured together, they cannot be featured together at all times, and therefore this answer choice is incorrect.

Answer choice (C) reflects a conditional relationship:

$$G \longrightarrow H$$

This cannot be true because G is featured on day 1, but H cannot be featured on day 1.

Answer choice (D) reflects a conditional relationship:

$$\cancel{R} \longrightarrow H$$

This answer choice is identical to stating that:

$$\begin{matrix} G \\ or \\ N \end{matrix} \longrightarrow H$$

As shown by an analysis of day 1, this cannot be true and therefore this answer can be eliminated.

Answer choice (E) reflects a conditional relationship:

$$\cancel{H} \longrightarrow R$$

This answer choice is identical to stating that:

$$\begin{matrix} M \\ \text{or} \\ S \end{matrix} \longrightarrow R$$

As shown by an analysis of day 1, this cannot be true and therefore this answer can be eliminated.

Question #24: Local, Could Be True. The correct answer choice is (D)

If H is not featured on day 7, then only Template #4 applies:

Template #4:

G	N	G/R	N/G	R/N	G	N
M/S	H	M/S	H	M/S	H	S/M
1	2	3	4	5	6	7

Answer choices (A), (B), (C), and (E) can each be quickly eliminated by examining the Template. Therefore, answer choice (D) is correct.

32

POWERSCORE®

33
PREPTEST

DECEMBER 2000 LOGIC GAMES SETUPS

PrepTest 33. December 2000 Game #1: *1. C   2. A   3. E   4. D   5. B*

This is a Pure Sequencing game.

Because Pure Sequencing is generally favorable for most test takers, this was an excellent way to begin the December 2000 LSAT. The scenario and rules create the following the following diagram:

H J L P Q S V[7]

```
                           P
                 J > Q > - - - -
         H > - - - - - - - - -  (S)
                 L > - - - - - - -
                           V
```

```
 H    J/L   ___   ___   ___   ___   P/V
 1     2     3     4     5     6     7
                                     8̸
```

In creating the sequence diagram, the most problematic television program is S. S is less popular than both Q and L, but Q and L are in separate branches. We have solved this problem by placing S at the terminus of the dotted line separator, and then circling S.

As with all Pure Sequencing games, this one is built on top of a linear base. H must be the most popular television program, and only J or L could be second. Since S cannot be seventh, P or V must be the least popular. With this information we can attack the questions, while watching the following two areas:

1. In Pure Sequencing games the test makers always check to see whether you will make unwarranted assumptions about the relationships between the variables.

2. The test makers typically introduce new relationships into the sequence to test your understanding of how the original relationships are affected.

Question #1: Global, Could Be True, List. The correct answer choice is (C)

Apply the rules and inferences in this order: the inference that H must be first, the fifth rule, the second rule, and, finally, the first, third, and fourth rules can be applied in any order since they are roughly equivalent in form.

Answer choice (A) is incorrect because H must be more popular than J.

Answer choice (B) is incorrect because J must be more popular than Q.

Answer choice (C) is the correct answer.

Answer choice (D) is incorrect because L must be more popular than V.

Answer choice (E) is incorrect because S cannot be seventh.

Question #2: Local, Must Be True. The correct answer choice is (A)

When examining the linear portion of the setup, take special note of the dual-options. A favorite trick of the test makers is to "take away" one of the variables in a dual-option to see if you recognize that the other variable is then forced into that position. Since either J or L must be second, and according to the question stem J is more popular than L, L cannot be second and J must be second. Answer choice (A) reflects that fact and is correct.

Question #3: Global, Cannot Be True. The correct answer choice is (E)

A program that cannot be ranked third is one that has either three or more variables ranked before it (such as S), or five or more variables ranked behind it (such as H). Applying the former criterion produces the following analysis:

H	minimum of 0 variables ranked ahead, cannot be ranked third since must be ranked first
J	minimum of 1 variable ranked ahead (H), can be ranked third
L	minimum of 1 variable ranked ahead (H), can be ranked third
P	minimum of 3 variables ranked ahead (H, J, Q), cannot be ranked third
Q	minimum of 2 variables ranked ahead (H, J), can be ranked third
S	minimum of 4 variables ranked ahead (H, J, Q, L), cannot be ranked third
V	minimum of 2 variables ranked ahead (H, L), can be ranked third

Accordingly, H, P, and S cannot be ranked third. Since only P appears among the answer choices, answer choice (E) is correct.

Note that this question does not require any writing. The listing above has been provided for the purposes of clarity. Because speed is a factor during the test, the number of variables ranked ahead should be visually scanned and counted.

Question #4: Local, Could Be True. The correct answer choice is (D)

The condition in the question stem produces the following diagram:

$$
\begin{array}{c}
\qquad\qquad\qquad J \\
H > L > \text{----}> Q > S > P \\
\qquad\qquad\qquad V
\end{array}
$$

S must be ranked ahead of P because otherwise S would be ranked seventh, a violation of the rules.

In a Could Be True question the correct answer choice can actually have the characteristic of Must Be True, but that usually does not occur on the LSAT. Consequently, since the correct answer will likely contain a scenario that is possible but not certain to occur, the best strategy is to look immediately for the uncertainty in the diagram and attack that area. Since the only uncertainty in this question involves J and V (J could be ranked ahead of V or V could be ranked ahead of J), immediately scan the answer choices for one that contains both J and V. In this case only answer choice (D) contains J and V. After a brief examination, it is apparent that answer choice (D) could be true and is therefore correct.

If the diagram to this question had more areas of uncertainty, the strategy above would still have been successful but might have taken more time to apply.

Question #5: Local, Must Be True, Except. The correct answer choice is (B)

Remember, *Must Be True EXCEPT* is the same as *Not Necessarily True*. The condition in the question stem produces the following diagram:

$$H > J > Q > \text{- - - - - - - - - - -} \begin{array}{c} P \\ \\ S \\ L > \text{- - - - -} \\ V \end{array}$$

H, J, and Q must be ranked first, second, and third, respectively. Answer choices (A), (D), and (E) can thereby be eliminated. The highest V can be ranked is fifth and that eliminates answer choice (C). Since P could be fourth, it follows that L does not have to be fourth and answer choice (B) is correct.

For most test takers the appearance of a Pure Sequencing game is cause for celebration. Remember, Pure Sequencing games can be easily identified since the majority of rules are relative in nature.

This is a Grouping: Undefined game.

The number of variables being selected—birds in this case—is left open, and so the game is classified as Undefined. Although a maximum of six birds can be in the forest (remember, there are only six birds total), prior to consideration of the rules there could be anywhere from zero to six birds in the forest. This uncertainty increases the difficulty of the game and is an element that must be tracked throughout the game. Of course, since it cannot be determined exactly how many birds are in the forest, there is no static "selection group" diagram as in a Defined game. Here is the setup:

G H J M S W[6]

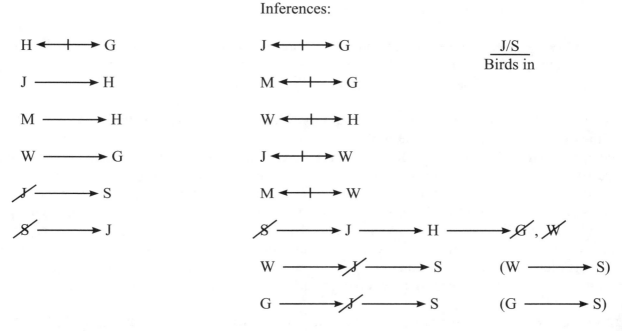

Like many Undefined Grouping games, this one contains a large number of conditional rules. By using basic linkage, we can draw a slew of inferences. Let us examine each in greater detail:

1. J ←—+—→ G. This inference results from linking the first two rules.

2. M ←—+—→ G. This inference results from linking the first two rules.

3. W ←—+—→ H. This inference results from linking the first and third rules.

4. J ←—+—→ W. This inference results from linking the first inference and the third rule. Note how the first inference has been recombined or "recycled" with the original rules.

5. M ←—+—→ W. This inference results from linking the second inference and the third rule. The third rule here refers to the rules as listed in the game.

6. S̸ ——→ J ——→ H ——→ G̸ , W̸. The final rule is tricky and bears further analysis. When J is not in the forest, then S must be in the forest. Via the contrapositive, when

S is not in the forest, then J must be in the forest. In each case, the absence of one of the birds forces the other bird to appear in the forest (hence J or S is always in the forest). This type of "omission" rule appears infrequently on LSAT games, but when it does, it tends to cause problems. It is easy to forget that the absence of a variable forces another variable to be present. In this case, when S is not in the forest, then J must be in the forest, and from the second rule, when J is in the forest, it follows that H must be in the forest. Of course, from the first rule and third inference, when H is in the forest, then G cannot be in the forest and W cannot be in the forest.

7. W $\longrightarrow\!\!\!\!\!/\!\!\!\longrightarrow$ S. From the fourth inference it is known that W and J cannot be in the forest together. Thus, when W is in the forest, then J cannot be in the forest, and from the last rule it follows that S must be in the forest (W $\longrightarrow$ S). This is another classic example of recycling an inference.

8. G $\longrightarrow\!\!\!\!\!/\!\!\!\longrightarrow$ S. Similar to the previous inference, when G is in the forest, then J cannot be in the forest, and from the last rule it follows that S must be in the forest (G $\longrightarrow$ S).

In light of all these inferences, the bigger question becomes, "When do you know you have made all of the inferences?" In this case the application of basic linkage creates a large number of inferences, and then the recycling of those inferences leads to even more inferences. At some point the time pressure of this section demands that you move on to the questions. Although in our diagram we could continue to make inferences (for example, if H is not in the forest, then J is not in the forest and S must be in the forest), there comes a point when you must ask yourself, "Do I have enough information to effectively attack the questions?" The answer here is undeniably "yes." It may be that you do not discover every inference in the game, but when you feel you have exhausted all the obvious routes of inference-making, it is time to move on to the questions. The challenge in the questions then becomes keeping track of all the information at your disposal.

Question #6: Global, Cannot Be True, List. The correct answer choice is (D)

In attacking this question, keep in mind that since each answer choice is supposed to be a complete and accurate list of the birds *not* in the forest, all of the birds not named on each list will be in the forest. Given the number of negative grouping rules in play, that is an important consideration. For example, in answer choice (B), when only H and G are not in the forest, J, M, S, and W are in the forest. But, according to the fourth inference, J and W cannot both be in the forest and therefore answer choice (B) is incorrect. Answer choice (E) can be eliminated by identical reasoning. Answer choice (C) can be eliminated because, via the third inference, H and W cannot both be in the forest. Answer choice (A) can be eliminated by applying the last rule. Answer choice (D) is therefore proven correct by process of elimination.

Question #7: Local, Must Be True. The correct answer choice is (E)

If H is in the forest, then G cannot be in the forest. If G cannot be in the forest, then W cannot be in the forest. At this point it has been established that H and M are in the forest and G and W are not in the forest. The only unaddressed birds are S and J, and at least one of them, possibly both, must be in the forest. Answer choices (A) and (B) are therefore incorrect because it is possible that both S and

J can be in the forest. Answer choice (C) is incorrect because, due to the final rule, the forest always contains at least S or J. Answer choice (D) is incorrect because it is possible there is only one other kind of bird in the forest (S or J). Answer choice (E) is thus correct because at most S and J can be in the forest in addition to M and H.

Question #8: Local, Cannot Be True, FTT. The correct answer choice is (D)

This question has been phrased in terms of falsity. Remember, always convert "false" questions into terms of "true." "Must Be False" is identical to "Cannot Be True," and so this question simply asks which one of the following Cannot Be True. If J is not in the forest, then according to the last rule, S must be in the forest, and answer choice (D) cannot be true and is therefore correct.

Question #9: Global, Must Be True, Maximum. The correct answer choice is (C)

In this question you must select the variables in such a way as to maximize the number of birds in the forest. This means that birds that tend to knock out several other birds must be removed. An examination of the list of inferences indicates that W must be removed since, when W is in the forest, then H, J, and M cannot be in the forest. The other bird that must be removed is G since, when G is in the forest, then H cannot be in the forest, and when H is not in the forest, then neither J nor M can be in the forest. If G and W are removed from consideration, then the remaining four birds are J, H, M, and S. Ultimately, four is the maximum number of birds in the forest, and answer choice (C) is correct.

Another approach to this question involves referring to work done on other questions. When this approach is used, hypotheticals are examined to eliminate certain answer choices. For example, in question #7 we were able to determine that four birds could be in the forest: M, H, S, and J. This hypothetical eliminates answer choices (A) and (B). To effectively use this approach, however, it would be best to skip this question and return after completing all other questions in order to have as many hypotheticals as possible.

A third approach involves considering the negative grouping rules in the setup. For example, since the first rule establishes that H and G cannot both be in the forest, answer choice (E) can be rejected. And since at least one of H and G cannot be in the forest and at least one of W and H (or W and J for that matter) cannot be in the forest, a case can also be made against answer choice (D). When you examine these rules, it is important to consider negative grouping rules that contain entirely different sets of variables. You cannot simply count all the negative rules and arrive at an answer because some of the rules will revolve around the same variables, and when those variable are removed the other variables can be selected.

Finally, let's take a moment to examine a mistake that is made by a number of test takers. Some students, upon encountering the final rule, make the classic error of assuming that the jays and the shrikes cannot be in the forest together. As discussed in the Avoiding False Inferences section, this is a false inference, and thus it is possible for J and S to be in the forest together. Let us take a moment to review:

Most LSAT Logic Game conditional rules place the "not" on the necessary condition, but in this rule, the "not" is on the sufficient condition. While that difference may seem minor, in effect it completely changes the meaning of the rule.

According to the rule, if J is not in the forest, then S must be in the forest, and via the contrapositive if S is not in the forest, then J must be in the forest. Essentially, this means that if either bird (S or J) is absent (not in the forest), then the other bird cannot also be absent (they cannot both be out of the forest at the same time; at least one must always be in the forest). In other words, all we know from the fourth rule is that they will never both be *out* of the forest, because as soon as one is out the other must be in. They could, however, both be in the forest at the same time. The rules never tell us anything about what happens when either J or S is *in* the forest, only what happens when J or S is not in the forest.

Since it is possible for both J and S to be in the forest at the same time, that possibility impacts the choices you have in questions #9 and #10. In #9, most people assume that one of J or S is always out of the forest. Obviously, that is not the case, and when arriving at the maximum number of birds in the forest you should include both J and S. In question #10, many people select answer choice (B) because they misinterpret the fourth rule. As explained above, J and S—the pair in answer choice (B) of question #10—can both be in the forest at the same time.

Question #10: Global, Cannot Be True. The correct answer choice is (A)

With Global Must Be True or Global Cannot Be True questions always make sure to check your inferences as the first step in attacking the question. Per inference #4 answer choice (A) is correct.

Note that this possibility is also discussed in the solution to question #9.

Question #11: Local, Must Be True. The correct answer choice is (A)

Per the final inference, when G is in the forest, then S must be in the forest, and answer choice (A) is proven correct. A review of the entire inference chain shows that, when G is in the forest, then H is not in the forest (from rule #1), and when H is not in the forest, then neither J or M is in the forest (from rule #2). When J is not in the forest, then S must be in the forest (from rule #4).

In this question, be sure to avoid making a Mistaken Reversal: although from the third rule we know that when W is in the forest then G must be in the forest, this does not mean that when G is in the forest that W must also be in the forest.

Question #12: Local, Could Be True. The correct answer choice is (B)

This is not a Suspension question because the rule is simply added on to the given information. In this way it acts like a normal Local question. The extra condition stipulates that S and H cannot both be in the forest. This affects both J and M because, when either J or M is in the forest, then H is in the forest. Thus, neither J and S nor M and S can be in the forest at the same time. This information is sufficient to reject answer choices (A) and (C). Answer choice (D) can also be rejected since, when J is not in the forest, then S must be in the forest, and when S is in the forest, then H is not in the forest, and when H is not in the forest, then neither J nor M is in the forest. Finally, answer choice (E) can be disproven since if H, for example, is in the forest, then G, S, and W are not in the forest. It follows that answer choice (B) is correct.

Despite the large number of inferences in this particular game, the typical student eventually comes to find this type of game completely reasonable, and certainly doable in the allotted time. As you develop the ability to make inferences more quickly, you will begin to see a game like this one as an opportunity to make up time, especially if you know how to handle the last rule.

This is a Grouping: Defined-Moving, Unbalanced: Overloaded, Numerical Distribution game.

This is a very challenging game. Initially, the game looks like a standard Overloaded Grouping game:

Ruby: F G H ^{3}
Saph: J K M ^{3}
Top: W X Y Z ^{4} Stone: ____ ____ ____ ____ ____ ____
                                            Type: ____ ____ ____ ____ ____ ____
                                                                      6 stones

Because each selection has two characteristics—type of stone (ruby, sapphire, topaz) and a specific name (F, G, etc)—there are two spaces for each of the six selections.

The first rule reserves at least two of the six selections for topazes:

Ruby: F G H ^{3}
Saph: J K M ^{3}
Top: W X Y Z ^{4} Stone: ____ ____ ____ ____ ____ ____
                                            Type: T   T   ____ ____ ____ ____
                                                                      6 stones

Note that the rule is somewhat open-ended as it specifies that *at least* two of the topazes are selected, so the above diagram only represents the minimum that must occur.

The second rule is conditional:

$$2S \longrightarrow 1R$$

Of course, if exactly two sapphires are selected, and exactly one ruby is selected, then the remaining three stones must be topazes:

$$2S \longrightarrow 1R \longrightarrow 3T$$

Thus, if exactly two sapphires are selected the six stone types are fully determined. More on this rule in a moment.

The third rule contains two negative grouping relationships:

$$W \longleftrightarrow\!\!\!\!| \longrightarrow H$$

$$W \longleftrightarrow\!\!\!\!| \longrightarrow Z$$

W and H are different types, so tracking this rule is a bit more challenging. W and Z are both topazes, and thus the maximum number of topazes that can be selected is three: X, Y, W/Z. In turn, this affects the second rule, which results in the topazes being selected. If the second rule is enacted, then the three topazes must include X and Y:

$$2S \longrightarrow 1R \longrightarrow 3T \ (X, Y, W/Z)$$

Note that because at least two topazes must be selected from the first rule, and W and Z cannot both be selected, we can infer that X or Y or both must always be selected.

The fourth rule is a simple conditional rule:

$$M \longrightarrow W$$

Of course, W appears in both the third and fourth rules, and combining those two rules leads to the following two inferences:

$$M \longleftrightarrow\!\!\!\!| \longrightarrow H$$

$$M \longleftrightarrow\!\!\!\!| \longrightarrow Z$$

Given that the first two rules address the number of each stone type in the game, a quick review of the numerical facts is worthwhile:

- Minimum 2 T (from the first rule)
- Maximum 3 T (W and Z won't go together, making 4 impossible)
- Maximum 3 R (there are only 3 Rs)
- Maximum 3 S (there are only 3 Ss)
- $2S \longrightarrow 1R \longrightarrow 3T$ (thus a 2-2-2 distribution is impossible)

Using these restrictions, the following Numerical Distributions can be identified:

Rubies	Sapphires	Topazes
1	3	2
3	1	2
1	2	3
2	1	3
3	0	3
0	3	3

The variety of distributions is one reason this game is difficult, but, fortunately, the distributions can be used to answer both question #14 and question #16.

Adding all of the information together produces the final setup:

Ruby: F G H ^{3}
Saph: J K M ^{3}
Top: W X Y Z ^{4}

$$\frac{X/Y}{T} \quad \frac{}{T} \quad \underline{\quad} \quad \underline{\quad} \quad \underline{\quad} \quad \underline{\quad}$$
6 stones

2S ⟶ 1R ⟶ 3T (X, Y, W/Z)   Grouping Inferences:

W ◄——► H   M ◄——► H

W ◄——► Z   M ◄——► Z

M ⟶ W   Either X or Y must be selected.

Rubies	Sapphires	Topazes
1	3	2
3	1	2
1	2	3
2	1	3
3	0	3
0	3	3

Question #13: Global, Could Be True, List. The correct answer choice is (D)

Answer choice (A) is incorrect because from the fourth rule if M is selected, W must be selected.

Answer choice (B) is incorrect because from the first rule at least two topazes must be selected.

Answer choice (C) is incorrect because two sapphires are selected (J and K) so only one ruby can be selected (but both F and G are selected here).

Answer choice (D) is the correct answer choice.

Answer choice (E) is incorrect because from the third rule W and Z cannot be selected together.

Question #14: Global, Must Be True. The correct answer choice is (E)

From the discussion of the distribution possibilities established by the rules, there must always be 3 rubies, 3 sapphires, or 3 topazes selected. Thus, answer choice (E) is correct.

Question #15: Local, Could Be True. The correct answer choice is (E)

If Z is selected, then from the third rule W is not selected. If W is not selected, then from the contrapositive of the fourth rule M is not selected. Thus, answer choices (A), (B), and (C), each of which contain M, are wrong.

Answer choice (D) is incorrect because it would result in an insufficient number of stones to make the six rings. If no ruby is selected, then all three sapphires must be selected. However, that means that M is selected, which from the fourth rule forces W to be selected. Since Z is already selected according to the question stem, this results in a violation of the third rule.

Answer choice (E) can be confirmed by the following hypothetical: X–Y–Z–F–G–H.

Question #16: Local, Must Be True. The correct answer choice is (D)

The question stem stipulates that *exactly* two rubies are selected. Of course, the first rule states that at least two topazes are selected, resulting in the following initial scenario:

Ruby: F G H ³
Saph: J K M ³
Top: W X Y Z ⁴

Stone: ___ ___ ___ ___ ___ ___
Type: R   R   T   T
                  6 stones

The last two stones appear to be undetermined, but because of the second rule, they *cannot* be two sapphires. That leaves only two apparent choices for the remaining two stones: two topazes, or one topaz and one sapphire. But, adding two topazes would mean all four topazes are selected, which is impossible due to the third rule. Thus, the remaining two stones must be one topaz and one sapphire, resulting in the following setup:

Ruby: F G H ³
Saph: J K M ³
Top: W X Y Z ⁴

Stone:						
Type:	R	R	T	T	T	S

6 stones

Hence, answer choice (D) is proven correct.

Question #17: Global, Must Be True. The correct answer choice is (D)

As discussed during the setup, because at least two Ts must be selected, and W and Z cannot both be selected, we can deduce that either X or Y or both must be selected. Answer choice (D) is therefore correct.

Question #18: Local, Could Be True. The correct answer choice is (B)

The condition in the question stem enacts the second rule: 2S $\longrightarrow$ 1R $\longrightarrow$ 3T. This leads to the following initial setup:

Ruby: F G H ³
Saph: J K M ³
Top: W X Y Z ⁴

Stone:	J	M		X	Y	W/Z
Type:	S	S	R	T	T	T

6 stones

However, more information can be derived. When M is selected, then from the fourth rule W is selected. When W is selected, from the third rule Z cannot be selected. And, from the third rule, when W is selected, H is not selected, and so only F or G remain for the ruby selection:

Ruby: F G H ³
Saph: J K M ³
Top: W X Y Z ⁴

Stone:	J	M	F/G	X	Y	W
Type:	S	S	R	T	T	T

6 stones

Thus, answer choice (B) could be true and is correct.

This is an Advanced Linear: Unbalanced: Underfunded game.

This game is reminiscent of the third game on the September 1995 LSAT. That game featured houses in one of three styles—ranch, split-level, and Tudor—on opposite sides of a street. In this game, stores on opposite sides of the street are decorated with lights of one of three colors, leading to the following initial setup:

G R Y [3]

<table>
<tr><td>___</td><td>___</td><td>___</td><td>___</td><td>___</td></tr>
<tr><td>1</td><td>3</td><td>5</td><td>7</td><td>9</td></tr>
</table>

<table>
<tr><td>___</td><td>___</td><td>___</td><td>___</td><td>___</td></tr>
<tr><td>2</td><td>4</td><td>6</td><td>8</td><td>10</td></tr>
</table>

Because only three colors of lights are available for each store, we can infer that when one color is unavailable there is only a dual-option remaining for that store. This realization is one of the keys to the game.

The first two rules establish that no adjacent stores have lights of the same color, and no stores facing each other have lights of the same color. This creates horizontal and vertical not-blocks for each color, which will be represented with "C" for color (this is a more efficient representation than drawing out all six not-blocks):

These two rules prove to have a significant effect on the game.

The third rule limits the use of yellow on each side of the street:

Side ⟶ Exactly 1 Yellow

The fourth and fifth rules both place specific colors on specific stores:

GRY[3]

		Y		
1	3	5	7	9

	R			
2	4	6	8	10

Applying the third rule, no other store on the north side of the street can be yellow. Applying the second rule, store 6 cannot be yellow and store 3 cannot be red. Applying the first rule, stores 2 and 6 cannot be red. These inferences can all be shown as Not Laws:

GRY[3]

		Y		
1	3	5	7	9
Y̸	Y̸		Y̸	Y̸
	R̸			

	R			
2	4	6	8	10
R̸		Y̸		
		R̸		

Of course, when one color is eliminated from consideration for a store, a dual-option remains. When two colors are eliminated, the store must be decorated in lights of the remaining color. Thus, store 3 must be green, and store 6 must be green. Consequently, from the first rule, store 1 cannot be green, and must therefore be red, and store 8 cannot be green:

GRY[3]

R	G	Y		
1	3	5	7	9
Y̸	Y̸		Y̸	Y̸
G̸	R̸			

	R	G		
2	4	6	8	10
R̸		Y̸	G̸	
		R̸		

Filling in the remaining dual-options brings us to the final setup for the game:

G R Y [3]

		R	G	Y	G/R	R/G
C/C		1	3	5	7	9
		G̶	X̶		X̶	X̶
C		X̶	R̶			
C						

	G/Y	R	G	R/Y	
	2	4	6	8	10
	R̶		R̶	G̶	
			X̶		

Side ⟶ Exactly 1 Yellow

Question #19: Global, Could Be True, List. The correct answer choice is (B)

Answer choice (A) is incorrect because there are no yellow lights, a violation of the third rule. On the flip side, answer choice (E) is incorrect because there are two yellow lights, also a violation of the third rule. Often when a rule has a specific number of items (such as the third rule), List questions will present one wrong answer with a fewer number of items than the number specified, and one wrong answer with a greater number of items than the number specified.

Answer choices (C) is incorrect because store 6 must be green.

Answer choice (D) is incorrect because store 4 must be red, and store 6 must be green.

Hence, answer choice (B) is correct.

Question #20: Local, Not Necessarily True, FTT. The correct answer choice is (D)

If store 7 has green lights, the following setup is produced:

R	G	Y	G	R
1	3	5	7	9

G/Y	R	G	R/Y	Y/G
2	4	6	8	10

Accordingly, answer choice (D) is correct.

Question #21: Global, Must Be True. The correct answer choice is (B)

Answer choice (B) reflects the store 1 inference discussed in the setup.

Question #22: Local, Must Be True. The correct answer choice is (E)

Due to the action of the first rule, a maximum of three stores on a side could possibly be green (this is the case without considering the other rules). Thus, to meet the condition in the question stem, three stores on one side must be decorated in green and two stores on the other side must be decorated in green.

If there are five stores decorated with green lights, and stores 3 and 6 are already green, then three stores remain to be decorated in green. On the north side of the street, store 3 is already decorated in green, and stores 1 and 5 are other colors. Only stores 7 and 9 are not fully determined, but, due to the first rule, only one of stores 7 and 9 can be green. Thus, the north side must be the side with two stores decorated in green. Those stores are store 3 and either store 7 or 9.

On the south side, store 6 is green, and, to meet the condition in the first rule, the other two stores decorated in green must be store 2 and store 10. With store 10 decorated in green, store 9 cannot be green and must be red; store 7 is therefore green. Store 8 must be yellow because store 8 is the only store remaining on the south side that is able to fulfill the stipulation in the third rule that exactly one store on each side is decorated in yellow. This information results in the following setup:

R	G	Y	G	R
1	3	5	7	9

G	R	G	Y	G
2	4	6	8	10

Answer choice (E) is therefore correct.

Question #23: Local, Must Be True, Suspension. The correct answer choice is (D)

The condition in the question stem—that two stores on the south side of the street are yellow—initially appears to require a new diagram. But, because stores 4 and 6 are still red and green, the two yellows can only decorate stores 2, 8 or 10. Because stores 8 and 10 are adjacent, only one of those stores can be yellow. Thus, we can then infer that store 2 must be yellow, and answer choice (D) is correct.

33

POWERSCORE®

34 PREPTEST

JUNE 2001 LOGIC GAMES SETUPS

This is a Basic Linear: Unbalanced: Underfunded, Identify the Templates game.

The game scenario indicates that five clerks must stock nine numbered aisles, creating an Underfunded Linear game:

J K L M O⁵

1	2	3	4	5	6	7	8	9

The information in the scenario and the first rule establishes that five clerks are in a fixed 2-2-2-2-1 Numerical Distribution of aisles stocked-to-clerks:

2	2	2	2	1
J	K	L	M	O

The second and third rules establish that K stocks aisle 2 and that M does not stock aisle 1:

J K L M O⁵

	K							
1	2	3	4	5	6	7	8	9
M̸								

The fourth rule creates a not-block for J:

J/J
(crossed out)

The fifth rule creates the following block:

M K M

While the initial thought may be to place this block in aisles 1-2-3, from the third rule M cannot stock aisle 1, and so this block must appear elsewhere in the setup. Thus, there are some limitations on which aisles K can stock, namely that K cannot stock aisles 1, 3, and 9:

J K L M O ^{5}

Note that while M cannot stock aisle 1, M could conceivably stock aisle 3 if K stocked aisle 4 and M stocked aisle 5.

The sixth rule establishes that *exactly one* of L's aisles is an end aisle:

J K L M O ^{5}

L ⟶ 1/9 not both

The seventh rule creates a sequence where O's aisle is numbered higher than both of K's aisles, but numbered lower than *at least one* of L's aisles. This rule can be combined with the block created in the fifth rule:

This rule has a dramatic effect on the game because it involves so many variables, and because the MKM block is limited in where it can be placed. Because M cannot stock aisle 1, the block can be placed no lower than aisles 3-4-5. And, because O and L must stock aisles behind M, the MKM block cannot be placed on aisle 8 or 9. Thus, the MKM block is either in aisles 3-4-5, 4-5-6, or 5-6-7. Consequently, O must stock aisle 6, 7, or 8. Because of the limited placement of the block, only three templates exist:

Template #1:	J/L	K	M	K	M				L/J
Template #2:	J/L	K	L/J	M	K	M	O/	/O	L/J
Template #3:	J	K	L/J	J/L	M	K	M	O	L
	1	2	3	4	5	6	7	8	9

In examining the above templates, certain limitations become apparent:

- Aisle 1 must be stocked by J or L. This occurs because M, K, and O cannot stock aisle 1.
- Aisle 5 must be stocked by K or M. This occurs because MKM block must be placed on aisle 5.
- Aisle 9 must be stocked by J or L. This occurs because M, K, and O cannot stock aisle 9.
- Template #3, with the MKM in 5-6-7, is the most restricted, with only two solutions.

With the three templates in hand, the game becomes considerably easier.

Question #1: Global, Could Be True. The correct answer choice is (C)

Answer choice (A) is incorrect due to the fourth rule.

Answer choice (B) is incorrect due to the fifth rule.

Answer choice (C) is the correct answer.

Answer choice (D) is incorrect due to the fifth rule.

Answer choice (E) is incorrect due to the first rule.

Question #2: Global, Cannot Be True. The correct answer choice is (E)

As referenced in the discussion of the templates, only K or M could stock aisle 5. Each of the four incorrect answers includes K or M. Only answer (E) does not include K or M, and thus answer choice (E) is correct.

Question #3: Global, Could Be True, List. The correct answer choice is (B)

There are two ways to solve this question:

1. Because neither K nor O can stock aisle 3, only J, L, and M could stock aisle 3.

2. As shown in the templates, only J, L, and M could stock aisle 3.

In each case, answer choice (B) is proven correct.

Question #4: Global, Could Be True, List. The correct answer choice is (D)

From the third rule, M does not stock aisle 1, and so answer choice (A) can be eliminated.

From the sequence created by the combination of the fifth and seventh rules, M cannot stock aisle 9, and so answer choice (B) can be eliminated.

The difference between answer choices (C), (D), and (E) is that (C) and (E) are incomplete lists of the aisles M could stock. As the question stem asks for a "complete list," and answer choice (D) contains the complete list, it is the correct answer.

Question #5: Local, Could Be True, Maximum. The correct answer choice is (A)

To separate L's two aisles by the maximum number of aisles while still meeting the requirements of the sixth rule would require placing L in aisles 1 and 8 or in aisles 2 and 9. But, because K stocks aisle 2 from the second rule, aisles 2 and 9 are not an option. Thus, you should create a hypothetical with L stocking aisles 1 and 8, or alternately refer to Templates #1 and #2 if you created those templates during your setup.

If L stocks aisles 1 and 8, then J must stock aisle 9, leaving the MKM block, and O and J to stock the middle aisles:

J K L M O [5]

L	K	(	MKM > O	,	J	)	L	J
1	2	3	4	5	6	7	8	9

Accordingly, answer choice (A) is correct.

Question #6: Local, Cannot Be True. The correct answer choice is (E)

If J stocks aisle 3, then the lowest-numbered aisles the MKM block could stock would be 4-5-6. Because O must stock a higher-numbered aisle than the MKM block, the lowest-numbered aisle O could stock would be aisle 7. Thus, O cannot stock aisle 6 and answer choice (E) is correct.

Question #7: Local, Cannot Be True, Suspension. The correct answer choice is (B)

The condition in the question stem specifies that L stocks aisles 1 and 9:

J K L M O [5]

$$\frac{L}{1} \quad \frac{K}{2} \quad \frac{(}{3} \quad \frac{MKM}{4} > \frac{O}{5} , \frac{J}{6} , \frac{J}{7} \quad \frac{)}{8} \quad \frac{L}{9}$$

Of course, the fourth rule regarding J not stocking consecutive aisles is still in force, and given the remaining unplaced variables above, is likely to play a role in this question.

If O stocks aisle 6, then J would have to stock aisles 7 and 8, causing a violation of the fourth rule. Thus, answer choice (B) cannot be true and is correct.

34

This is a Basic Linear: Unbalanced: Overloaded, Identify the Possibilities game.

This is an unusually simple game. Five lectures are given over the course of five weeks, instilling a Linear aspect in the game. While the five lectures are given by speakers with different specialties, the speakers are only referred to as "the first week's speaker" etc, meaning that the 1-2-3-4-5 week base equally serves to refer to the speakers. Thus, the five weeks/speakers are the base, and the specialties are placed above the base.

And, as opposed to rules establishing various placements or limitations on variables, here the majority of rules simply indicate which lectures can be given each week. The third, fourth, fifth, and sixth rules reveal the following information about the speaker's specializations:

K L M N O P [6]

K/L/M	K/L/M/N	M/N	M/N	N/O/P
1	2	3	4	5

The second rule leads to the powerful inference that because the third and fourth speakers must lecture on M and N, *no other speaker can lecture on N and M*, leading to the following setup:

K/L	L/K	M/N	N/M	O/P
1	2	3	4	5

This setup can be used as-is, or four basic templates can be created:

Template #4:	L	K	N	M	O/P

Template #3:	L	K	M	N	O/P

Template #2:	K	L	N	M	O/P

Template #1:	K	L	M	N	O/P
	1	2	3	4	5

These four templates contain just eight possibilities. With this setup the game is very easy.

Question #8: Global, Could Be True. The correct answer choice is (E)

As noted in the main setup and every template, the fifth speaker could lecture on O, and thus answer choice (E) is correct.

Question #9: Local, Must Be True, Maximum. The correct answer choice is (A)

The question stem requires you to provide the maximum number of different orders when the philosophers discussed are in alphabetical order. Only Template #1 is in alphabetical order, and as there are two solutions in that template—both of which meet the alphabetical requirement—answer choice (A) is correct.

Question #10: Global, Justify. The correct answer choice is (C)

The question stem asks you to identify the philosophers that, if you knew their scheduled weeks, would allow you to fully determine the schedule for the five weeks. Consider again the diagram for the game:

$$\frac{K/L}{1} \qquad \frac{L/K}{2} \qquad \frac{M/N}{3} \qquad \frac{N/M}{4} \qquad \frac{O/P}{5}$$

In this setup, K and L form one group, M and N form a second group, and O and P form a third group. As each group is fully independent of the other two groups, if you can ascertain the schedule for one member of each group, then you can determine the schedule of the other member. For example, if K is the philosopher lectured on in the first week, then L would have to be the philosopher lectured on in the second week. Thus, we need an answer that contains one of K and L, one of M and N, and one of O and P. Answer choice (C) contains one from each of the three groups, and thus answer choice (C) is correct.

Question #11: Local, Could Be True, Except. The correct answer choice is (D)

The question stem divides the philosophers by nationality:

German: K, N

British: L, M, O

The diagram and templates show that the third and fourth speakers lecture once on a German philosopher and once on a British philosopher. Thus, answer choice (D) cannot be true and is correct.

Question #12: Local, Could Be True, Except. The correct answer choice is (B)

The question stem adds a new philosopher to the mix for the third week:

$$\underset{1}{\underline{K/L/M}} \qquad \underset{2}{\underline{K/L/M/N}} \qquad \underset{3}{\underline{M/N/S}} \qquad \underset{4}{\underline{M/N}} \qquad \underset{5}{\underline{N/O/P}}$$

This additional philosopher eliminates the inference pattern we used to arrive at the four templates. Thus, you should use the information above to attack the answer choices.

Each answer choice addresses M and N, which is beneficial because the fourth week is the most restricted week and it must always be M or N. Thus, you should expect the correct answer to play on that relationship.

Answer choice (B) places M second and N third, which would leave no philosopher available for the fourth week. Thus, answer choice (B) cannot be true and is correct.

This is a Basic Linear: Balanced, Identify the Templates game.

The game scenario and first rule establish that seven trains arrive in order, creating a Basic Linear: Balanced setup:

Q R S T V W Y [7]

$$\underline{}\ \ \underline{}\ \ \underline{}\ \ \underline{}\ \ \underline{}\ \ \underline{}\ \ \underline{}$$
$$\ \ 1\qquad 2\qquad 3\qquad 4\qquad 5\qquad 6\qquad 7$$

The second rule creates a W/Y dual-option on the fourth train:

Q R S T V W Y [7]

$$\underline{}\ \ \underline{}\ \ \underline{}\ \ \overset{\text{W/Y}}{\underline{}}\ \ \underline{}\ \ \underline{}\ \ \underline{}$$
$$\ \ 1\qquad 2\qquad 3\qquad 4\qquad 5\qquad 6\qquad 7$$

The third rule creates the following chain sequence:

$$W > S > Y$$

This chain results in six Not Laws, but we will eschew showing Not Laws for the moment.

The fourth rule creates a double-branched sequence:

$$R > \begin{matrix} T \\ \text{------} \\ V \end{matrix}$$

This sequence creates four Not Laws, but again we will refrain from diagramming the Not Laws until all of the rules have been considered.

The fifth rule creates a rotating not-block:

The second rule naturally sends the game in two separate directions. This rule, combined with the fact that the third rule connects both of the variables in the second rule, and the fact that there are two other rules, indicates that there is a limited number of solutions in this game. The best approach is to create two templates, one based on when W is fourth, and one based on when Y is fourth.

Template #1: Y arrives fourth

When Y arrives fourth, both W and S must arrive ahead of Y. The placement of the R, T, V sequence now becomes a problem. If R arrives fifth, then T and V would have to arrive sixth and seventh, a violation of the last rule. Thus, R must arrive before Y. We can now infer that the three trains arriving before Y are W, S, and R, not necessarily in that order. Both T and V must arrive after Y. Because T and V cannot arrive consecutively, either T or V must arrive fifth, and the remainder must arrive seventh. Q, the random, must arrive sixth.

Template #1: $\underline{(\ W > S\ ,\ R\ )}\quad \underline{Y}\quad \underline{T/V}\quad \underline{Q}\quad \underline{V/T}$
                    1   2   3   4   5   6   7

Template #2: W arrives fourth

When W arrives fourth, both S and Y must arrive after W. As in the previous template, the placement of the R, T, V sequence now becomes a problem. R, T, and V cannot all arrive before W, and thus either T or V must arrive after W. Consequently, R and the remainder of T/V must arrive before W. Q is also forced to arrive before W.

Template #2: $\underline{(\ Q\ ,\ R > V/T\ )}\quad \underline{W}\quad \underline{(\ S > Y\ ,\ T/V\ )}$
                    1   2   3   4   5   6   7

The prior information can be combined to produce the final setup for the game:

Q R S T V W Y [7]
*

W > S > Y

R > ------
       T
       V

Template #2:   (Q , R > V/T)   W   (S > Y , T/V)

Template #1:   (W > S , R)   Y   T/V   Q   V/T

1	2	3	4	5	6	7

Question #13: Global, Could Be True, List. The correct answer choice is (C)

Answer choice (A): From the last rule T and V are not consecutive, so this answer choice is wrong.

Answer choice (B): From the third rule S must arrive at some time before Y, and so this answer choice is incorrect.

Answer choice (C): This is the correct answer choice.

Answer choice (D): The second rule stipulates that W or Y is fourth, and so this answer choice is incorrect.

Answer choice (E): The fourth rule indicates that T arrives at some time after R, and so this answer choice is incorrect.

Question #14: Local, Could Be True. The correct answer choice is (A)

W can arrive before R only under Template #1. With the added condition that W > R, there are four possible orders:

	1	2	3	4	5	6	7
#4:	W	S	R	Y	V	Q	T
#3:	W	S	R	Y	T	Q	V
#2:	W	R	S	Y	V	Q	T
#1:	W	R	S	Y	T	Q	V

Accordingly, answer choice (A) is correct.

34

Question #15: Global, Must Be True. The correct answer choice is (E)

This type of question can easily be attacked using the two templates. In both templates, W arrives earlier than Y, and so answer choice (E) is correct.

Question #16: Global, Could Be True. The correct answer choice is (B)

This is another question that can easily be attacked using the two templates. In Template #1 (and as shown in question #14), R can immediately follow S, and so answer choice (B) is correct.

Question #17: Local, Could Be True. The correct answer choice is (E)

The question stem forms a W ___ Y block. This block can occur under either template:

#2:	(Q , R > V/T)	W	S	Y	T/V		
#1:	R	W	S	Y	T/V	Q	V/T
	1	2	3	4	5	6	7

As R can arrive first, answer choice (E) is correct.

Question #18: Global, Must Be True. The correct answer choice is (C)

The question stems forms a Q > R sequence, which can only occur under Template #2. In Template #2 W arrives fourth, and so answer choice (C) is correct.

This game serves as another excellent example of the power of rule linkage and interaction. The second and third rules link together in a limiting way, and the fourth and fifth rules also link together in a limiting way. When the two sets of rules are combined, their interaction produces a limited number of possibilities, and thus produce two templates. If you have been carefully studying our materials, you should now understand the importance of the Identify the Templates and Identify the Possibilities approach. If you know these techniques and you understand when to apply them, you give yourself a tremendous advantage over other test takers.

34

This is a Grouping: Defined-Moving, Balanced, Identify the Templates game.

The game scenario indicates that six doctors are at exactly one of two clinics:

J K L N O P ^{6}

$$\overline{} \quad \overline{}$$
$$S \qquad R$$

Because each doctor must be at either Souderton or Randsborough, this game features a two-value system. Thus, if a doctor is not at Souderton, he or she must be at Randsborough; if a doctor is not at Randsborough, he or she must be at Souderton. The two-value system leads to a number of interesting contrapositives. Ultimately, the game is sufficiently restricted to lead to four templates. First, let's examine each rule, with the rule diagram presented first, followed by the contrapositive, which will be translated in order to account for the effects of the two-value system:

First rule: $J_S \longrightarrow K_R$

$K_S \longrightarrow J_R$

Second rule: $J_R \longrightarrow O_S$

$O_R \longrightarrow J_S$

Third rule: $L_S \longrightarrow \begin{array}{c} N_R \\ + \\ P_R \end{array}$

$\begin{array}{c} N_S \\ \text{or} \\ P_S \end{array} \longrightarrow L_R$

Fifth rule: $N_R \longrightarrow O_R$

$O_S \longrightarrow N_S$

Sixth rule:

$$P_R \longrightarrow \begin{array}{c} K_S \\ + \\ O_S \end{array}$$

$$\begin{array}{c} K_R \\ \text{or} \\ O_R \end{array} \longrightarrow P_S$$

Of course, several of these rules and contrapositives can be combined, such as $J_R \longrightarrow O_S \longrightarrow N_S \longrightarrow L_R$. With the application of the rules and contrapositives, the game seems only moderately difficult. However, most students fail to apply to two-value system and they will find the game rather hard. You can also take the rule relationships a step further, and show four templates containing six total possibilities:

Template #1: O at R

	/N
N/	K
P	L
J	O
S	R

Template #2: O at S, K at S, J at R

P/	
K	/P
N	J
O	L
S	R

Template #3: O at S, K at R, J at S

P	
J	
N	K
O	L
S	R

Template #4: O at S, K at R, J at R

P	K
N	J
O	L
S	R

Note that the templates reveal one of the challenging inferences of the game: L can never be at Souderton, and thus L must always be at Randsborough.

Question #19: Global, Could Be True, List. The correct answer choice is (B)

Template #1 indicates that J, P, and N could be at Souderton. Template #2 adds O to the list. Accordingly, answer choice (B) is correct.

Question #20: Local, Must Be True. The correct answer choice is (A)

If P is at R, then only Template #2 applies:

Template #2: O at S, K at S, J at R, P at R

$$
\begin{array}{cc}
\underline{K} & \underline{P} \\
\underline{N} & \underline{J} \\
\underline{O} & \underline{L} \\
S & R
\end{array}
$$

Accordingly, answer choice (A) is correct.

Question #21: Global, Must Be True, Minimum. The correct answer choice is (C)

As shown in Template #1, the minimum number of doctors that could be at Souderton is two: J and P. Thus, answer choice (C) is correct.

Question #22: Local, Must Be True. The correct answer choice is (A)

If N and O are at different clinics, then only Template #1 applies:

Template #1: O at R, N at S

$$
\begin{array}{cc}
\underline{N} & \underline{K} \\
\underline{P} & \underline{L} \\
\underline{J} & \underline{O} \\
S & R
\end{array}
$$

Accordingly, answer choice (A) is correct.

Question #23: Global, Cannot Be True. The correct answer choice is (E)

Having the templates makes this Global Cannot Be True considerably easier.

Answer choice (A): Template #4 shows that J and K can both be at Randsborough.

Answer choice (B): Template #2 shows that J and P can both be at Randsborough.

Answer choice (C): Template #1 shows that K and O can both be at Randsborough.

Answer choice (D): Template #1 shows that N and O can both be at Randsborough.

Answer choice (E): This is the correct answer choice. None of the Templates shows that N and P can both be at Randsborough.

Question #24: Local, Must Be True. The correct answer choice is (B)

If K is at Souderton, then only Template #2 applies:

Template #2: O at S, K at S, J at R

$$
\begin{array}{cc}
\underline{P/} & \\
\underline{K} & \underline{/P} \\
\underline{N} & \underline{J} \\
\underline{O} & \underline{L} \\
S & R
\end{array}
$$

Accordingly, answer choice (B) is correct.

34

278 THE POWERSCORE LSAT LOGIC GAMES SETUPS ENCYCLOPEDIA II

POWERSCORE®

PREPTEST 35

OCTOBER 2001 LOGIC GAMES SETUPS

35

This is a Grouping: Defined-Fixed, Unbalanced: Overloaded game.

This is a Profile Charting game, a variation on a Grouping game that we discuss in our LSAT courses. From a Grouping standpoint the game is Defined-Fixed, Unbalanced: Overloaded. The selection pool is subdivided.

The game initially sets up as eight candidates for four spaces:

F J K L M N P T ^{8}

‾‾‾‾ ‾‾‾‾ ‾‾‾‾ ‾‾‾‾
4 astronauts

However, the eight candidates each have two characteristics. The simplest way to handle all of the information is to create a chart that profiles each candidate:

Profile Chart:

	E/I	G/R
F	E	G
J	E	R
K	E	R
L	E	R
M	I	G
N	I	R
P	I	G
T	I	G

The first two rules specify the composition of the group that must be selected:

F J K L M N P T ^{8}

‾‾‾‾ ‾‾‾‾ ‾‾‾‾ ‾‾‾‾
2E/2I
2G/2R

The third rule establishes that either P or L, or both are selected. This produces the setup that most students have as their final setup.

F J K L M N P T [8]

Profile Chart:

	E/I	G/R
F	E	G
J	E	R
K	E	R
L	E	R
M	I	G
N	I	R
P	I	G
T	I	G

P/L _____ _____ _____
           2E/2I
           2G/2R

While the above setup is accurate, it is incomplete. In Profile Charting games, the most critical step is to examine the profile chart to determine which candidates have identical characteristics. The search for identical pairs must be done because often these identical pairs have natural "opposite" pairs within the game, and consequently powerful hypotheticals can be created. This game contains several such hypotheticals.

From the profile chart, we can determine that J, K, and L are identical, each with the characteristics *ER*. M, P, and T are also identical, each with the characteristics *IG*. Thus, the two groups are perfect opposites, and as long as the rule regarding "either P or L or both are selected" is considered, we can quickly make hypotheticals from the two groups:

Hypotheticals:

J	L	M	P
J	L	M	T
J	L	P	T
K	L	M	P
K	L	M	T
K	L	P	T
J	K	M	P
J	K	P	T

The hypotheticals above solve, or can be used to help solve, question #1 and question #4. The hypotheticals also have the additional benefit of instilling confidence since they contain so much information about the game.

It is also notable that the two remaining variables, F and N, are perfect opposites, and, because they

35

are unique in the game, if one appears then the other *must* appear. Both question #3 and question #5 hinge on this inference.

Because F and N are opposites, the remaining two variables that are selected with F and N must also have opposite characteristics. Hence, one variable from the group J, K and L must be selected, and one variable from the group M, P, and T must be selected:

$$\underline{\text{\ \ F\ \ }} \quad \underline{\text{\ \ N\ \ }} \quad \underline{\text{J/K/L}} \quad \underline{\text{M/P/T}}$$

Of course, the P/L rule must still be obeyed.

There are a few simple lessons taught by this game:

1. You must be able to recognize the game type you are facing. Students who recognized this game as a Profile Charting game had a distinct advantage over students who did not recognize the game.

2. When attacking a Profile Charting game you must examine the chart for variables that are identical and variables that are perfect opposites. Use the results of this search to construct hypotheticals.

3. Use the hypotheticals to attack the questions. When you do so, the game becomes incredibly easy.

Question #1: Global, Could Be True, List. The correct answer choice is (D)

As shown in the discussion of hypotheticals, J-L-M-T is possible, and thus answer choice (D) is correct.

Question #2: Local, Must Be True. The correct answer choice is (A)

The question stem establishes the following:

$$\underline{\text{\ \ F\ \ }} \quad \underline{\text{\ \ P\ \ }} \quad \underline{\text{\ \ \ \ \ }} \quad \underline{\text{\ \ \ \ \ }}$$

This selection satisfies the P/L rule, and so the only conditions that must be met are the selection criteria regarding the characteristics of each of the candidates in the group.

As both F and P are geologists, the remaining two selections must be radiobiologists. This information eliminates answer choices (B) and (C).

F is an experienced astronaut and P is an inexperienced astronaut, and so the remaining two selections must consist of one experienced astronaut and one inexperienced astronaut. This information eliminates answer choices (D) and (E), and thus answer choice (A) is correct.

Question #3: Local, Must Be True. The correct answer choice is (D)

Note that any hypothetical that can be created containing F and J will allow some answer choices to be eliminated because if a variable isn't in the hypothetical, then it does not *have* to be selected when F and J are selected. Thus, we can refer back to the last hypothetical created in the setup discussion:

F	N	J/K/L	M/P/T

Accordingly, the correct answer must be N, as N would have to be selected when F and J are selected.

Of course, as noted in the setup and again in question #6, when F is selected, N must also be selected.

Question #4: Local, Could Be True. The correct answer choice is (B)

The question stem establishes the following:

M	T	___	___

Both M and T are inexperienced geologists, so the remaining two selections must be experienced radiobiologists. Thus, two from the group of J, K, and L must be selected. However, due to the third rule, L must be selected, resulting in the following setup:

M	T	L	J/K

Accordingly, answer choice (B) is correct.

Question #5: Local, Must Be True. The correct answer choice is (A)

As discussed during the setup, F and N are perfect opposites, and, due to the characteristics of the other six candidates, when one of F and N is selected, the other must also be selected. Thus, answer choice (A) is correct.

35

This is a Grouping: Defined-Fixed, Unbalanced: Underfunded, Numerical Distribution game.

The game scenario indicates that six new cars are each equipped with *at least one* of three options. Prior to reading the rules, either the cars or the three options could be chosen as the base of the game. However, after reviewing the rules—each of which starts by listing a car and its related options—the cars are the better choice:

P L S[3]

T	V	W	X	Y	Z

The first two rules establish options for V and W:

P L S[3]

		S	L			
		P	P			
	T	V	W	X	Y	Z

The third rule indicates that W and Y do not have any options in common. Because W already has two options from the second rule, Y must then have the remaining option, S. The combination of the second and third rules also numerically sets W's options at 2, and Y's options at 1:

P L S[3]

W ←——|——→ Y

			2		1	
		S	L			
		P	P		S	
	T	V	W	X	Y	Z

X ←——|——→ Y

The fourth rule states that X has more options than W:

$$\#X \quad > \quad \#W$$

Because W already has two options, X must have all three options:

P L S[3]

$$W \longleftarrow | \longrightarrow Y$$

$$\#X \quad > \quad \#W$$

		2	3	1		
				S		
		S	L	L		
	P	P	P	P	S	
T	V	W	X	Y	Z

$$X \longleftarrow | \longrightarrow$$

The fifth rule indicates that V and Z have exactly one option in common:

P L S[3]

$$W \longleftarrow | \longrightarrow Y$$

$$\#X \quad > \quad \#W$$

$$V \longleftarrow_{1} \longrightarrow Z$$

		2	3	1		
				S		
		S	L	L		
	P	P	P	P	S	P/S
T	V	W	X	Y	Z

$$V \longleftarrow \quad X \longleftarrow | \longrightarrow \quad \longrightarrow Z$$

1 only

The operational effect of this rule is that Z cannot have all three options (otherwise Z would have both P and S, a violation of the rule).

The sixth rule is another numerical rule, this time indicating that T has fewer options than Z:

$$\#Z \quad > \quad \#T$$

Because each car has at least one option, T must have at least one or two options under this rule. But, if T has two options, Z would have to have three options, which is not possible as discussed in the analysis of the fifth rule. So, Z must have two options, and T must have exactly one option. Because Z has two options, and can only have one of P and S, we can also infer that Z must have L as an option. Finally, because Z has two options, by applying the fifth rule we can infer that V cannot have all three options, and thus has only two options. Combining all of the prior information results in the final setup:

35

PLS³

W ◄——|——► Y

#X > #W

V ◄——1——► Z

#Z > #T

1	2	2	3	1	2
			S		
	S	L	L		P/S
	P	P	P	S	L
T	V	W	X	Y	Z

V ◄————— X —————► Z
(1 only)

Because the Numerical Distribution is so critical, let's review the steps that create the distribution:

1. Since W has at least two options, and W and Y have no options in common, it follows that W must have exactly two options and Y must have exactly one option.

2. Since X has more options than W, X must have exactly three options.

3. Since T has fewer options than Z, Z must have at least two options. And since V has at least two options and V and Z have only one option in common, it follows that Z cannot have three options. Therefore, Z must have exactly two options. Because of the VZ rule it follows that V cannot have three options and therefore V must have exactly two options.

4. Since Z must have two options, it follows that T must have exactly one option.

5. The above steps create the 1-2-2-3-1-2 Fixed Distribution.

With the distribution, determining most of the options is simple. The only uncertainty in the game is what option T will have, and whether Z will have P or S.

Question #6: Global, Must Be True. The correct answer choice is (C)

In our setup we determined the exact options for cars V, W, X and Y, and thus the correct answer is answer choice (C).

Note that this question does not ask for the *number* of options determined for each car, but rather the number of cars for which we have an exact list of options.

Question #7: Local, Cannot Be True, FTT. The correct answer choice is (A)

Because we have already determined that cars V and Y do not have leather interiors, the maximum number of cars that can have leather interiors is four, and thus answer choice (A) cannot be true and is correct.

35

Question #8: Local, Cannot Be True, FTT. The correct answer choice is (E)

The question stem creates the following conditional relationship:

$$L \longrightarrow P$$

This rule establishes that Z, which already has L, must also have P:

			S		
	S	L	L		P
	P	P	P	S	L
T	V	W	X	Y	Z

As Z has power windows, Z cannot have a sunroof and answer choice (E) is correct.

Question #9: Local, Cannot Be True, FTT. The correct answer choice is (D)

If Z has no options in common with T, then T cannot have L. If Z also has at least one option in common with every other car, then Z must have S (Y has only S, so Z must also have S). Since Z has S, then T cannot have S, and we can infer that T has P, leading to the following setup:

			S		
	S	L	L		S
P	P	P	P	S	L
T	V	W	X	Y	Z

Because only three cars have L, answer choice (D) cannot be true and is correct.

Question #10: Local, Could Be True, Except. The correct answer choice is (C)

If no two cars have exactly the same options, then Z must have S because W already has L and P. In addition, T cannot have S because Y already has just S. This information leads to the following setup:

			S		
	S	L	L		S
L/P	P	P	P	S	L
T	V	W	X	Y	Z

Because four of the cars already have S, answer choice (C) cannot be true and is correct.

Question #11: Local, Must Be True, Except. The correct answer choice is (D)

If exactly four of the cars have L, those cars must be T, W, X, and Z, and if exactly four of the cars have P, those cars must be V, W, X, and Z. This information leads to the following setup:

			S		
	S	L	L		P
L	P	P	P	S	L
T	V	W	X	Y	Z

Because W and Z have the exact same two options, answer choice (D) cannot be true and is the correct answer.

Question #12: Local, Cannot Be True, FTT, Suspension. The correct answer choice is (D)

The impact of the rule suspension is to create uncertainty over whether X has two or three options. W must still have two options since W and Y have no options in common. If X has two options, then X must have options L and P so as to have exactly two options in common with W; if X has three options, then X must of course have options L, P, and S. All other relationships and options remain identical:

1	2	2	2/3	1	2
			S/		
	S	L	L		P/S
	P	P	P	S	L
T	V	W	X	Y	Z

Because X and Z must have at least one option in common, answer choice (D) cannot be true and is correct.

Note the heavy presence of False To True (FTT) questions and Except questions in this game. This likely occurs because the game setup contains so much information, leading to a situation where the test makers want to create greater difficulty in the questions (a result usually caused by the False To True wording and the use of Except).

This is an Advanced Linear: Unbalanced: Underfunded game.

The game scenario establishes that five members of the Kim family attend an opera. There are six seat options, with three seats in two rows. Thus, this is an Advanced Linear game. As there are only five family members for the six seats, the game is Underfunded, and one seat will always be empty, which can be designated with an "E". This maneuver transforms the game from Unbalanced: Underfunded to Balanced. E is then treated like any other variable.

Q R S T U⁵ E

G: _____   _____   _____

H: _____   _____   _____
     1   2   3

The first rule is a bit difficult to parse, but the operational result is that the empty seat cannot be the middle seat in either row:

Q R S T U⁵ E

| K̸EK |

G: _____   _____   _____
               E̸

H: _____   _____   _____
     1   2   3
               E̸

This rule effectively means a KEK block ("K" stands for Kim) is impossible, and that each Kim family member is always next to at least one other family member (shown as a KEK not-block).

The second rule assigns T and U to row H, so two side Not Laws can be shown on row G:

Q R S T U⁵ E

| K̸EK |

G: _____   _____   _____   T̸ Ʉ̸
     T̸   E̸   S̸

H: _____   _____   _____
     1   2   3
               E̸

The third rule creates a sequence:

$$
\begin{array}{c}
S \\
\text{- - - - } > T \\
U
\end{array}
$$

This sequence eliminates T from sitting in seat 1 in either row, and S and U from sitting in seat 3 in either row. Because T cannot sit in row G or seat H1 (row H, seat 1), T must be in seat H2 or H3:

Q R S T U⁵ E

K K̶ K

$$
\begin{array}{c}
S \\
\text{- - - } > T \\
U
\end{array}
$$

G: ___T̶___ ___E̶___ ___S̶___ T̶ U̶

H: ___1___ __T/__ 2 __/T__ 3
      T̶   E̶   S̶ U̶

The fourth rule creates a block involving R:

R Q/S
or both

Because T and U both sit in row H, we can infer that R, and Q or S or both, must sit in row G. When this inference is combined with the fifth rule, which states that R sits in seat 2, we can infer that R sits in seat G2. And, because R, S, T, and U cannot sit in seat G3, only Q or the empty seat can be seat G3. This results in this setup for the game:

Q R S T U⁵ E

K K̶ K

$$
\begin{array}{c}
S \\
\text{- - - } > T \\
U
\end{array}
$$

R Q/S
or both

G: ___T̶___ __R__ E̶ __Q/E__ S̶ T̶ U̶

H: ___1___ __T/__ 2 __/T__ 3
      T̶   E̶   S̶ U̶

Several important inferences remain, based on the placement of certain family members:

- T must sit in seat H2 or H3. Thus, by applying the second and third rules, if T sits in H2, then U must sit in H1 and S must sit in G1.

- Seat H3 cannot be occupied by R, S, or U, and thus H3 is occupied by Q, T, or E.

- If E is in seat G3, then seat G1 is Q or S; If E is in seat G1, then seat G3 is Q.

Combining all of the prior information results in the final setup for the game:

Q R S T U⁵ E

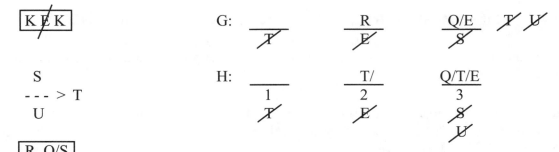

Question #13: Global, Could Be True. The correct answer choice is (A)

The Not Laws eliminate every answer choice except answer choice (A), the correct answer.

Question #14: Global, Could Be True. The correct answer choice is (B)

Answer choice (A) is incorrect because R sits in seat G2.

Answer choice (B) is the correct answer.

Answer choice (C) is incorrect because this answer forms a QS or SQ block, and thus neither Q nor S could sit in the same row as R, a violation of the fourth rule.

Answer choices (D) and (E) are incorrect because R sits in row G, whereas T and U sit in row H.

Question #15: Local, Not Necessarily True, FTT. The correct answer choice is (C)

If T sits in seat 2, he must sit in seat H2. From the second and third rules, U must then sit in seat H1, and S must sit in seat G1:

S	R	Q/E
U	T	E/Q
1	2	3

Accordingly, answer choice (C) is correct.

Question #16: Global, Must Be True, List. The correct answer choice is (E)

There are a number of ways to do this question, including referring to the main diagram or by using hypotheticals.

Perhaps the easiest way to solve this question is to use the hypothetical from question #15. That solution shows that G3 and H3 could be empty, and only answer choice (E) contains both those seats. Thus, answer choice (E) is correct.

Question #17: Global, Must Be True, List. The correct answer choice is (E)

The hypothetical in question #15 already established that T could sit in seat H2, so answer choices (A), (B), and (C) can be eliminated. There is nothing precluding Q from sitting in seat H2, and so answer choice (E) is correct.

This is a Basic Linear: Balanced-Moving, Numerical Distribution game.

The game scenario indicates that seven professors were hired over a period of seven years. That sounds like a recipe for a simple Linear game, but the second-to-last sentence in the scenario indicates that two professors can be hired in the same year and therefore the game is not necessarily in a 1-to-1 assignment ratio. To break down the setup for this game, first we will examine the professors that are hired, then the specialties, and finally the various restrictions governing the hiring and the specialties.

The first rule places M and R, and part of the fifth rule places O:

M N O P R S T⁷

	O	R		M		
89	90	91	92	93	94	95

The second, third, and fifth rules address the specialties (Sp) of the professors, grouping them as follows:

$$\boxed{M\ O\ T}_{Sp}$$

$$\boxed{N\ R}_{Sp}$$

$$\boxed{O\ S}_{Sp}$$

Note that these are not linear blocks, but rather a method to show the grouping of the professors according to shared specialties, and that professors can have other specialties. These specialty groupings have a significant impact on the game when considered in light of the restrictions stated in the game scenario. We will examine those restrictions in a moment.

The fourth rule creates a sequence:

$$N > \begin{array}{c} P \\ \text{----} \\ S \end{array} > M$$

This rule generates its own set of Not Laws and inferences, but we will examine that in connection with the restriction about the specialties.

The game scenario contains two not-block rules involving the specialties:

These extremely restrictive rules about the specialties create a plethora of Not Laws, but also make this game relatively easy. The final setup is created by taking the following steps:

1. Because T shares a specialty with M and O, T cannot be hired in years 89, 90, 91, 92, 93, or 94. It follows that T must be hired in 95:

$$\underline{}\quad\underset{89}{}\quad\underset{90}{O}\quad\underset{91}{R}\quad\underset{92}{}\quad\underset{93}{M}\quad\underset{94}{}\quad\underset{95}{T}$$

	O	R		M		T
89	90	91	92	93	94	95

2. Due to the sequence, N must be hired in before M; but because N shares a specialty with R, N cannot be hired in years 90, 91, or 92. Therefore, N must be hired in 89:

N	O	R		M		T
89	90	91	92	93	94	95

3. Due to the sequence, S must be hired after N but before M; since S shares a specialty with O, S cannot be hired in years 90 or 91. Therefore, S must be hired in 92:

N	O	R	S	M		T
89	90	91	92	93	94	95

Thus, the only uncertainty in the game is the hiring of P. Since P must be hired after N but before M, P can only be hired in 90, 91, or 92. With so few possibilities, the game is quite easy. This is the final setup:

MNOPRST⁷

			P/	P/	P/			
	N	O	R	S	M		T
	89	90	91	92	93	94	95

MOT ₛₚ

NR ₛₚ

OS ₛₚ

$$N > \underset{S}{\overset{P}{----}} > M$$

Note that although this game has only three solutions, this isn't technically an Identify the Possibilities game because there is no decision to show the possibilities; instead, the natural process of making the setup organically results in all of the variables except one being placed.

Question #18. Global, Could Be True, List. The correct answer choice is (C)

Note that this question asks for a list of the professors who could have been hired in the three named years. Thus, the professors in each answer choices are not given in chronologically correct order, but rather in alphabetical order. Thus, you simply need to find the answer choice that contains all of the professors who could have been hired at some point in those three years.

We have already established that N, O, and R were hired in 1989, 1990, and 1991, respectively, so any answer choice that does not include those three professors must be eliminated. This removes answer choices (B), (D), and (E) from consideration. The remaining two answer choices—(A) and (C)—differ only in that answer choice (C) contains P whereas (A) does not. As established previously, P could have been hired in 1990 or 1991, and thus P must be included in the correct answer if the list is to be a complete and accurate list. Hence, answer choice (C) is correct.

Question #19: Local, Could Be True. The correct answer choice is (A)

The condition in the question stem establishes that P must be hired in 1990 or 1992.

Answer choice (A) could be true and is correct because if P was hired in 1990, then P and M are not subject to the specialty restriction rules, and sharing a specialty would not cause any other violations.

Answer choice (B) is incorrect because R and S were hired in consecutive years, and thus cannot have a specialty in common.

Answer choice (C) is incorrect because this answer would require P to be hired in 1991, which is impossible according to the condition in the question stem.

Answer choice (D) is incorrect because the initial setup establishes that no professor was hired in 1994.

Answer choice (E) is incorrect because the initial setup establishes that two professors cannot be hired in 1993.

Question #20: Global, Cannot Be True, FTT. The correct answer choice is (E)

The analysis of the game setup proves that answer choice (E) cannot be true and is thus correct.

Question #21: Global, Must Be True. The correct answer choice is (D)

The game setup shows that R was hired in 1991 and S was hired in 1992, and thus answer choice (D) is correct.

Question #22: Local, Could Be True. The correct answer choice is (A)

The question stem establishes that P was hired in 1992. Thus, O, P, and T could share a specialty, and answer choice (A) is correct. Note that the rule that states that M, O, and T must share a specialty can easily be met if M, O, and T share a different specialty than O, P, and T (and the rules allow for this because the idea of multiple specialties is stated clearly in the game scenario: "Each professor has one or more specialties").

Question #23: Local, Must Be True. The correct answer choice is (E)

The condition in the question stem establishes that P cannot be hired in 1992 and thus must have been hired in 1990 or 1991. This information provides the basis for selecting answer choice (E).

POWERSCORE®

36

PREPTEST

DECEMBER 2001 LOGIC GAMES SETUPS

This is a Grouping: Undefined game.

Because the scenario does not establish any numerical information about the number of kinds of fruit carried by the stand (other than that at least one must be carried), this game is Undefined. Thus, our diagram will consist of a single space for the group:

F K O P T W [6]

$$\overline{\quad\quad\quad\quad}$$
Fruit

Each of the four rules is conditional in nature, and the diagram for each is as follows:

Rule #1:   K ←——|——→ P

Rule #2:   F̷ ————→ K

The contrapositive of this rule is notable: K̷ ————→ T

Rule #3:   O ————→ P
                              +
                              W

Rule #4:   W ————→ F
                              or
                              T

Of course, the rules allow for a number of inferences. The first and second rules can be combined:

F̷ ————→ K ————→ P̷

This chain reduces to:

F̷ ————→ P̷

The contrapositive of this rule leads to the big inference of the game:

$$P \longrightarrow T$$

This inference allows the third rule to be restated:

$$O \longrightarrow \begin{matrix} P \longrightarrow T \\ + \\ W \end{matrix}$$

In addition, we can combine the first and third rules:

$$O \longrightarrow \begin{matrix} P \longleftarrow\!\!+\!\!\longrightarrow K \\ + \\ W \end{matrix}$$

Allowing us to draw the inference that $O \longleftarrow\!\!+\!\!\longrightarrow K$.

Note that the second rule forces at least K or T to *always* be carried by the fruit stand, and thus we can place a K/T dual-option in the single space representing the group. This leads to the complete setup for this game:

F K O P T W [6]

$$K \longleftarrow\!\!+\!\!\longrightarrow P$$

$$\cancel{T} \longrightarrow K$$
$$\cancel{K} \longrightarrow T$$

$$O \longrightarrow \begin{matrix} P \longrightarrow T, \cancel{K} \\ + \\ W \end{matrix}$$

$$W \longrightarrow \begin{matrix} F \\ or \\ T \end{matrix}$$

$$\dfrac{K/T}{Fruit}$$

Inferences:

$$P \longrightarrow T$$

$$O \longleftarrow\!\!+\!\!\longrightarrow K$$

36

Question #1: Global, Could Be True, List. The correct answer choice is (B)

As we determined from our discussion of the inferences, when P is carried then T must be carried. This relationship eliminates answer choices (A), (C), and (E).

Also, when O is carried then P and W must be carried, which eliminates answer choices (A) (again) and (D).

Of course, K and P cannot be carried together, and this eliminates (E) as well.

Consequently, answer choice (B) is proven correct by process of elimination.

Question #2: Global, Could Be True. The correct answer choice is (D)

Because the second rule indicates that if the stand does not carry T then it must carry K (and by the contrapositive, if the stand does not carry K then it must carry T), the answer must be either K or T. For example, if the fruit stand attempts to carry only F, then by application of the second rule the stand does not carry T and therefore it must carry K. Thus, F cannot be the only kind of fruit that the stand carries. Since the answer must be K or T, and only T appears among the answers, answer choice (D) is correct. An alternate way of looking at the answers is to consider that O, P, and W are all sufficient conditions; that is, their occurrence automatically indicates that other kinds of fruit are carried by the stand. Thus, none of those fruits could be the only fruit carried by the stand.

Question #3: Global, Cannot Be True, List. The correct answer choice is (E)

The answer requires you to find a grouping of fruits that violates at least one of the rules. As you might expect, the more fruits listed in an answer choice, the more likely that the answer will violate one or more of the rules. Answer choice (E) lists the greatest number of fruits, and violates two of the rules. First, from the first rule, K and P cannot both be carried by the stand. Second, from the inferences, when the stand carries P it must also carry T. Thus, answer choice (E) cannot be a viable list of fruits carried by the stand, and answer choice (E) is thus correct.

Question #4: Local, Must Be True. The correct answer choice is (C)

If the stand does not carry W, then by the contrapositive of the third rule the stand cannot carry O. The only remaining fruits that could be carried by the stand are then F, T, K, and P. However, from the first rule K and P cannot be carried at the same time, and the only fruits that can then be carried are F, T, and the choice of K or P, or a maximum of three fruits. Answer choice (C) is therefore correct.

Answer choice (B) is incorrect because although the stand can carry two kinds of fruit, it does not have to carry at least two kinds of fruit (it could carry only one kind of fruit, K or T).

Answer choices (D) and (E) are incorrect because although the stand cannot carry O, it could carry P or K.

Question #5: Local, Cannot Be True, FTT. The correct answer choice is (E)

Oddly, in this Cannot Be True question the Local condition has no effect on the correct answer. From the discussion of inferences, we know that when P is carried then T must be carried. Thus, the statement in answer choice (E), that P is carried but T is not carried, cannot be true and answer choice (E) is correct. Clearly, the test makers felt this inference was extremely challenging to make, and so it is tested repeatedly in this game.

Question #6: Local, Cannot Be True, List, Suspension. The correct answer choice is (C)

The condition in the question stem suspends the second rule. With the second rule suspended, only three rules remain in effect: the first, third, and fourth rules. As none of the answer choices contain K, the first rule is inapplicable.

Two of the answer choices—(C) and (E)—contain O, but both of those answer choices also contain P and W, so there is no violation of the third rule.

Two answers—(C) and (E)—contain W, but while (E) also contains F, (C) contains neither F nor T, and thus answer choice (C) violates the fourth rule and is therefore the correct answer.

This is an Advanced Linear: Balanced, Identify the Templates game.

The initial setup made by most students appears as follows:

F G H I M ⁵
L T ²
V V S S K ⁵

L/T:	___	___	T	___	___	
City:	___	___	K	___	___	V V S S K
Caller:	I/M	M/I	H	F/G	G/F	F G H I M
	1	2	3	4	5	

S ——————▶ [L / S]

G
H > - - - - - -
F

[S / M] [S / F]

However, there is more that can be done with the setup because the linkage among the rules ultimately leads to a set of powerful and limiting inferences. Let's review the setup first:

Because I and M are the first two calls aired, and F and G's calls air after H, H must call third, and F and G call fourth and fifth, not necessarily in that order:

Caller:	I/M	M/I	H	F/G	G/F
	1	2	3	4	5

Note that for the callers there are only four possible orders. By itself this does not suggest that you should draw out all four orders. The diagram thus far captures them well, and without the other pieces placed, there are still far too many overall solutions to attempt to show them all.

Continuing on, because H must call third, H calls from K and is taped:

L/T:	___	___	T	___	___
City:			K		
Caller:	I/M	M/I	H	F/G	G/F
	1	2	3	4	5

The last rule can now be applied in decisive fashion. If neither M or F calls from S, and H is the one call from K, then M and F must both call from V. Further, G and I must then call from S, and, from the third rule, both calls from S are live.

These connections create the following vertical blocks:

V		V		L		L
M		F		S		S
				G		I

The placement options for these blocks are so limited, and they provide so much additional information, as to make it obvious that we should Identify the Possibilities based on the order of the callers, and adding in the block information:

Template #1:

	L	T	L	
V	S	K	S	V
M	I	H	G	F
1	2	3	4	5

Template #2:

L		T	L	
S	V	K	S	V
I	M	H	G	F
1	2	3	4	5

Template #3:

	L	T		L
V	S	K	V	S
M	I	H	F	G
1	2	3	4	5

Template #4:

L		T		L
S	V	K	V	S
I	M	H	F	G
1	2	3	4	5

Further, since there is only the option of L or T in the open spaces, each template encompasses four solutions, and thus these four templates hold the sixteen possibilities of this game (we will not show the L/T dual-option in each remaining open space in order to preserve clarity since the diagrams are already so info-laden).

Question #7: Global, Could Be True, List. The correct answer choice is (E)

H must be the third call aired, and thus answer choices (A), (B), and (D) can be eliminated. G must be the fourth or fifth call aired, and thus answer choice (C) (and (D) again)can be eliminated. Thus, answer choice (E) is proven correct by process of elimination.

Question #8: Global, Must Be True. The correct answer choice is (A)

As indicated in Template #1, F's call could air fifth, and thus answer choice (A) is correct.

Question #9: Local, Could Be True. The correct answer choice is (C)

If the first call aired is from Seattle, then only Templates #2 and #4 apply. As shown in Template #2, H's call could be the call aired after M's call, and so answer choice (C) could be true and is correct.

Question #10: Local, Cannot Be True. The correct answer choice is (C)

If the first call aired is taped, then only Templates #1 and #3 can apply. In both templates a live call airs second, and so answer choice (C) cannot be true and is therefore correct.

Question #11: Global, Must Be True. The correct answer choice is (A)

In the discussion of the blocks, we established via the last rule that M and F do not call from Seattle, and that therefore G and I do call from Seattle. And, from the third rule, we know that both Seattle calls are live. Thus, G's call is live, and answer choice (A) is correct.

Question #12: Local, Must Be True. The correct answer choice is (A)

The conditions in the question stem specify that no two consecutive calls are live or taped. Thus, no LL blocks or TT blocks can appear in the L/T stack, and the result is that L and T must alternate in this stack (regardless of which is first). Let's examine each template and see which ones can meet these conditions:

Template #1: If the first and last calls are taped, then the conditions in the question stem are met. Thus, the order in Template #1 is viable.

Template #2: Because L is first and T is third, there is no call that can be aired second that will not cause a violation of the conditions in the question stem. Thus, this template cannot produce an order that satisfies the question.

Template #3: Because T is third and L is fifth, there is no call that can be aired fourth that will not cause a violation of the conditions in the question stem. Thus, this template cannot produce an order that satisfies the question.

Template #4:   Because L is first and T is third and L is fifth, there are no calls that can be aired second or fourth that will not cause a violation of the conditions in the question stem. Thus, this template cannot produce an order that satisfies the question.

Thus, the only template that can meet the conditions in the question stem is Template #1, and so only one order of the callers meets the conditions, and answer choice (A) is correct.

Question #13: Local, Cannot Be True. The correct answer choice is (B)

If the second call aired is taped, then only Templates #2 and #4 apply. As shown in both templates, the first call is from Seattle, and so answer choice (B) cannot be true and is correct.

36

This is an Advanced Linear: Balanced game.

The game scenario indicates that six people ride a bus together. The bus seats are divided into three rows of two seats each. This creates an Advanced Linear: Balanced scenario:

G H I K L M [6]

The first rule indicates that G and H form a block in the aisle seats:

$$\boxed{\text{G H}}_A$$

This rule eliminates G and H from sitting in the window seats, and additionally eliminates H from sitting in row 1 and G from sitting in row 3. Because the GH block must occupy the aisle seats in rows 1-2 or rows 2-3, either G or H always sit in the aisle seat in row 2:

G H I K L M [6]

The second rule states that if M occupies an aisle seat, then H and L sit in the same row, with H in the aisle seat according to the first rule:

$$M_A \longrightarrow \boxed{\begin{array}{c} L \\ \text{G H} \end{array}}$$

The third rule is another odd rule, and states that when G and K sit in the same row, then M is in the seat *directly behind* I's seat. The phrase "directly behind" indicates that they are both in window seats or both in aisle seats; however, I and M cannot be in aisle seats because that would not leave room for the GH block, and so I and M would have to be in window seats:

$$\boxed{\begin{array}{l} K_{\,W} \\ G\,H \end{array}}_{A} \longrightarrow \boxed{I\ M}_{\,W}$$

More on this rule shortly.

The fourth rule states that when K occupies a window seat, M sits in row 3:

$$K_{\,W} \longrightarrow M_{\,3}$$

The fifth rule states that when K occupies a seat in row 3, I sits in row 1:

$$K_{\,3} \longrightarrow I_{\,1}$$

You may have noted that the rules in this game are extremely varied. This makes remembering the rules more difficult, and increases the difficulty of applying the rules. Not surprisingly, most students feel that this is the most difficult game of the test.

With the basic diagram of each rule in place, let's consider some of the inferences that can be drawn when the rules are linked together.

The third rule can only be enacted if K and G sit in row 1. Otherwise, there is no room for the IM block. In fact, the rules are so restrictive that when the K and G rule is enacted there is only one solution to the game:

K	I	M
G	H	L
1	2	3

The second rule also produces a severely limited scenario. When M sits in an aisle seat, M must be in row 1 or 3 in order to accommodate the GH block. However, with the aisle seats filled, K must sit in a window seat. This enacts the fourth rule, which stipulates that when K sits in a window seat, M must sit in row 3:

```
                    L
 ____             ____            ____
   G                H                M
   1                2                3
```

Further, the third rule ultimately prohibits K from sitting in row 1, and thus K must sit in row 3. Finally, I must sit in row 1:

```
   I                L                K
 ____             ____            ____
   G                H                M
   1                2                3
```

At this point, you might be coming to the realization that there are a limited number of solutions to this game. In fact, only seven templates containing fourteen possibilities exist in this game. Although one approach would be to identify each of these templates, there are likely too many templates to be able to show each within the time limits of the game. Normally, we would prefer to draw out four or five templates at most.

With the variety of rules, you should remember that using hypotheticals can be a very effective weapon. If you find yourself unable to identify the inferences in a game, draw out a few solutions to the game; this approach allows you to work with the rules and at the same time increase your knowledge of the game. For example, the following hypothetical proves correct answer choice (E) on Question #14 and answer choice (A) on question #15:

```
   I                L                K
 ____             ____            ____
   G                H                M
   1                2                3
```

Before moving on to the questions, here is the final setup for the game:

$$\boxed{GH}_A$$

W: ___ ___ ___ $\cancel{G}$ $\cancel{H}$

$$M_A \longrightarrow \boxed{\begin{array}{c} L \\ G\,H \end{array}}$$

A: $\underset{\cancel{H}}{\underline{\quad\quad}}$ $\underset{2}{\underline{G/H}}$ $\underset{\cancel{G}}{\underline{\quad\quad}}$
$\quad\quad\quad 1$

$$\boxed{\begin{array}{c} K_W \\ G\,H \end{array}}_A \longrightarrow \boxed{I\,M}_{W\,2-3}$$

$$K_W \longrightarrow M_3$$

$$K_3 \longrightarrow I_1$$

Question #14: Global, Could Be True. The correct answer choice is (E)

As mentioned during the setup, the following hypothetical proves that answer choice (E) could be true and is thus correct:

I	L	K
G	H	M
1	2	3

Question #15: Local, Could Be True. The correct answer choice is (A)

The hypothetical in question #14 above proves that answer choice (A) could be true, and thus (A) is the correct answer.

Question #16: Local, Must Be True. The correct answer choice is (D)

If M sits in row 1, it *initially* appears that M can sit in the aisle or window seat. But, if M occupies the aisle seat in row 1, a violation of the fourth rule results, as explained below.

When M sits in the row 1 aisle seat, G and H then sit in rows 2 and 3:

```
        ___        ___        ___
        M          G          H
        1          2          3
```

From the second rule, L must then sit in row 3:

```
                              L
        ___        ___        ___

        M          G          H
        1          2          3
```

However, this forces K (and I) into a window seat, enacting the third rule which cannot then be satisfied. Thus, M cannot sit in the aisle seat and M must sit in the window seat in row 1:

```
        M          ___        ___

        ___        ___        ___
        1          2          3
```

When M sits in row 1, from the contrapositive of the fourth rule K cannot occupy a window seat, and must then occupy an aisle seat. Thus, the three aisle seats are occupied by K, G, and H, and the three window seats are occupied by M, I, and L.

In the aisle seats, K appears to have the choice of row 1 or 3. But, because of the fifth rule, in this question if K sits in row 3, then I would have to occupy the row 1 window seat, which is impossible because M sits in that seat. Thus, K cannot sit in row 3, and must instead sit in row 1, leading to the following diagram:

```
        M          I/L        L/I

        K          G          H
        1          2          3
```

Accordingly, answer choice (D) is correct.

36

Question #17: Local, Must Be True, Except. The correct answer choice is (B)

If K occupies the aisle seat in row 3, then the fifth rule is activated and I must sit in row 1. However, because the GH block occupies rows 1 and 2 of the aisle seats, I must sit in the row 1 window seat, leaving L and M as the other two window seats:

I	L/M	M/L
G	H	K
1	2	3

Accordingly, answer choice (B) is not necessarily true and therefore correct.

Questions #18: Local, Could Be True. The correct answer choice is (C)

If G does not sit in row 1, from the first rule G must sit in row 2 and H must sit in row 3. I must then occupy a window seat in row 2 or 3:

	I/	/I
	G	H
1	2	3

This information eliminates answer choices (A) and (D).

The only remaining aisle seat is in row 1, and if M were to occupy that seat, then K would have a window seat, which would lead to a violation of the fourth rule. Thus, M cannot sit in the row 1 aisle seat, which eliminates answer choice (E).

The remaining two answer choices—answer choices (B) and (C)—address row 2, of which the window seat is the only remaining seat available. If K sits in the row 2 window seat, then from the fourth rule M would have to sit in the row 3 window seat, forcing I to sit in row 1. But, this causes a violation of the condition in the question stem, and thus K cannot sit in row 2. This information eliminates answer choice (B), and thus answer choice (C) is correct.

The following hypothetical shows that answer choice (C) is possible:

L	M	I
K	G	H
1	2	3

This is an Advanced Linear: Balanced, Identify the Templates game.

The game scenario and first rule establish the following Advanced Linear scenario:

P: F G K L ⁴

CP: R S T U ⁴

P: __   __   __   __
CP: __   __   __   __
     1   2   3   4

The second rule creates a sequence:

                    min
        F > ___ > G

This rule creates several Not Laws: G cannot pilot the first two flights, and F cannot pilot the last two flights. We will hold off on diagramming those Not Laws, and instead consider the other rules first.

The third rule assigns K, a pilot, to flight 2:

P: F G K L ⁴

CP: R S T U ⁴

P: __   K   __   __
CP: __   __   __   __
     1   2   3   4

            min
    F > ___ > G

When this rule is combined with the second rule, a powerful inference can made: F must pilot flight 1. From the second rule, F cannot pilot the last two flights, and from the third rule K pilots the second flight. Thus, only flight 1 is available for F, leaving G and L to pilot flights 3 and 4:

P: F G K L ⁴

CP: R S T U ⁴

P: F   K   G/L   L/G
CP: __   __   __   __
     1   2   3   4

            min
    F > ___ > G

The fourth rule creates a vertical block with U and L:

$$\boxed{\begin{array}{c} \text{L} \\ \text{U} \end{array}}$$

The placement options for this block are limited. Because L must pilot flight 3 or 4, U must co-pilot flight 3 or 4. Adding that information to the diagram, as well as the fact that co-pilots R, S, and T are randoms, results in the final diagram for the game:

P: F G K L [4]

CP: R S T U [4]
      * * *

P:	F	K	G/L	L/G
CP:			/U	U/
	1	2	3	4

min
$$\boxed{\text{F} > \underline{} > \text{G}}$$

$$\boxed{\begin{array}{c} \text{L} \\ \text{U} \end{array}}$$

The limitation on the pilot orders and the block creates two basic templates:

P:	F	K	L	G
CP:			U	
	1	2	3	4

P:	F	K	G	L
CP:				U
	1	2	3	4

Question #19: Global, Could Be True. The correct answer choice is (A)

The pilot for flight 1 must be F, which eliminates answer choices (C), (D), and (E).

Because U must co-pilot flight 3 or 4, U cannot co-pilot flight 1, eliminating answer choice (B).

Thus, answer choice (A) is correct.

Question #20: Local, Cannot Be True. The correct answer choice is (C)

If R's flight is later than U's flight, then U must co-pilot flight 3 and R must co-pilot flight 4. This results in L piloting flight 3 and G piloting flight 4:

```
P:    F     K     L     G
CP:  S/T   T/S    U     R
      1     2     3     4
```

Thus, answer choice (C) cannot be true and is correct.

Question #21: Local, Not Necessarily True, FTT. The correct answer choice is (D)

If L pilots an earlier flight than G, then L pilots flight 3 and G pilots flight 4:

```
P:    F     K     L     G
CP:  ___   ___    U    ___
      1     2     3     4
```

Because S could co-pilot flight 4, answer choice (D) is not necessarily true and therefore correct.

Question #22: Global, Must Be True, Maximum. The correct answer choice is (C)

Only L or G can pilot flight 4, and when L pilots flight 4, from the fourth rule U must co-pilot flight 4. When G pilots flight 4, any of the three randoms (R, S, or T) could co-pilot the flight. Thus, the four different pilot and co-pilot teams that could be assigned to flight 4 are:

```
L      G      G      G
U      R      S      T
```

Accordingly, answer choice (C) is correct.

Question #23: Local, Not Necessarily True, FTT. The correct answer choice is (D)

If L pilots an earlier flight than S, then L pilots flight 3 and S co-pilots flight 4:

```
P:    F     K     L     G
CP:  R/T   T/R    U     S
      1     2     3     4
```

Accordingly, answer choice (D) is not necessarily true and is therefore correct.

This game is quite easy, and this test, like the December 2000 LSAT, serves as another example of the most difficult game appearing third and the easiest game appearing fourth.

POWERSCORE®

37

PREPTEST

JUNE 2002 LOGIC GAMES SETUPS

This is an Advanced Linear: Balanced game.

The game scenario and first two rules create an Advanced Linear scenario:

M M M / F F F F F ^{8}

North: ____ ____ ____ ____

South: ____ ____ ____ ____
            R   T   V   W

The third rule helpfully assigns females to two of the eight wings:

M M M / F F F F F ^{8}

North: _F_ _F_ ____ ____

South: ____ ____ ____ ____
            R   T   V   W

The fourth rule indicates that if males are assigned to a wing, the other wing must be assigned females. Operationally, this means that males can never be assigned to both wings of a dormitory, which results in a vertical not-block:

$$\frac{\boxed{M}}{\boxed{M}}$$

The fifth rule is conditional:

$$VS_M \longrightarrow WN_M$$

Of course, if the fifth rule is enacted, and both those wings are assigned males, then by applying the fourth rule, the other wings in those dormitories would be assigned females:

$$VS_M \longrightarrow \begin{array}{c} VN_F \\ + \\ WN_M \\ + \\ WS_F \end{array}$$

Thus, if Veblen South is assigned males, the Veblen and Wisteria dormitories are fully assigned.

This game also contains a two-value system: each dormitory is assigned either male or female students. Thus, if a dormitory does not have male students, then the dormitory must have female students. As is so often the case, the two-value system can be applied to a conditional rule to create greater insight. Consider the contrapositive of the final rule:

$$\cancel{WN}_M \longrightarrow \cancel{VS}_M$$

The same contrapositive reinterpreted by applying the two-value system:

$$WN_F \longrightarrow VS_F$$

This inference is directly tested in question #3.

Another point of restriction in the game is the males. Because males cannot be assigned to both wings of a dormitory, at most males can be assigned to one wing of a dormitory. At the same time, the rules state that there must be exactly three wings with males. Because there are only four dormitories, the situation is restricted, and the following inferences can be drawn:

1. If a dormitory has female students assigned to both wings, then the males must be assigned to one wing in each of the other three dormitories. For example, if Tuscarora South is assigned females (as in question #5), then males must be assigned to Richards South, Veblen North or South, and Wisteria North or South. In question #5, this inference is sufficient to eliminate answer choices (A), (B), and (E). Answer choice (C) can be eliminated by the contrapositive of the final rule, leaving answer choice (D) as correct.

    Another way to look at this inference is to assert that only one dormitory can be all-female, and the other three dormitories must each have one male and one female wing.

2. Among any two dormitory pairs, males must *always* be assigned to at least one wing. For example, with Veblen and Wisteria, at least one of the four wings must always be male.

    This inference is directly tested in question #2. With Richards and Tuscarora (only South is relevant since the North wings are assigned to females), at least one must always be male, otherwise there will not be a sufficient number of wings available to house the males. Hence, answer choice (B) is correct.

The final setup to the game appears as follows, but keep in mind the points made in the analysis of the two-value system:

M M M / F F F F F [8]

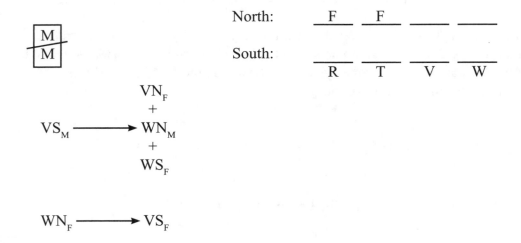

North: F   F   ___ ___

South: ___ ___ ___ ___
            R   T   V   W

VN_F
+
$VS_M \longrightarrow WN_M$
+
WS_F

$WN_F \longrightarrow VS_F$

After a careful consideration of the rules, the only two active rules are the fourth and fifth rules. Obviously, you should pay close attention to these rules as you work through the questions, and indeed, the interaction of these rules creates several powerful inferences that are tested throughout the game. In fact, the inferences are so powerful that only a limited number of templates exist for this game, and one approach would be to show the three basic templates:

    Template #1: Veblen South is male. Two total solutions.
    Template #2: Wisteria North is female, Veblen South is female. Four total solutions.
    Template #3: Veblen South is female, Wisteria North is male. Three total solutions.

The choice to show the templates is yours because the game can be done quickly with either approach.

Question #1: Local, Could Be True. The correct answer choice is (D)

If females are assigned to Veblen South and Veblen North, then four of the wings are assigned to females:

North: F   F   F   ___

South: ___ ___ F   ___
            R   T   V   W

The remaining four wings must then be assigned as follows: three wings to males and one wing to females. Because Wisteria cannot have males assigned to both wings (per the fourth rule), at most one of the Wisteria wings can be assigned males, and by Hurdling the Uncertainty we can deduce that Richards South and Tuscarora South are assigned males, resulting in the following setup:

North:	F	F	F	F/M
South:	M	M	F	M/F
	R	T	V	W

Accordingly, answer choice (D) is correct.

Question #2: Global, Cannot Be True. The correct answer choice is (B)

As discussed during the setup analysis, with Richards and Tuscarora, at least one must always be male otherwise there will not be a sufficient number of wings available to house the remaining males. Hence, answer choice (B) is correct.

Question #3: Local, Must Be True. The correct answer choice is (D)

As explained during the discussion of the contrapositive of the final rule, when Wisteria North is assigned females, then Veblen South must be assigned females. Accordingly, answer choice (D) is correct.

Question #4: Local, Cannot Be True. The correct answer choice is (D)

The information in the question stem enacts the last rule, and creates the following setup:

North:	F	F	F	M
South:	F/M	M/F	M	F
	R	T	V	W

Accordingly, answer choice (D) is correct.

Question #5: Local, Could Be True. The correct answer choice is (D)

This question is explained during the discussion of the restriction of the males. Answer choice (D) is correct.

This is an Advanced Linear: Balanced game.

The game scenario establishes that seven trucks arrive in order at a warehouse, and that each truck is either red or green, but not both. This creates a Balanced Advanced Linear setup:

S T U W X Y Z ^{7}
R G ^{2}

R/G: ____ ____ ____ ____ ____ ____ ____
Trucks: ____ ____ ____ ____ ____ ____ ____
          1   2   3   4   5   6   7

The first rule prohibits two red trucks from arriving consecutively:

$$\boxed{R\!\!\!/\!R}$$

The second and third rules can be combined to create a super-sequence:

$$
\begin{array}{ccc}
R & & T \\
\text{- - - -} > Y > \text{- - - -} \\
R & & W
\end{array}
$$

More on this sequence in a moment.

The fourth rule assigns S to the sixth position:

S T U W X Y Z ^{7}
R G ^{2}

R/G: ____ ____ ____ ____ ____ ____ ____
Trucks: ____ ____ ____ ____ ____ S   ____
          1   2   3   4   5   6   7

The fifth rule is another sequential rule:

$$Z > U$$

The key to this setup is Y. Because Y must arrive before both T and W, and because S must arrive sixth, the latest that Y can arrive is fourth:

$$
Y > \quad
\begin{array}{c}
S \\
- - - - - \\
T \\
- - - - - \\
W
\end{array}
$$

In addition, because exactly two red trucks arrive before Y, and these red trucks cannot be consecutive, the earliest Y can arrive is fourth:

$$
\begin{array}{c}
\text{min} \\
\boxed{R \underline{\quad} R}
\end{array} > Y
$$

Consequently, because Y can arrive no earlier and no later than fourth, Y must arrive fourth.

Because Y arrives fourth, and S arrives sixth, T and W must arrive fifth and seventh, not necessarily in that order:

R/G:	___	___	___				
Trucks:	___	___	___	Y	T/W	S	W/T
	1	2	3	4	5	6	7

Because exactly two red trucks arrive before Y, and these red trucks cannot be consecutive, they must arrive first and third. The second and fourth trucks must be green in order to comply with the first rule:

R/G:	R	G	R	G			
Trucks:	___	___	___	Y	T/W	S	W/T
	1	2	3	4	5	6	7

The color of the fifth, sixth, and seventh trucks cannot be determined. The remaining three variables, U, X, and Z, must arrive first, second, and third, not necessarily in that order. The combination of the above leads to the final diagram for the game:

S T U W X Y Z ^{7}

$*$

R G ^{2}

$$\boxed{R / R}$$ ⟋

$$\begin{array}{ccc} R & & T \\ ----&> Y >&---- \\ R & & W \end{array}$$

Z > U

R/G:	R	G	R	G			
Trucks:	(Z > U ,	X)	Y	T/W	S	W/T
	1	2	3	4	5	6	7
	~~X~~	~~X~~	~~X~~		~~X~~	~~X~~	~~X~~
		~~U~~		~~Z~~			

Question #6: Global, Could Be True, List. The correct answer choice is (A)

Answer choices (B), (C), (E) can each be eliminated because Y does not arrive fourth (there are also other reasons for eliminating (B), (C) and (E)).

Answer choice (D) can be eliminated since T arrives ahead of Y, a violation of the second rule.

Hence, answer choice (A) is correct.

Question #7: Global, Cannot Be True. The correct answer choice is (B)

Answer choice (B) is correct because T and S must be consecutive (5-6 or 6-7), and if they are both red then the first rule would be violated.

Question #8: Local, Must Be True. The correct answer choice is (C)

If X arrives third, then according to our diagram Z must arrive first and U must arrive second:

R/G:	R	G	R	G			
Trucks:	Z	U	X	Y	T/W	S	W/T
	1	2	3	4	5	6	7

Hence, U must be green and answer choice (C) is correct.

37

Question #9: Local, Must Be True. The correct answer choice is (A)

If exactly three trucks are green, then four trucks must be red, and the Separation Principle applies, forcing trucks 1-3-5-7 to be red and trucks 2-4-6 to be green:

R/G:	R	G	R	G	R	G	R
Trucks:	(Z > U ,	X)	Y	T/W	S	W/T
	1	2	3	4	5	6	7

Hence, S must be green and answer choice (A) is correct.

Question #10: Global, Must Be True. The correct answer choice is (B)

In our initial diagram, only Y and S are fixed, and these are the only two trucks that are exactly fixed. Consequently, answer choice (B) is correct.

Question #11: Global, Cannot Be True. The correct answer choice is (E)

Because Z must arrive before U from the fifth rule, and U must arrive before Y per our inferences, and inherent Z > U > Y sequence is present in the game. Thus, Z and Y cannot arrive consecutively, and answer choice (E) is correct.

Note that the hypothetical produced in question #6 eliminates answer choices (A) and (D).

This is a Grouping: Defined-Fixed, Balanced, Identify the Templates game.

The game scenario establishes that six books (of three different types) occupy spaces on three different shelves, resulting in a Balanced Grouping game:

Grammar: F H [2]
Linguistics: P S [2]
Novels: V W [2]

1 ____

2 ____ ____

3 ____ ____ ____

The three rules appear relatively simple, and they establish a set of blocks and not-blocks:

Rule #1: | F V/W |

Rule #2: | P/S |

Rule #3: | V̸/P |

             | V̸/S |

Note that the first rule establishes that F cannot occupy the first shelf, and must therefore be on the second or third shelf.

The key to this game is the interaction of the last two rules. Because no two books from the group of V, P, and S can be on the same shelf, each book must be on a different shelf. And, since there are only three shelves, we can infer that one book from the group of V, P, and S must be on each shelf:

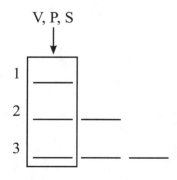

Thus, the first shelf is occupied by one of V, P, or S; the second shelf is occupied by one of V, P, or S, and one other book; and the third shelf is occupied by one of V, P, or S, and two other books.

The interaction of V, P, and S also affects the other three variables, F, H, and W. Using Hurdle the Uncertainty, because the first shelf is occupied, F, H, and W must be on the second and third shelf:

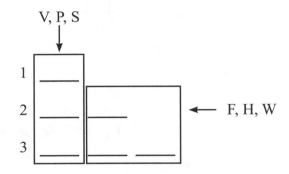

The only remaining "active" rule is the first rule. Thus, the placement of F must be carefully tracked, and in fact, depending on the placement of F and W, there are only three possible templates:

Template #1: F on the second shelf

1	P/S		
2	V	F	
3	S/P	H	W

Because F must be on the same shelf as V or W, V must be on the second shelf. P and S form dual-options on the first and third shelves.

Template #2: F on the third shelf, W on the second shelf

1	P/S		
2	S/P	W	
3	V	F	H

Because F must be on the same shelf as V or W, V must be on the third shelf. P and S form dual-options on the first and second shelves.

<u>Template #3: F on the third shelf, W on the third shelf</u>

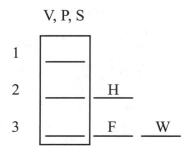

V, P, S

Because F and W are on the same shelf, the first rule is satisfied, and thus V can be assigned to any one of the three shelves.

In total, these three templates contain ten solutions, and using these templates makes the game considerably easier. However, the game is still time-consuming because there are seven questions.

Question #12: Global, Could Be True, List. The correct answer choice is (B)

Answer choice (A) can be eliminated because V and S are on the same shelf, a violation of the third rule.

Answer choice (B) is the correct answer.

Answer choice (C) can be eliminated because F is not on the same shelf as V or W.

Answer choices (D) and (E) can be eliminated because P and S are on the same shelf, a violation of the second rule.

Question #13: Global, Cannot Be True. The correct answer choice is (A)

From the discussion above, we know that only V, P, or S can be on the first shelf. Hence, no grammar is on the first shelf and answer choice (A) is correct.

Question #14: Global, Must Be True. The correct answer choice is (D)

Template #1 can be used to disprove answer choice (A).

Template #2 can be used to disprove answer choice (B).

Template #2 can be used to disprove answer choice (C).

Template #2 can be used to disprove answer choice (E).

Hence, answer choice (D) is correct.

37

Question #15: Local, Could Be True. The correct answer choice is (E)

Only Template #2 meets the criterion in the question stem, and Template #2 proves answer choice (E) is correct. Note that, in Template #2, only P and S are uncertain; hence, in a Could Be True question you should look for answers that include P or S or both. Only answer choices (A) and (E) include P or S, and looking at those two answers first would reduce the amount of time spent completing the question.

Question #16: Global, Must Be True. The correct answer choice is (E)

From the setup discussion, W must always be on the second or third shelf. Hence, answer choice (E) is correct.

Question #17: Local, Could Be True. The correct answer choice is (C)

Only Template #1 meets the criteria in the question stem, and Template #1 proves answer choice (C) is correct. Also, in Template #1, only P and S are uncertain; hence, as mentioned above in question #15, in a Could Be True question you should look for answers that include P or S or both. Only answer choices (A) and (C) include P or S, and looking at those two answers first would reduce the amount of time spent completing the question.

Question #18: Local, Must Be True. The correct answer choice is (E)

Both Template #1 and Template #3 meet the condition in the question stem. An examination of the two templates reveals that the only constant between the two is that W is always on the third shelf. Thus, given that this is a Must Be True question, you should immediately look for W on the third shelf as an answer.

Correspondingly, answer choice (E) is correct. Here are both possibilities with H and P on the same shelf:

1	S/V				1	S		
2	P	H			2	V	F	
3	V/S	F	W		3	P	H	W

37

This is an Advanced Linear: Balanced, Identify the Templates game.

The game scenario and rules combine to form the following main diagram:

J K L M O⁵

K/L

M > O J

1	2	3	4	5
$\cancel{O}$	$\cancel{J}$	$\cancel{O}$	$\cancel{J}$	$\cancel{M}$
				$\cancel{L}$

6	7	8	9	10
$\cancel{O}$	$\cancel{J}$	$\cancel{O}$	$\cancel{J}$	$\cancel{M}$
				$\cancel{L}$

The game scenario indicates that laps 1 and 6; 2 and 7; 3 and 8; 4 and 9; and 5 and 10 are all paired, so that a member who swims one lap in the pair automatically swims the other lap in the pair. For example, if a member swims lap 1, he or she also swims lap 6, and if a member swims lap 6, he or she also swims lap 1. Consequently, if a member cannot swim one of the laps in a pair, he or she cannot swim the other lap in the pair. For example, the rules state that J cannot swim lap 9. By deduction, J also cannot swim lap 4.

The pairing of the laps also has an unusual effect on the last rule. The last rule is rather carefully worded to say, "*At least one* of J's laps is immediately after one of O's laps" (italics added). In a regular linear game, a rule like this would normally create an OJ block where J cannot swim lap 1 and O cannot swim lap 5. In this game, however, because laps 5 and 6 are consecutive, J *can* swim lap 1 and O can swim lap 5, as in the following hypothetical:

J	L	M	K	O
1	2	3	4	5

J	L	M	K	O
6	7	8	9	10

In the above hypothetical, J in lap 6 swims immediately after O in lap 5, meeting the specification in the last rule.

In the main diagram, there are several Not Laws worth considering. The last rule produces Not Laws for O on laps 3 and 8. If J cannot swim laps 4 or 9, then O cannot swim laps 3 or 8.

The third rule, M > O, creates two Not Laws because the rule applies to the first lap O swims. Hence,

O cannot swim lap 1 (and lap 6) and M cannot swim lap 5 (and lap 10). And, if O cannot swim laps 1 or 6, by applying the last rule we can deduce that J cannot swim laps 2 or 7.

The only remaining Not Law is L on laps 5 and 10. If L swims laps 5 and 10, the OJ block must swim laps 2-3 and 7-8. M must then swim laps 1 and 6. The only remaining laps for K to swim are laps 4 and 9, and thus K would swim immediately before L, a violation of the first rule.

A close examination of the game reveals that the placement options of the OJ block are limited. In fact, O and J can only be placed into three separate positions: 2-3 and 7-8; 4-5 and 9-10; 5-6 and 1-10. One approach to the game would be to Identify the Templates:

Template #1: O swims lap 2, J swims lap 3

$$
\begin{array}{ccccc}
\underline{\text{M}} & \underline{\text{O}} & \underline{\text{J}} & \underline{\text{L}} & \underline{\text{K}} \\
1 & 2 & 3 & 4 & 5
\end{array}
$$

$$
\begin{array}{ccccc}
\underline{\text{M}} & \underline{\text{O}} & \underline{\text{J}} & \underline{\text{L}} & \underline{\text{K}} \\
6 & 7 & 8 & 9 & 10
\end{array}
$$

Template #2: O swims lap 4, J swims lap 5

$$
\begin{array}{ccccc}
\underline{(\text{M},\ \boxed{\text{K}/\text{L}})} & & \underline{\text{O}} & \underline{\text{J}} \\
1 \quad 2 & 3 & 4 & 5
\end{array}
$$

$$
\begin{array}{ccccc}
\underline{(\text{M},\ \boxed{\text{K}/\text{L}})} & & \underline{\text{O}} & \underline{\text{J}} \\
6 \quad 7 & 8 & 9 & 10
\end{array}
$$

Template #3: O swims lap 5, J swims lap 6

$$
\begin{array}{ccccc}
\underline{\text{J}} & \underline{(\text{M},\ \boxed{\text{K}/\text{L}})} & & \underline{\text{O}} \\
1 & 2 \quad 3 & 4 & 5
\end{array}
$$

$$
\begin{array}{ccccc}
\underline{\text{J}} & \underline{(\text{M},\ \boxed{\text{K}/\text{L}})} & & \underline{\text{O}} \\
6 & 7 \quad 8 & 9 & 10
\end{array}
$$

Although the above templates make the game quite easy, the original setup to the game can also be used to attack the game effectively.

Question #19: Global, Could Be True, List. The correct answer choice is (A)

Answer choice (A) is the correct answer.

Answer choice (B) can be eliminated because J swims lap 4, a violation of the implications of the second rule.

Answer choice (C) can be eliminated because at least one of J's laps is not immediately after one of O's laps.

Answer choice (D) can be eliminated because O's first lap is before M's first lap.

Answer choice (E) can be eliminated because K's lap is immediately before L's lap.

Question #20: Local, Must Be True. The correct answer choice is (A)

If J swims lap 8, then, according to Template #1, all ten lap assignments are determined. Hence, answer choice (A) is correct.

Question #21: Local, Could Be True. The correct answer choice is (D)

If O swims lap 4, then J must swim lap 5 (Template #2). Accordingly, answer choices (A), (B), (C), and (E) are incorrect. By process of elimination, answer choice (D) must be correct.

Question #22: Global, Could Be True. The correct answer choice is (B)

By applying the Not Laws on our initial diagram, answer choices (A), (C), (D), and (E) can be eliminated. Hence, answer choice (B) is correct.

Question #23: Global, Cannot Be True. The correct answer choice is (B)

The Not Laws on our initial diagram prove answer choice (B) correct. Note that answer choices (A) and (D) are functionally identical (they reference the same lane pairing), and therefore incorrect.

Question #24: Global, Could Be True, List. The correct answer choice is (C)

Answer choice (A) can be eliminated because at least one of J's laps is not immediately after one of O's laps.

Answer choice (B) can be eliminated because K's lap is immediately before L's lap.

Answer choice (C) is the correct answer.

Answer choice (D) can be eliminated because J swims lap 9, a violation of the second rule.

Answer choice (E) can be eliminated because O's first lap is before M's first lap.

POWERSCORE®

38

PrepTest

OCTOBER 2002 LOGIC GAMES SETUPS

This is a Pure Sequencing game.

The game scenario establishes that eight clowns get out of a car in order, according to a set of rules that are all sequential in nature. The sequence is a tricky one, so let's walk through the rules in order to evaluate how the final diagram is created.

The first rule indicates that V gets out some time before both Q and Y:

$$V > \begin{array}{l} Q \\ \text{- - -} \\ Y \end{array}$$

The second rule indicates that Z gets out some time before Q. This relationship is best added to the diagram with an arrow:

$$\begin{array}{l} Z \leftarrow \!\!\lnot \\[4pt] V > \begin{array}{l} Q \\ \text{- - -} \\ Y \end{array} \end{array}$$

The third rule states that T gets out before V but after R:

$$\begin{array}{l} Z \leftarrow \!\!\lnot \\[4pt] R > T > V > \begin{array}{l} Q \\ \text{- - -} \\ Y \end{array} \end{array}$$

The fourth rule complicates matters, and adds another clown, S, behind V:

$$\begin{array}{l} Z \leftarrow \!\!\lnot \\[4pt] Q \\ \text{- - -} \\ R > T > V > Y \\ \text{- - -} \\ S \end{array}$$

The fifth and final rule may be the one that poses the most difficulty. R, who already gets out of the car ahead of T, also gets out of the car ahead of W. This creates a double-branched vertical, leading to the final diagram:

Q R S T V W Y Z [8]

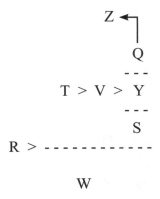

As in all Sequencing games, always evaluate which variables could be first or last: only R or Z could get out of the car first, and only Q, S, W, or Y could exit the car last.

Question #1: Global, Could Be True, List. The correct answer choice is (E)

Answer choice (A) is incorrect because T and V cannot get out of the car before R.

Answer choice (B) is incorrect because Q cannot get out of the car before T.

Answer choice (C) is incorrect because Q cannot get out of the car before Z.

Answer choice (D) is incorrect because W cannot get out of the car before R.

Answer choice (E) is the correct answer.

Question #2: Global, Could Be True. The correct answer choice is (D)

Answer choice (A) is incorrect because the earliest Y could exit the car is fourth.

Answer choice (B) is incorrect because the latest R could exit the car is second.

Answer choice (C) is incorrect because the earliest Q could exit the car is fifth (don't forget about Z > Q).

Answer choice (D) is the correct answer.

Answer choice (E) is incorrect because the latest V can exit the car is fifth.

Question #3: Local, Could Be True. The correct answer choice is (C)

If Z is the seventh clown to get out of the car, then Q must be the last clown to get out of the car. This information eliminates answer choice (E). With Z and Q placed, the remaining relationship controls the variables:

$$
\begin{array}{c}
 \text{Y} \\
\text{T} > \text{V} > \text{- - -} \\
 \text{S} \\
\text{R} > \text{- - - - - - - - - - -}
\end{array}
$$

$$
\text{W}
$$

Thus, R must be the first clown to get out of the car, eliminating answer choice (A).

Answer choice (B) is incorrect because T must be the second or third clown to get out of the car.

Answer choice (C) is correct because W can exit the car after any of R, T, V, Y, and S.

Answer choice (D) is incorrect because the latest V can get out of the car is fourth.

Question #4: Local, Must Be True. The correct answer choice is (D)

When T gets out of the car fourth, R, W, and Z must get out of the car in the first three spaces:

$$
\underbrace{ (\ R > W\ ,\ Z\ )\ \ }_{1 \qquad 2 \qquad 3} \quad \underset{4}{\underline{\text{T}}} \quad \underset{5}{\underline{}} \quad \underset{6}{\underline{}} \quad \underset{7}{\underline{}} \quad \underset{8}{\underline{}}
$$

Thus, V, Q, S, and Y are the last four clowns to get out of the car. Because V must exit ahead of Q, S, and Y, V must get out of the car fifth, and Q, S, and Y are the last three clowns to exit the car:

$$
\underbrace{(\ R > W\ ,\ Z\ )}_{1 \quad 2 \quad 3} \quad \underset{4}{\underline{\text{T}}} \quad \underset{5}{\underline{\text{V}}} \quad \underbrace{(\ Q\ ,\ S\ ,\ Y\ )}_{6 \quad 7 \quad 8}
$$

Accordingly, answer choice (D) is correct.

Question #5: Local, Could Be True, Except. The correct answer choice is (D)

If Q gets out of the car fifth, then S, W, and Y *must* be the last three clowns to exit the car:

				Q		(S , W , Y)
1	2	3	4	5	6	7	8

This information proves that answer choice (D) is correct

Question #6: Local, Must Be True. The correct answer choice is (E)

If R is the second clown to get out of the car, then Z must be the first clown to get out of the car (remember, R and Z are the only two clowns who could exit first):

Z	R						
1	2	3	4	5	6	7	8

Because Z gets out of the car first, we can ascertain that answer choice (E) is correct.

Question #7: Local, Could Be True. The correct answer choice is (E)

The question stem adds a new condition: V > Z. This new rule affects the initial diagram, producing the following controlling chain:

$$Z > Q$$
$$- - - - - -$$
$$T > V > Y$$
$$- - - - - -$$
$$S$$
$$R > - - - - - - - - - - - - - - -$$
$$W$$

This condition actually simplifies the initial chain, eliminating the confusion caused by the possible movement of Z.

Answer choice (A) is incorrect because without the possibility of Z getting out of the car first, R must be the first clown to get out of the car.

Answer choice (B) is incorrect because T must exit the car no later than third.

Answer choice (C) is incorrect because the earliest Q could exit the car is fifth.

Answer choice (D) is incorrect because the latest V could get out of the car is fourth.

Answer choice (E) is the correct answer.

This is an Advanced Linear: Balanced game.

The game scenario indicates that six tasks will be demonstrated at a farm exhibition. Each task is demonstrated one after the other, giving the game a Linear aspect, and each demonstration is given by one of three volunteers. The initial scenario appears as follows:

H M P S T W [6]

F F G G L L [6]

Task: ＿＿ ＿＿ ＿＿ ＿＿ ＿＿ ＿＿

Volunteer: ＿＿ ＿＿ ＿＿ ＿＿ ＿＿ ＿＿
                1   2   3   4   5   6

The first rule, which involves F and G, has a powerful effect, and creates exactly two possible sequences for F and G:

Sequence 1:   F > G > G > F

Sequence 2:   F > G > F > G

Note that this eliminates G from demonstrating the first task. More on the limitations produced by this rule later.

The second rule creates F Not Laws on the first and last demonstrations, leaving only L available to demonstrate the first task, and G or L for the last task. With L demonstrating the first task, by applying the first rule a G Not Law can be placed on the second demonstration as well (creating a F/L dual-option):

H M P S T W [6]

F F G G L L [6]

Task: ＿＿ ＿＿ ＿＿ ＿＿ ＿＿ ＿＿

Volunteer: 　L　 　F/L　 ＿＿ ＿＿ ＿＿ 　G/L
             1   2   3   4   5   6
            G̶   F̶
            F̶   G̶

The third and fourth rules are similar, and each removes two tasks from a volunteer:

When combined, these rules eliminate both G and L from harvesting, resulting in the inference that F must demonstrate harvesting:

And, because from the second rule F can perform neither first nor last, we can deduce that harvesting is demonstrated neither first nor last. In addition, because L must demonstrate the first task, T cannot be demonstrated first (H has already been eliminated):

H M P S T W ^{6}

F F G G L L ^{6}

F > G > G > F
F > G > F > G

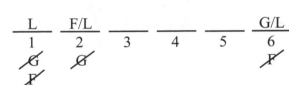

The fifth and final rule creates a standard block:

T M

The application of this block eliminates T from being demonstrated last, M from being demonstrated first and second (remember, L already demonstrates the first task and L cannot demonstrate T from the fourth rule, which means that the earliest T could be demonstrated is second). Adding in the randoms, we near the final setup:

H M P S T W [6]
   * *   *
F F G G L L [6]

Task:

H̶	M̶				H̶
P̶					P̶
M̶					

F > G > G > F
F > G > F > G

Volunteer:

L	F/L				G/L
1	2	3	4	5	6
F̶	G̶				F̶
G̶					

H̶/G M̶/G   H̶/L T̶/L

H
F

T M

Before moving on to the questions, let's revisit the possible orderings of F, G, and L. The first rule, which involves F and G, has a controlling effect on the performances of the three volunteers. As stated earlier, the rule creates exactly two possible sequences for F and G:

Sequence 1:   F > G > G > F

Sequence 2:   F > G > F > G

Because, as discussed during the setup, L must perform first, the only wild card in the two sequences above is L's second performance. In the case of Sequence 1, because F cannot perform last, L must perform last, producing just one acceptable ordering of the volunteers:

L	F	G	G	F	L
1	2	3	4	5	6

In the case of Sequence 2, L's second performance can be second, third, fourth, fifth, or sixth, producing five acceptable orderings of the volunteers:

38

L's second performance is second:	L	L	F	G	F	G
L's second performance is third:	L	F	L	G	F	G
L's second performance is fourth:	L	F	G	L	F	G
L's second performance is fifth:	L	F	G	F	L	G
L's second performance is sixth:	L	F	G	F	G	L
	1	2	3	4	5	6

Although these six orders limit the possibilities in the game, there are too many combinations of the tasks-to-volunteers to make it worthwhile to Identify the Possibilities or Templates.

Question #8: Global, Could Be True, List. The correct answer choice is (C)

Answer choice (A) is incorrect because F cannot perform first.

Answer choice (B) is incorrect because F must perform exactly once prior to G's first performance.

Answer choice (C) is the correct answer.

Answer choice (D) is incorrect because G cannot demonstrate harvesting.

Answer choice (E) is incorrect because threshing and milling must be performed consecutively.

Question #9: Global, Must Be True. The correct answer choice is (A)

As mentioned during the setup discussion, because neither G nor L can demonstrate harvesting, F must demonstrate harvesting. Hence, answer choice (A) is correct.

Question #10: Local, Could Be True. The correct answer choice is (B)

If L performs fourth, the application of the first rule (as discussed during the setup) forces the volunteers into the following performance order:

L	F	G	L	F	G
1	2	3	4	5	6

Because F must demonstrate harvesting, we can infer that harvesting is demonstrated either second or fifth. Hence, answer choice (B) is correct.

Question #11: Local, Must Be True. The correct answer choice is (A)

The condition in the question stem creates the following block:

$$\begin{array}{|ccc|} \hline P & T & M \\ G & F & \_\_ \\ \hline \end{array}$$

Because this block places F after G, by applying the first rule we can infer that F's other performance must come before the block:

$$\begin{array}{|c|} \hline H \\ F \\ \hline \end{array} \quad > \quad \begin{array}{|ccc|} \hline P & T & M \\ G & F & \_\_ \\ \hline \end{array}$$

Consequently, G's other performance must come after F's first performance, and thus either before or after the block. Adding the inference that L performs first creates the following scenario:

$$\begin{array}{|cc|} \hline S/W & H \\ L & F \\ \hline \end{array} \quad > \quad \begin{array}{|ccc|} \hline P & T & M \\ G & F & L \\ \hline \end{array}$$

$$\begin{array}{|c|} \hline W/S \\ G \\ \hline \end{array}$$

Thus, the only two possible performance orderings of volunteers are:

L-F-G-G-F-L

or

L-F-G-F-L-G

In both scenarios, F will demonstrate harvesting second, and thus answer choice (A) is correct.

Question #12: Global, Must Be True. The correct answer choice is (D)

As mentioned during the setup, because neither F nor G can perform first, L must perform first. Hence, answer choice (D) is correct.

Question #13: Global, Could Be True. The correct answer choice is (E)

The Not Laws created during the setup of this game eliminate answer choices (A), (B), (C), and (D). Thus, by process of elimination, answer choice (E) is proven correct.

This is a Grouping: Defined-Fixed, Balanced, Identify the Templates game.

The game scenario creates a classic Grouping scenario where seven applicants are hired for positions in three different departments:

F G H I W X Y [7]

_____	_____
_____	_____
_____	_____	_____
M	P	S

The fourth rule is the easiest to diagram, and it assigns F to a position in P:

F G H I W X Y [7]

_____	_____
_____	_____
_____	F	_____
M	P	S

The first rule establishes that H and Y are a block:

```
┌───┐
│ H │
│ Y │
└───┘
```

Because H and Y fill two positions, they cannot be assigned to the management department, and must be assigned to either the production or sales department:

F G H I W X Y [7]

```
┌───┐
│ H │
│ Y │
└───┘
```

	┌─H─/│	/─┌─H─┐
	│ Y │/	/│ Y │
_____	F	_____
M	P	S

The second rule establishes a vertical not-block:

Consequently, when the fourth rule is considered, G cannot fill a production position and must instead fill a position in management or sales:

F G H I W X Y [7]

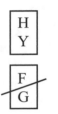

G/
―――
 M
 H̶
 X̶

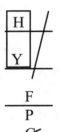

F
―――
P
G̶

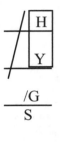

/G
―――
 S

The third rule is conditional:

$$X_S \longrightarrow W_P$$

Combining the previous information, and adding in the fact that I is a random, results in the following diagram:

F G H I W X Y [7]
        *

$$X_S \longrightarrow W_P$$

G/
―――
 M
 H̶
 X̶

F
―――
P
G̶

/G
―――
 S

38

Because of the restrictions resulting from pairing H and Y together (and the implications that result from the other rules), templates can be made based on their placement. The first placement to consider is when H and Y are together in P:

Template #1 (H and Y in P):

		Y	I
		H	G
	X	F	W
	M	P	S

Because H and Y in P completely fills the production department, you can apply the contrapositive of the third rule to determine that X cannot fill a position in S. That means that X must go fill the position in M, and the other three variables—W, G, and I—are all hired in S.

The next template possibility involves the placement of H and Y in S. Unfortunately this will not completely fill group S, so more movement is allowed. Because of the additional spaces available to the other variables, a secondary consideration must be applied. In this case, you should look at the next most restricted variable: G. Because G cannot go in group P, create two templates: one template with G in M, and another with G in S.

Template #2 (H and Y in S, G in M):

		I/X/W	I/X/W
		I/X/W	Y
	G	F	H
	M	P	S

Template #3 (H and Y in S, G in S):

	I/X/W	G
	I/X/W	Y
I/X/W	F	H
M	P	S

Question #14: Global, Could Be True, List. The correct answer choice is (E)

Answer choice (A) is incorrect because if X is in S, W must be in P.

Answer choice (B) is incorrect because F must be in P.

Answer choice (C) is incorrect because G and F cannot be in the same group.

Answer choice (D) is incorrect because H and Y must be in the same group.

Answer choice (E) is the correct answer choice.

Question #15: Global, Cannot Be True, List. The correct answer choice is (D)

From the main diagram only G is restricted from group P, so the correct answer is (D).

Question #16: Global, Justify. The correct answer choice is (C)

By looking at the templates, you should be able to quickly determine which answer choice would place all seven variables without allowing any possible additional movement.

Answer choice (C) is correct because it can only exist in Template #1, where all seven variables are placed. The other four answers either allow movement within a single template, or could occur in both Template #2 and Template #3 (so they do not produce a single, fixed outcome).

Question #17: Global, Could Be True, Except, List. The correct answer choice is (B)

Again, the templates reveal that G and X can never be together in S, so answer choice (B) is correct.

Question #18: Local, Could Be True, Except. The correct answer choice is (B)

If F is hired with X, then either Template #2 or #3 applies.

Answer choice (A) is incorrect because G could be in S (Template #3).

Answer choice (B) is the correct answer choice. H must be in S.

Answer choice (C) is incorrect because I could be in S (Template #2).

Answer choice (D) is incorrect because W could be in M (Template #3).

Answer choice (E) is incorrect because W could be in P (either template).

Question #19: Local, Could Be True. The correct answer choice is (C)

All three templates are possible if X is not in P. Thus, P is either filled by F, H and Y, or F, I and W.

Answer choice (A) is incorrect because F cannot be in S.

Answer choice (B) is incorrect because if H is in S then W must be in P (Templates #2 and #3) for this question.

Answer choice (C) is the correct answer choice (Template #1).

Answer choice (D) is incorrect because G cannot be in P.

Answer choice (E) is incorrect because if H is in P it must be with F and Y, not W.

This is an Advanced Linear: Balanced, Identify the Templates game.

The game scenario and two rules combine to form the following diagram:

N O S T V⁵

N: F L
O: H M
S: G H
T: F G
V: L M

Instrument: ___ ___ ___ ___ ___
Instrument: ___ ___ ___ ___ ___
Piece: ___ N/T ___ ___ ___
             1   2   3   4   5

This can be a challenging game due to the heavy Pattern element of the instruments. In order to effectively attack this game, you must thoroughly analyze the first rule. The rule is very carefully worded to state, "Each piece shares one instrument with the piece performed immediately before it *or* after it (or both)" (italics added). Thus, although a piece can share an instrument with the piece before it *and* with the piece after it, this is not a requirement. Therefore, there can be "breaks" within the performance order where two consecutive pieces do not share an instrument. However, these "breaks" can only appear between certain pieces, namely between the second and third pieces, and between the third and fourth pieces. Let us examine why:

Because each piece must share an instrument with another piece, we can infer that the first piece must share an instrument with the second piece, and that the fifth piece must share an instrument with the fourth piece.

The only other consecutive pieces are the second and third pieces, and the third and fourth pieces. A "break" is possible between the second and third pieces: the first and second pieces share an instrument, and then the third piece shares an instrument with the fourth, and the fourth piece shares an instrument with the fifth piece.

A "break" is also possible between the third and fourth pieces: the first and second pieces share an instrument, the second and third pieces share an instrument, and then the fourth piece shares an instrument with the fifth piece.

The restriction of the first rule, in combination with the second rule, ultimately sparks the decision to Identify the Templates. Because there are only two options for the second performance, and we know from the first rule that the first piece must share an instrument with the second piece, there seems to be an inherent limitation in the pieces that can be performed first and second. There are, in fact, only four possibilities:

When N is performed second: Because N is performed with fiddle and lute, the first piece must also be performed with fiddle or lute, and thus only T or V can be performed first.

38

When T is performed second: Because T is performed with fiddle and guitar, the first piece must also be performed with fiddle or guitar, and thus only N or S can be performed first.

We can now create the following four templates for the pieces:

Template	1	2	3	4	5
Template #4:	S	T	(N,	O,	V)
Template #3:	N	T	(O,	S,	V)
Template #2:	V	N	(O,	S,	T)
Template #1:	T	N	(O,	S,	V)

Within each template, there are also a limited number of possibilities for the pieces performed third, fourth, and fifth; that is, there are not six options in each template as might originally appear to be the case. Let us examine this in more detail, using the first template as an example:

Template #1 features T and N as the first two pieces. Initially, the remaining three pieces—O, S, and V—appear to have six possible orders: O-S-V; O-V-S; S-O-V; S-V-O; V-O-S; and V-S-O. However, due to the restriction of the first rule, only three of these possibilities are valid:

T-N-O-S-V: this possibility fails because V does not share an instrument with S
T-N-O-V-S: this possibility fails because S does not share an instrument with V
T-N-S-O-V: this possibility is a valid solution with no "break"
T-N-S-V-O: this possibility fails because S does not share an instrument with either N or V
T-N-V-O-S: this possibility is a valid solution with no "break"
T-N-V-S-O: this possibility is a valid solution with a "break" between the third and fourth piece

This same type of analysis can be applied to each of the other templates, and each of the other templates also contains three possible solutions:

Template #2. The three solutions are:

V-N-T-O-S
V-N-T-S-O
V-N-O-S-T

Template #3. The three solutions are:

N-T-S-O-V
N-T-S-V-O
N-T-V-O-S

Template #4. The three solutions are:

S-T-N-O-V
S-T-N-V-O
S-T-O-V-N

An examination of the solutions for each template reveals an interesting pattern: the remaining three pieces in each template contain one piece that shares an instrument with each of the other two pieces, but those two other pieces do not share an instrument with each other. For example, in Template #2, S shares an instrument with both O and T, but O and T do not share an instrument with each other. In Template #3 (and Template #1), O shares an instrument with both S and V, but S and V do not share an instrument with each other. In Template #4, V shares an instrument with both N and O, but N and O do not share an instrument with each other. This pattern in part limits the total number of solutions since the two pieces that do not share an instrument cannot be performed fourth and fifth.

In total, the game contains twelve solutions, but it would be quite time-consuming to list each possibility at the start of the game. We recommend that you instead proceed with the four templates, and make note of the basic relationships among the remaining three variables in each template. The templates prove critical to answering several of the questions.

Question #20: Global, Could Be True, List question. The correct answer choice is (D)

An analysis of the templates above reveals that answer choice (D) is correct.

Question #21: Global, Cannot Be True. The correct answer choice is (A)

At first, this question appears to require more work because you are asked to analyze the instruments played with each piece. However, we know from the second rule that either N or T must be second. N and T have the fiddle in common, so it follows that a fiddle is always used with the second performance. Since each instrument only appears twice among the five pieces (the fiddle is used twice, the guitar is used twice, the harp is used twice, the lute is used twice, and the mandolin is used twice) and the fiddle must be played second, we can infer that the fiddle can never be played in both the third and fourth pieces. Hence, answer choice (A) is correct.

Question #22: Local, Could Be True. The correct answer choice is (A)

The hypothetical V-N-T-S-O can be used to prove answer choice (A) correct.

Question #23: Global, Could Be True, Except. The correct answer choice is (B)

From our discussion of the four templates, we know that only N, S, T, or V could be the first piece performed. Therefore, answer choice (B) is correct.

Question #24: Local, Could Be True. The correct answer choice is (D)

This is a classic final game question—time-consuming and frustrating. If S is performed fifth, then either O or T must apparently be performed fourth. But, T cannot be performed fourth because there is no workable hypothetical with T fourth and S fifth (N must then be performed second, V must be performed first, and then O is left to be performed third, creating a V-N-O-T-S hypothetical that violates the first rule). Hence, O must be performed fourth, and this inference eliminates answer choices (B) and (C). Now that we have established that O will be performed fourth and S will be performed fifth, we can examine the templates to see if any possibilities have been eliminated. Because Template #4 features S as the first performance, we can eliminate Template

#4 from consideration. The remaining three templates each feature N as either the first or second performance, and thus we can eliminate answer choice (A). The only remaining answer choices are (D) and (E)—V performed either first or second. Of our three templates (#1, #2, and #3), only Template #2 features V as either the first or second performance, and thus Template #2—which features V as the first performance—proves answer choice (D) correct.

DECEMBER 2002 LOGIC GAMES SETUPS

This is an Advanced Linear: Balanced game.

The game scenario specifies that eight files will be ordered from first to eighth. This lends the game a Linear aspect. Each file is one of three colors, and so one row must be made for the files, and another row must be made for the colors, creating an Advanced Linear game:

Red: H M O ^{3}

Green: P V X ^{3}

Yellow: T Z ^{2}

Color:	___	___	___	___	___	___	___	___
File:	___	___	___	___	___	___	___	___
	1	2	3	4	5	6	7	8

Let's first present the final diagram for the game, and then discuss some of the more interesting facets of the game:

Red: H M O ^{3}

Green: P V X ^{3}
        *
Yellow: T Z ^{2}
        *

H > O

$\boxed{H\cancel{O}}$

X > V

$\boxed{H > O} = \boxed{X > V}$

$\boxed{Z\,M}$

Color:	G/Y	___	___	___	___	___	___	___
	R̶							
File:								
	1	2	3	4	5	6	7	8
	H̶	Ø̶	Ø̶				H̶	H̶
	M̶	V̶	V̶				X̶	X̶
	Ø̶							Z̶
	V̶							

This game is fairly standard, except for the third rule, which is unusual. There are a number of different possible representations of this rule, but we have chosen a diagram that features blocks around the sequences in order to make sure the rule is clear. In our estimation, this representation:

$$\boxed{H > O} = \boxed{X > V}$$

is clearer than:

$$H > O = X > V$$

39

There are several inferences that can be drawn from this rule, namely:

1. Because the file separation must be equal for both pairs, if X is placed first, V cannot be placed eighth, and if V is placed eighth, then X cannot be placed first. The same relationship applies to H and O (although the last rule already established that H cannot be placed first). Also, V cannot be placed second (since H and O must always be separated by at least one space, therefore if X was first the earliest V could be placed would be third).

2. Because $\boxed{H\!/\!O}$, we can infer that $\boxed{X\!/\!V}$.

There are also some interesting Not Laws within the diagram:

1. <u>O cannot be placed second</u>. Because H cannot be placed first, and O must be placed in some position after H, we can infer that O cannot be placed second.

2. <u>O cannot be placed third.</u> The earliest that H can be placed is second. But, because O cannot immediately follow H, we can infer that O cannot be placed third.

3. <u>H cannot be placed seventh</u>. If H is placed seventh, then O must be placed eighth, and that would cause a violation of the rule that states that H cannot immediately precede O.

Question #1: Global, Could Be True, List. The correct answer choice is (D)

Answer choice (A) is incorrect because H cannot be placed first.

Answer choice (B) is incorrect because Z must immediately precede M.

Answer choice (C) is incorrect because H cannot immediately precede O.

Answer choice (D) is the correct answer.

Answer choice (E) is incorrect because X and V must be separated by the same number of files as separate H and O.

Question #2: Global, Must Be True, Maximum. The correct answer choice is (C)

This is a perfect question to attack with a hypothetical. Either of the following two hypotheticals proves answer choice (C) correct:

	1	2	3	4	5	6	7	8
Hypothetical #2:	X	H	V	O	P	T	Z	M
Hypothetical #1:	Z	M	X	P	V	H	T	O

Question #3: Local, Must Be True. The correct answer choice is (A)

The condition in the question stem produces three red-green blocks:

$$\boxed{\text{RG}} \qquad \boxed{\text{RG}} \qquad \boxed{\text{RG}}$$

Consequently, a green file can never be placed first. This inference, in combination with the last rule, proves answer choice (A).

Question #4: Global, Must Be True, Maximum. The correct answer choice is (C)

From our initial analysis of the third rule, we know that if X is placed first, then V cannot be placed eighth. However, if X is placed first, perhaps V could be placed seventh. The following hypothetical template proves this is possible:

Hypothetical #1:
$$\underset{1}{\text{X}} \quad \underset{2}{\text{H}} \quad \underset{3}{(} \quad \underset{4}{\text{P, T,}} \quad \underset{5}{\boxed{\text{ZM}}} \quad \underset{6}{)} \quad \underset{7}{\text{V}} \quad \underset{8}{\text{O}}$$

This hypothetical, one of several possible hypotheticals, proves answer choice (C) correct.

Question #5: Local, Could Be True, List. The correct answer choice is (C)

This question is quite easy. From the Not Laws, we know that H cannot be placed first or seventh, and this information eliminates answer choices (A), (B), and (E). Next, the local condition in the question stem establishes that Z is in the fifth position. From the fourth rule, if Z is in the fifth position, them M must be in the sixth position. This information eliminates answer choice (D), and thus answer choice (C) is correct.

As you review the game, closely examine questions #2 and #4 as they both can be effectively attacked by using hypotheticals.

This is a Grouping: Partially Defined game.

At first, this game appears to be fairly standard: nine sessions are being filled, and three employees are available to fill those sessions. The first rule then establishes that each employee can attend only two of the sessions. This rule makes the game appear Underfunded, which is not a concern because we can create three empty spaces (E) to balance out the game. But, the final rule reveals that employees can attend sessions together, and this leaves the number of sessions attended by the employees uncertain. Because we can determine that the employees attend a maximum of six different sessions or a minimum of four sessions, this game is Partially Defined.

Because the employees can attend a maximum of six different sessions, at least three of the nine sessions will be "empty" for our purposes. These can be designated with "E," leading to the initial setup, which is based on the game scenario and the first rule:

M M S S T T [6]

    min 3 E's

    2 sessions per employee

R: ____ ____ ____

I: ____ ____ ____

H: ____ ____ ____
    1   2   3

The second rule eliminates M and S from attending an investing session. This information is best shown with side Not Laws. The third rule eliminates T from attending any session on the third day, which can be shown as a standard Not Law. Of course, the combination of these two rules causes a problem for the investing session on the third day: neither M, nor S, nor T can attend that session. Thus, that session must be unattended, which will be designated with an E. The consequences of these two rules are shown below, along with a note regarding the fourth rule:

M M S S T T [6]

    min 3 E's

    2 sessions per employee

    max 2 employees together

R: ____ ____ ____

I: ____ ____ E ~~M~~ ~~S~~

H: ____ ____ ____
    1   2   3
                ~~T~~

Question #6: Global, Must Be True, Maximum. The correct answer choice is (D)

As mentioned in the discussion above, six is the maximum number of sessions that the Capital employees can attend. Thus, answer choice (D) is correct. Here is one hypothetical that proves the point:

R: $\underline{\text{E}}$ $\underline{\text{S}}$ $\underline{\text{M}}$

I: $\underline{\text{E}}$ $\underline{\text{T}}$ $\underline{\text{E}}$

H: $\underline{\text{T}}$ $\underline{\text{M}}$ $\underline{\text{S}}$
    1   2   3

Question #7: Global, Cannot Be True, FTT. The correct answer choice is (E)

Because M and S can never attend an investing session, and T cannot attend a session on the third day, we were able to deduce in the setup that investing on the third day is empty. Answer choice (E) is impossible and therefore correct.

Question #8: Local, Must Be True. The correct answer choice is (C)

Because T cannot attend a session on the third day, for employees to attend two sessions on the third day then M and S must separately attend the hiring and regulations sessions:

R: ____ ____ M/S

I: ____ ____ E

H: ____ ____ S/M
    1   2   3

This inference allows us to prove that answer choice (C) is correct. For example, if M attends the regulations session on day three and S attends the hiring session on day three, then M cannot attend another regulation session and S cannot attend another hiring session. So, if M and S were to attend a session together, they would have to do so at an investing session. But we know from the second rule that M and S cannot attend an investing session. Thus, we can infer that M and S do not attend any session together.

This discussion allows us to make an inference that will be useful later in the game, on question #10: when M and S attend different session topics, i.e. one attends a hiring session and one attends a regulations session (regardless of the day attended), they cannot attend a session together at any point in the game.

Question #9: Global, Could Be True, Except. The correct answer choice is (B)

Like the other Global questions in this game (#6 and #7), this question can be time-consuming. Remember, on many Global questions using hypotheticals is a fast and effective method of attack.

Answer choice (A) is proven incorrect by the hypothetical provided in question #6.

Answer choice (B) is the correct answer choice. If the condition in the answer choice is true, then only three sessions would be attended by the employees (two sessions per employee and two employees at each session equals three sessions of two employees each). However, there is no acceptable scenario where this can occur because none of the employees can repeat a session topic.

Answer choice (C) is proven incorrect by the following hypothetical:

R:	T	MS	E
I:	E	T	E
H:	MS	E	E
	1	2	3

Answer choices (D) and (E) are functionally identical, and therefore both are incorrect. M and S are basically interchangeable, and these two answers simply pair S with T, and then M with T. If S can pair with T, then logically M can pair with T. According to the Uniqueness Theory of Answer Choices, each correct answer choice is identifiably unique, and so any pair of functionally identical answer choices must be incorrect.

Question #10: Local, Cannot Be True, FTT. The correct answer choice is (A)

The condition in the question stem leads to the following basic scenario:

R:	M/S	___	___
I:	T	___	E
H:	S/M	___	___
	1	2	3

As discussed in question #8, when M and S attend different session topics (as on the first day in this question), they cannot attend a session together at any point in the game. Hence, answer choice (A) is correct.

Question #11: Local, Could Be True, Except. The correct answer choice is (A)

If M and T are the only employees to attend a session on the first day, we can infer that S must attend sessions on both the second day and the third day. And because T cannot attend a session on the third day, T must attend a session on the second day. Thus, M and T attend a session on the first day, S and T attend a session on the second day, and S attends a session on the third day. This information is sufficient to prove answer choice (A) correct.

This is an Advanced Linear: Unbalanced, Identify the Templates game.

Here is the full setup as produced by the game scenario and rules. A discussion follows thereafter.

S T U W Z⁵ E E

L L L R R⁵ E E

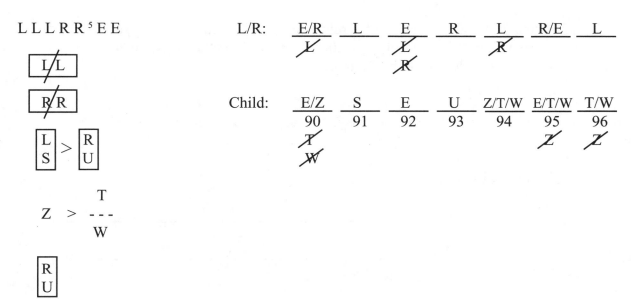

Because there are seven years and only five children, this linear game is Unbalanced. However, this imbalance is easily corrected by creating two empty years, designated by the "E's" above. Since an E in either the L/R row or the child row means that the entire year is empty, we can show the two empty years as:

| E | and | E |
| E | | E |

This game requires a series of related steps to create the complete setup above:

Step 1. The combination of the first rule and the fifth rule allows us to infer that a left-handed child was not born in 1990 or 1992.

Step 2. U, a right-handed child, was born in 1993. Thus, a right-handed child was not born in 1992 or 1994. Further, from the third rule we can infer that S, a left-handed child, was born in 1990, 1991, or 1992. However, when this inference is combined with step 1, we can infer that S was born in 1991.

Step 3. Since neither a left-handed nor a right-handed child can be born in 1992, 1992 must be an empty year. Since a left-handed child cannot be born in 1990, 1990 must be either an empty or a right-handed year.

Step 4. From the first three steps above, we have placed one right-handed child, one left-handed child, and one empty year. Further, 1990 has been established as either an empty or a right-handed year.

Consequently, two left-handed children must be born in the years 1994, 1995, and 1996. Because of the first rule, we can therefore infer that the two left-handed children are born in 1994 and 1996. From that inference we can deduce that 1995 is the remainder of the right-handed/empty dual-option from 1990. At this point, the entire L/R row is complete, and the only uncertainty is in 1990 and 1995.

Step 5. Due to steps 1 though 4 above, all the rules are "dead" except the fourth rule. The fourth rule is the only remaining active rule, and even then there are limitations, as shown by the dual- and triple-options in the child row of the diagram.

The discussion above reveals the deep restrictions in this game. In fact, there are only two basic templates that exist:

Template #1: Z born in 1990

L/R:	R	L	E	R	L	E	L
Child:	Z	S	E	U	T/W	E	W/T
	90	91	92	93	94	95	96

Template #2: Z born in 1994

L/R:	E	L	E	R	L	R	L
Child:	E	S	E	U	Z	T/W	W/T
	90	91	92	93	94	95	96

Either the original diagram or these two templates can be used to effectively attack this game.

Question #12: Global, Could Be True, List question. The correct answer choice is (E)

Answer choice (A) is incorrect because S was born in 1991, not 1990. (A) is also incorrect because no one was born in 1992.

Answer choice (B) is incorrect because Z was born before both T and W.

Answer choice (C) is incorrect because U was born in 1993, not 1992.

Answer choice (D) is incorrect because one of 1990 or 1995 was an empty year.

Answer choice (E) is the correct answer.

Question #13: Local, Cannot Be True. The correct answer choice is (D)

If S was born before Z, then Z must have been born in 1994, as in Template #2:

L/R:	E	L	E	R	L	R	L
Child:	E	S	E	U	Z	T/W	W/T
	90	91	92	93	94	95	96

Consequently, answer choice (D) is proven correct. Also, please note that in this template, the E in the 1990 child row forces a corresponding E in the L/R row, and in turn you can infer that in 1995 a right-handed child was born.

Question #14: Global, Cannot Be True, FTT. The correct answer choice is (C)

Our original diagram proves answer choice (C) correct. If your setup was incomplete, please be aware that you could have used the answer to question #12 to eliminate answer choices (B) and (D).

Question #15: Local, Must Be True, Maximum. The correct answer choice is (B)

The question is specific in requesting the number of different sequential orderings, not the number of different orders of children and years. If W > T, there are two possible sequential orderings:

Order #1: $Z > S > U > W > T$

Order #2: $S > U > Z > W > T$

Hence, answer choice (B) is correct.

Question #16: Local, Must Be True. The correct answer choice is (D)

The condition in the question stem creates the following scenario, identical to Template #1:

L/R:	R	L	E	R	L	E	L
Child:	Z	S	E	U	T/W	E	W/T
	90	91	92	93	94	95	96

Therefore, answer choice (D) is correct.

Again, if you had difficulty creating the scenario above, the solution from question #12 can be used to eliminate answer choices (B) and (E).

Question #17: Local, Cannot Be True, Except, FTT. The correct answer choice is (D)

If T is right-handed, then the only year T could have been born is 1995. If 1995 is a right-handed year, then 1990 is an empty year, and we can conclude that Z was born in 1994:

L/R:	E	L	E	R	L	R	L
Child:	E	S	E	U	Z	T	W
	90	91	92	93	94	95	96

Thus, answer choice (D) is proven correct.

Question #18: Local, Cannot Be True, FTT. The correct answer choice is (D)

If Z > U, then Z was born in 1990, as in Template #1:

L/R:	R	L	E	R	L	E	L
Child:	Z	S	E	U	T/W	E	W/T
	90	91	92	93	94	95	96

Hence, answer choice (D) is correct.

Once again, if you had difficulty creating the scenario above, the solution from question #12 can be used to eliminate answer choices (A) and (B).

This game is a model example of an Advanced Linear game. Our organized attack features two key pieces: first, we created two "E" placeholders to compensate for the Unbalanced aspect of the game; second, we attacked the rules by linkage, and we kept a close watch on the two not-blocks, especially the LL not-block as the game contained three L's. These two steps reduced the game to a simple exercise in tracking the fourth rule, the only remaining active rule (a quick survey of the questions reveals that every Local question references either T, W, or Z). Students able to recognize the restriction inherent in the fourth rule can then create two templates to attack the game.

This is a Grouping: Undefined game.

At first this game appears to be a fairly standard Grouping game, but the test makers throw a slight twist into the mix with the last rule that specifies the number of Os selected. Fortunately, this is the only numerical rule, and thus it is easy to remember throughout the game.

Because there is no specified number of fish selected, there is no representation for the group.

The seven rules can be diagrammed as follows:

J K L M N O P⁷
*   *

First rule:	K ◄——┼——► O
Second rule:	M ◄——┼——► N
Third rule:	M ————► O
Fourth rule:	N ————► O
Fifth and sixth rules:	O ◄————► P
Seventh rule:	O_1 ————► O_2

Because of the large number of rules, there are also a large number of inferences:

1. M ◄——┼——► K. This inference is produced by the combination of the first and third rules.

2. N ◄——┼——► K. This inference is produced by the combination of the first and fourth rules.

3. M ————► P. This inference is produced by the combination of the third and fifth rules.

4. N ————► P. This inference is produced by the combination of the fourth and fifth rules.

5. P ◄——┼——► K. This inference is produced by the combination of the first and sixth rules.

6. M ————► O_2. This inference is produced by the combination of the third and last rules.

7. N ————► O_2. This inference is produced by the combination of the fourth and last rules.

8. P ————► O_2. This inference is produced by the combination of the sixth and seventh rules.

Two additional notes:

1. In the rule diagrams, the fifth and sixth rules were combined to create the double-arrow representation, which perfectly captures the relationship between O and P.

2. J and L are both randoms, which in an Undefined game means that their appearance has no effect unless a number is specified for the group. Hence, your focus in this game should be almost entirely on K, M, N, O and P.

Here is the complete setup for the game:

J K L M N O P [7]
*   *

Rules	Inferences
K ←—+—→ O	M ←—+—→ K
M ←—+—→ N	N ←—+—→ K
M ——→ O	M ——→ P
N ——→ O	N ——→ P
O ←——→ P	P ←—+—→ K
O_1 ——→ O_2	M ——→ O_2
	N ——→ O_2
	P ——→ O_2

39

Question #19: Global, Could Be True, List. The correct answer choice is (C)

Answer choice (A) is incorrect because M and K cannot be selected together; alternately, if M is selected, than at least two Os must be selected.

Answer choice (B) is incorrect because K and O cannot be selected together.

Answer choice (C) is the correct answer.

Answer choice (D) is incorrect because if one O is selected, than at least two Os must be selected.

Answer choice (E) is incorrect because M and N cannot be selected together

Question #20: Local, Could Be True. The correct answer choice is (A)

If P is not selected, then O cannot be selected. Via the contrapositive, if O is not selected, then N and M cannot be selected. This information is sufficient to eliminate answer choices (B), (C), (D), and (E). Thus, by process of elimination, answer choice (A) is proven correct.

Question #21: Local, Cannot Be True. The correct answer choice is (A)

To solve this question, we must first determine which fish species should be included; that is, which fish species are necessary to allow other fish species to be chosen. In this game, one fish species stands out as the strongest candidate: O. Because O is a necessary condition for M, N, and P, if O is not selected, then via the contrapositive M, N, and P cannot be selected, a loss of four fish species (O, M, N, P). On the other hand, if O is selected, then O, P, and the choice of M or N can be selected, a total of three selected fish species (O, P, M/N). Clearly, the selection of O has a dramatic positive effect on the maximum number of fish species selected. Hence, if we accept that O should be one of the selected fish species, then from the first rule we can establish that K cannot be selected. Answer choice (A) is therefore correct.

Question #22: Global, Cannot Be True, FTT. The correct answer choice is (C)

Answer choice (A) is proven incorrect by the following hypothetical: J J J J.

Answer choice (B) is proven incorrect by the following hypothetical: L L L L.

Answer choice (C) is the correct answer. If M is selected, then O must be selected, and if O is selected, then two Os must be selected. Also, if O is selected then P must be selected. So, at a minimum, if M is selected, then at least four fish must be selected.

Answer choice (D) is proven incorrect by the following hypothetical: O O P.

Answer choice (E) proven incorrect by the following hypothetical: P O O.

Please note that answer choices (A) and (B) are functionally identical since they both hinge on a random. Thus, answer choices (A) and (B) are both incorrect. A similar, but slightly different relationship exists between answer choices (D) and (E). The same hypothetical eliminates each answer choice, so once you determine one answer choice is incorrect, you can eliminate the other answer choice.

Question #23: Local, Must Be True, Maximum-Minimum. The correct answer choice is (B)

If Barbara selects at least one fish species for her aquarium, the minimum number of fish species she can select is one—she can select either J or L (again, the randoms). Because answer choices (D) and (E) indicate that the minimum number of fish selected is two, both answer choices can be eliminated.

From our discussion in question #21, we know that O is a fish species that should be selected. If O is selected, we must then also select P. We can also select M or N, but not both. In addition, since J and L are both randoms, we can also select those two species. However, we cannot select K. Thus, the maximum number of fish species Barbara can select is five:

$$\underline{\quad O \quad} \quad \underline{\quad P \quad} \quad \underline{\quad M/N \quad} \quad \underline{\quad J \quad} \quad \underline{\quad L \quad}$$

Therefore, answer choice (B) is proven correct.

POWERSCORE®

PREPTEST

40

JUNE 2003 LOGIC GAMES SETUPS

This is a Basic Linear: Balanced game.

This game—a Balanced Basic Linear game—provides a great start to the June 2003 LSAT. The game features six foods added one at a time, and thus yields a diagram with six spaces. Because no food can be added more than once, the variables are in a one-to-one relationship with the spaces:

K L M O T Z[6]

$$\underline{\quad} \quad \underline{\quad} \quad \underline{\quad} \quad \underline{\quad} \quad \underline{\quad} \quad \underline{\quad}$$
$$\quad 1 \qquad 2 \qquad 3 \qquad 4 \qquad 5 \qquad 6$$

The first two rules are conditional, and we will examine those after addressing the third and fourth rules.

The third rule creates two Not Laws on the fifth position:

K L M O T Z[6]

$$\underline{\quad} \quad \underline{\quad} \quad \underline{\quad} \quad \underline{\quad} \quad \underline{\quad} \quad \underline{\quad}$$
$$\quad 1 \qquad 2 \qquad 3 \qquad 4 \qquad 5 \qquad 6$$

The last rule is sequential, but contains an element of uncertainty because you cannot determine the exact relative order of the variables. There are only two possible orders that result from the rule:

$$T > M > K$$
or
$$K > M > T$$

Regardless of the exact order, we can infer that M is never added first or last (this will be shown on our diagram with Not Laws). Additionally, if M is added second, either T or K must be added first; if M is added fifth, either T or K must be added sixth.

T/K > M > T/K

1	2	3	4	5	6
~~M~~				~~T~~	~~M~~
				~~K~~	

As noted previously, the first two rules of this game are conditional, and Linear games that feature conditional rules often are slightly harder than games that feature only Not Law, block, and sequencing rules. The diagrams for the two rules are as follows:

First rule: $M_3 \longrightarrow L_6$

Second rule: $Z_1 \longrightarrow L > O$

A close examination of the first two rules yields some useful inferences:

When Z is added first, L must be added before O. Thus, when Z is added first, L cannot be added sixth and O cannot be added second:

$$Z_1 \longleftarrow\!\!\!| \longrightarrow L_6$$

$$Z_1 \longleftarrow\!\!\!| \longrightarrow O_2$$

From the first rule, we know that when M is added third, L must be added sixth. Thus, if M is added third, then L could not come before O, and therefore when M is third, Z cannot be first:

$$Z_1 \longleftarrow\!\!\!| \longrightarrow M_3$$

Clearly, when Z is added first, the number of solutions to the game is limited. These scenarios are tested in question #5 and will be discussed in more detail then.

Combining the third and fourth rules, we can infer that if M is added fourth, then T or K must be added sixth.

$$M_4 \longrightarrow T/K_6$$

If we combine the first and last rule, we can infer that if M is added third, then either T or K must be added fourth.

$$M_3 \longrightarrow T/K_4$$

The discussion should help you focus on M and Z as the key variables in this game. Of additional note is the fact that there are no randoms in this game. Here is the final setup for the game:

K L M O T Z^6

$M_3 \longrightarrow L_6$

$Z_1 \longrightarrow L > O$

$T/K > M > T/K$

1	2	3	4	5	6
$\cancel{M}$				$\cancel{T}$	$\cancel{M}$
				$\cancel{K}$	

$Z_1 \longleftrightarrow\!\!\!| \longrightarrow L_6$

$Z_1 \longleftrightarrow\!\!\!| \longrightarrow O_2$

$Z_1 \longleftrightarrow\!\!\!| \longrightarrow M_3$

$M_4 \longrightarrow T/K_6$

$M_3 \longrightarrow T/K_4$

Question #1: Global, Could Be True, List. The correct answer choice is (D)

Answer choice (A) is incorrect because T cannot be added fifth.

Answer choice (B) is incorrect because if M is added third then L must be added sixth.

Answer choice (C) is incorrect because either K or T must be added before M.

Answer choice (D) is the correct answer.

Answer choice (E) is incorrect because if Z is added first then L must be added before O.

Question #2: Global, Cannot Be True. The correct answer choice is (C)

From the Not Laws we know that M cannot be added first, and thus answer choice (C) is correct.

Question #3: Local, Must Be True. The correct answer choice is (A)

If L is added last, from the first inference we know that Z cannot be added first. Thus, as stated in answer choice (A), at least one of the foods is added at some time before Z.

Question #4: Global, Could Be True, List. The correct answer choice is (C)

This is an unusual partial List question.

Answer choice (A) is incorrect because when M is added third then L must be added sixth.

Answer choice (B) is incorrect because the proposed scenario would force K or T to be added fifth, and that would be a violation of the third rule.

Answer choice (C) is the correct answer.

Answer choice (D) is incorrect because if Z is added first then L cannot be added last.

Answer choice (E) is incorrect because if Z is added first then M cannot be added second.

Note that answer choices (B), (D), and (E) are all violations of the inferences discussed previously.

Question #5: Local, Cannot Be True. The correct answer choice is (D)

This question tests the limited scenarios that result when Z is added first. When Z is added first, M cannot be second, third, or last. Hence, we can create two hypotheticals based on the position of M:

Hypothetical #2: Z ___ ___ ___ M ___

Hypothetical #1: Z ___ ___ M ___ ___
          1   2   3   4   5   6

Because the position of M is restricted, we should first apply the last rule (and the third rule because it affects K and T) :

Hypothetical #2: Z (K/T, ___ ___) M T/K

Hypothetical #1: Z (K/T,) M ___ T/K
          1   2   3   4   5   6

Finally, by applying the second rule, we can fill in each hypothetical:

Hypothetical #2: Z (K/T, L > O) M T/K

Hypothetical #1: Z (K/T, L) M O T/K
          1   2   3   4   5   6

When applying the second rule, in Hypothetical #1 we can infer that O must be added fifth by taking the following steps:

1. There are only three open spaces: the second, third, and fifth.

2. Since K/T > M, we know that K/T must be added second or third.

3. Since L > O, L cannot be added fifth, and thus must be added second or third.

4. Thus, because O cannot be added second or third, the only remaining space for O is the fifth space.

Both hypotheticals must be considered when answering the question. Answer choice (D) is correct: in Hypothetical #1 we know M is fourth, and in Hypothetical #2 we know L cannot be fourth because L > O. Thus, L cannot be added fourth when Z is added first.

Question #5 is probably the most difficult question of the game, and the only effective way to attack the question is to use hypotheticals. Hopefully, by quickly answering questions #1 through #4 you will build enough time to comfortably work through question #5.

This is a Grouping/Linear Combination game.

This game requires you to focus on two separate functions: establishing the group and then ordering the group:

F G H I K L M [7]

$$\underline{\hspace{3em}}\ \ \underline{\hspace{3em}}\ \ \underline{\hspace{3em}}\ \ \underline{\hspace{3em}}\ \ \underline{\hspace{3em}} \quad \longrightarrow \quad \underset{1}{\underline{\hspace{2em}}}\ \ \underset{2}{\underline{\hspace{2em}}}\ \ \underset{3}{\underline{\hspace{2em}}}\ \ \underset{4}{\underline{\hspace{2em}}}\ \ \underset{5}{\underline{\hspace{2em}}}$$

The group of five   The order of the five

Any variable that is in the group of five must then be ordered, and we have shown that relationship with an arrow from the group to the order.

As the first three rules are applied, we can begin to fill in the diagram:

$$\underline{F/G}\ \ \underline{L}\ \ \underline{I}\ \ \underline{\hspace{2em}}\ \ \underline{\hspace{2em}} \quad \longrightarrow \quad \underset{1}{\underline{F/G}}\ \ \underset{2}{\underline{L}}\ \ \underset{3}{\underline{\hspace{2em}}}\ \ \underset{4}{\underline{\hspace{2em}}}\ \ \underset{5}{\underline{\hspace{2em}}}$$

The last three rules are more complex, and must be discussed in detail:

The fourth rule can be diagrammed as follows:

$$GH \longrightarrow H > G$$

This rule can be difficult to apply. Some students make the mistake of assuming that the rule implies that G can never be first and that H can never be fifth; this is true only if *both* G and H are tested. If only G or only H is tested, then the sufficient condition of the rule would not be enacted and the rule would not apply.

If we link the fourth rule with the second rule, we can make the inference that if H is tested then F must be ranked first. Here is why: if H is tested, then if G is tested we know from the fourth rule that H would be ranked ahead of G; according to the second rule, either F or G must be ranked first, so if H is tested, then G could never be first and we can infer that F would have to be first:

$$H \longrightarrow F_1$$

Because the fifth rule is identical in structure to the fourth rule, a similar analysis can be applied. The fifth rule can be diagrammed as follows:

$$FK \longrightarrow K > F$$

As with the fourth rule, some students make the mistake of assuming that the rule implies that F can never be first and that K can never be fifth; this is true only if *both* F and K are tested. If only one is tested, then the sufficient condition of the rule would not be enacted and the rule would not apply.

If we combine the fifth rule with the second rule, we can make the inference that if K is tested then G must be ranked first. Here is why: if K is selected, then when F is selected (and we will discover below that F must be selected) we know from the fourth rule that K must be ranked ahead of F; according to the second rule, either F or G must be ranked first, so if K is tested, then F could never be first and we can infer that G would have to be first:

$$K \longrightarrow G_1$$

The final rule can be diagrammed as follows:

$$M \longrightarrow \begin{matrix} F \\ + \\ H \end{matrix}$$

This rule is extremely restrictive because the selection of M automatically adds two other members to the group. And, because the group already includes L and I, the selection of M yields only one possible group of five cold medications: M-F-H-L-I. When this group is ordered, F must be ranked first, and, of course, L must be second.

One final inference remains, and this inference is tricky indeed. An examination of the rules reveals that F is a critical variable: F appears in three of the six rules while no other variable appears in more than two of the rules. In fact, F is so critical that F must be one of the five cold medications that are tested. Consider the following: if F is not selected to be tested, then by the contrapositive of the last rule we know that M cannot be selected for testing. This situation forces the remaining five cold medications—G, H, I, K, and L—to comprise the entire testing group. Because both G and H are included in this group, the fourth rule is enacted, and we know H must rank better than G. This causes a violation of the second rule, which requires either F or G to be ranked first. Hence, because an acceptable group cannot be selected when F is not included, we can infer that F must be included in the group of five cold medications tested in the study. The group of cold medications is therefore as follows:

$$\underline{\text{F}} \quad \underline{\text{L}} \quad \underline{\text{I}} \quad \underline{\quad} \quad \underline{\quad}$$

The group above is not given in order; although F can be first, if G is also tested then G could be first instead of F. Please note also that because F must be selected, from the action of the fifth rule we can deduce that K can never be ranked last.

Of additional note is that there are no randoms in this game.

Question #6: Global, Could Be True, List. The correct answer choice is (D)

Answer choice (A) is incorrect because L must be ranked second.

Answer choice (B) is incorrect because when both G and H are tested, H must rank better than G.

Answer choice (C) is incorrect because when M is tested both F and H must be tested.

Answer choice (D) is the correct answer.

Answer choice (E) is incorrect because when both F and K are tested, K must rank better than F.

Question #7: Global, Could Be True. The correct answer choice is (C)

This is a challenging Global question. Both answer choice (A) and answer choice (E) can be eliminated because M and G can never be in the same group of five ranked products (see the discussion of the last rule). Answer choices (B) and (D) have an identical structure: they each play on relationships created by combining the second rule with the fourth or fifth rule. For answer choice (B), as discussed above, when H is selected for testing then F must rank first. For answer choice (D), also as discussed above, when K is selected for testing then G must rank first. Hence, both answer choice (B) and answer choice (D) can be eliminated because each is impossible. By process of elimination, answer choice (C) is correct.

Question #8: Global, Must Be True. The correct answer choice is (A)

As discussed above, F must selected for the study, and therefore answer choice (A) is correct.

Question #9: Global, Could Be True, List. The correct answer choice is (E)

The initial rules indicate that L can never be tested last. From our discussion of F, we were also able to deduce that K cannot be last. Ultimately, K and L are the only two variables that cannot be ranked last, and therefore F, G, H, I, and M can all be ranked last. Answer choice (E) is thus correct.

Question #10: Local, Could Be True, Except. The correct answer choice is (B)

The condition in the question stem leads to the following two basic scenarios, based on whether F or G is first:

	1	2	3	4	5
Scenario #2:	G	L	I		
Scenario #1:	F	L	I		

In Scenario #1, K cannot be selected because F is first (this inference was discussed above: when K is selected, G must be first). Thus, only G, H, and M remain to fill the final two spaces. If both G and H are selected, then H must rank better than G. If M is selected, then H must be selected.

In Scenario #2, neither H nor M can be selected: M cannot be selected with G, and H cannot be selected when G is first (when H is selected, F must be first). Thus, only K and F remain to fill the final two spaces. And because of the fifth rule, K must rank ahead of F.

The information above yields the following completed scenarios:

	1	2	3	4	5
Scenario #2:	G	L	I	K	F
Scenario #1:	F	L	I	(G, H, M)	

Consequently, answer choice (B) is correct.

This is a Grouping: Partially Defined game.

Most students attempt to set up this game as a map, with connections between each of the cities. But, a map setup makes it difficult to display the rules. Instead, this game is properly represented with a Grouping setup, as follows:

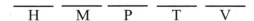

$$\underline{\quad} \quad \underline{\quad} \quad \underline{\quad} \quad \underline{\quad} \quad \underline{\quad}$$
$$\text{H} \qquad \text{M} \qquad \text{P} \qquad \text{T} \qquad \text{V}$$

In this setup, each letter represents the corresponding city. There is a space above each letter where the connecting cities will be placed. At the moment, only a single space is placed above each city because we know that, at a minimum, each city is connected with at least one other city. But, each city can have multiple connections (except Montreal) so there can be more spaces added to each city as needed.

In using this setup you must remember that the nature of the connections creates an unusual effect: because each connection has two cities, when a connection is made then each city must reflect that connection. Literally, each connection creates the placement of two variables. For example, let us say that Montreal and Vancouver are connected. In the Montreal space, we would place a V, and in the Vancouver space we would place an M, as follows:

$$\underline{\quad} \quad \overset{\text{V}}{\underline{\quad}} \quad \underline{\quad} \quad \underline{\quad} \quad \overset{\text{M}}{\underline{\quad}}$$
$$\text{H} \qquad \text{M} \qquad \text{P} \qquad \text{T} \qquad \text{V}$$

Thus, regardless of the city or number of connections, we can see all the relationships by examining the variables above the city.

If two cities cannot be connected, Not Laws must be placed under each city. For example, we know from the second rule that Honolulu and Toronto cannot be connected. Thus, we need to place a "T" Not Law under Honolulu, and an "H" Not Law under Toronto, as follows:

$$\underline{\quad} \quad \underline{\quad} \quad \underline{\quad} \quad \underline{\quad} \quad \underline{\quad}$$
$$\text{H} \qquad \text{M} \qquad \text{P} \qquad \text{T} \qquad \text{V}$$
$$\cancel{T} \qquad \qquad \qquad \qquad \cancel{H}$$

It is critical that you remember that any connection will produce the placement of two separate variables (one for each city). When you know that two cities cannot be connected, that will produce two Not Laws.

In the final analysis, although this game may initially appear to be a Mapping game, it is really a Grouping game. The game is Partially Defined because we know there are a minimum number of connections and a maximum number of connections (to be discussed in question #16), but the exact number is not fixed by the rules.

Let us take a look at the complete setup and then discuss each of the rules:

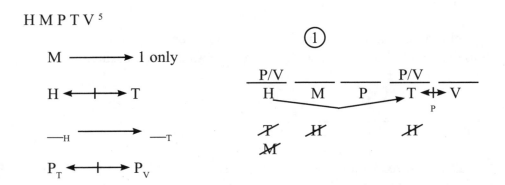

First Rule: The first rule restricts the number of connections with Montreal. As soon as any connection is made with Montreal, we can then infer that no other city will be able to connect to Montreal. We have shown this restriction by placing a "1" in a circle above the M space. If the setup was done vertically, we could put a bar at the end of the Montreal space to indicate that only one connection can be made.

Second Rule: This rule produces a "T" Not Law under Honolulu, and an "H" Not Law under Toronto.

Third Rule: We have shown this rule on the diagram itself with the arrow from H to T. By internally diagramming the rule in this fashion, we can be sure we will not forget the rule during the course of the game. This rule also allows us to infer that Montreal cannot be connected to Honolulu (M would also then be connected to T, violating the first rule). Hence, an "M" Not Law is placed under Honolulu, and an "H" Not Law is placed under Montreal.

Because H cannot be connected to M or T, we can infer that H must, at the least, be connected to P or V; hence, we have placed a P/V dual option above H, and of course because of this third rule we then know that P or V at the minimum must be connected to T.

Fourth Rule: We have internally diagrammed this rule by placing a double-not arrow between T and V, with a sub-P to indicate that Philadelphia cannot be connected to both cities.

Because this game does not yield a tremendous number of inferences, heading into the questions your focus must be on the rules and how they apply to the connections for each city.

Question #11: Global, Could Be True, List. The correct answer choice is (A)

Answer choice (A) is the correct answer.

Answer choice (B) is incorrect because M can only have one connection.

Answer choice (C) is incorrect because H and M cannot be connected, as established in the discussion above about the third rule.

Answer choice (D) is incorrect because P cannot be connected to both T and V.

Answer choice (E) is incorrect because H and T cannot be connected.

Question #12: Local, Could Be True. The correct answer choice is (B)

From the basic physical constraints of the game, Philadelphia can only connect with four other cities: Honolulu, Montreal, Toronto, and Vancouver. From the fourth rule, we know that Philadelphia cannot connect to both Toronto and Vancouver, and thus, the options for Philadelphia are H, M, and V/T. The question stem in #12 indicates that exactly three cities are connected with Philadelphia. Hence, we know we are selecting from the group of H, M, and V/T. But, because of the action of the third rule, when Philadelphia is connected with Honolulu, then Philadelphia must also be connected with Toronto. We can then determine in question #12 that Philadelphia is connected only to H, M, and T, as follows:

$$\frac{P}{H} \quad \frac{P}{M} \quad \frac{\begin{matrix}T\\M\\H\end{matrix}}{\underset{\cancel{V}}{P}} \quad \frac{P}{T} \quad \frac{}{\underset{\cancel{P}}{V}}$$

Because P cannot connect with V, we can eliminate answer choice (E). Also, because M is now connected to P, from the second rule we know that M cannot connect with any other city. Thus, answer choices (A), (C), and (D) can be eliminated. Therefore, answer choice (B) is proven correct by process of elimination.

Question #13: Global, Cannot Be True. The correct answer choice is (A)

From our discussion of the third rule, we were able to establish that H and M cannot be connected. Hence, answer choice (A) is correct.

Question #14: Global, Could Be True. The correct answer choice is (A)

In this Global question it is useful to note that each answer choice is given in the same form. In each answer choice, a pair of cities is given and the question is whether the pair can only be connected to each other, and not to any other city. Because any city connected with Honolulu must also be connected with Toronto, attempting to connect Toronto with only one other city is not feasible. For example, as in answer choice (B), if Montreal and Toronto are only connected to each other, there will be a violation because any city then connected to Honolulu will have to be connected to Toronto. Using this line of reasoning, we can eliminate each of the answers that contains Toronto, namely answer choices (B), (C), and (E).

Answer choice (D) is tricky, but when Philadelphia and Vancouver are only connected to each other, the result is that no other city is available to connect to Honolulu, a violation of the game scenario. As indicated in our discussion of the third rule, we know that neither M nor T can connect to H. Thus, H must be connected to at least P or V. However, in answer choice (D) neither of those two cities is available to H. Hence, answer choice (D) cannot occur and is incorrect. Therefore, answer choice (A) is correct.

Question #15: Local, Could Be True. The correct answer choice is (D)

The condition in the question stem yields the following scenario (Not Laws from the original diagram are included):

At this point, we can see that Honolulu has become quite restricted, and therefore H and V must be connected, with the further implication that because V is connected to H, then V must also be connected to T:

From this information, we can eliminate answer choices (A), (B), (D), and (E). Therefore, answer choice (D) is correct.

Note that answer choice (E) is impossible because of the action of the second rule.

Question #16: Global, Must Be True, Maximum. The correct answer choice is (B)

Note that Maximum questions are automatically Must Be True questions (because the maximum number is an absolute). Because there are only five cities, the maximum number of theoretical connections is ten (the first city connects to the other four, the next city connects to the remaining three, the following city connects to the last two, and the second to last city connects to the last city; $4 + 3 + 2 + 1 = 10$).

However, the rules limit the number of actual connections:

The first rule eliminates three possible connections.
The second rule eliminates one connection.
The fourth rule eliminates one connection.

Thus, the rules eliminate five of the possible ten connections, leaving only five actual connections that could be made. Answer choice (B) is correct.

Question #17: Local, Must Be True. The correct answer choice is (C)

The question stem stipulates that one city is connected to the other four cities. From the first rule, we can eliminate M from the list of possible cities connected to all the others. From the second rule, we can eliminate H and T from the list. From the fourth rule we can eliminate P from the list. Thus, V is the only city that can be connected to every other city. Answer choice (C) is the only answer choice that contains V, and therefore answer choice (C) is correct.

This is a Grouping: Defined-Fixed, Unbalanced: Overloaded game.

The initial scenario, rules, and inferences can be diagrammed as follows:

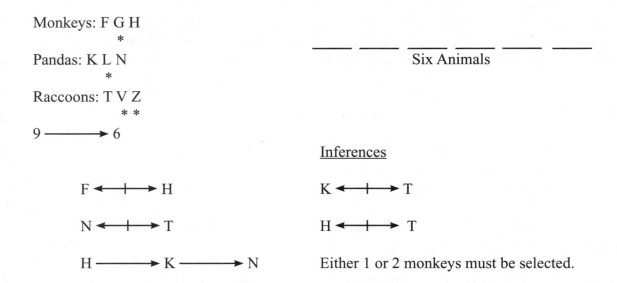

Monkeys: F G H

Pandas: K L N

Raccoons: T V Z

9 ⟶ 6

Six Animals

Inferences

F ⟵—⟶ H   K ⟵—⟶ T

N ⟵—⟶ T   H ⟵—⟶ T

H ⟶ K ⟶ N   Either 1 or 2 monkeys must be selected.

In the setup, some students create a second row within the group to show the type of animal—monkey, panda, or raccoon. While there is nothing wrong with this decision, operationally it has little effect as the questions focus more on the individual animals than on their type, and also, the questions can easily be answered without adding a second row.

There are more inferences in this game than might appear at first. Let us take a moment to examine the inferences that can be drawn.

First, at the group level, we can deduce from the first rule that if two monkeys are selected, then G must be one of those monkeys (we know this by Hurdling the Uncertainty—since F and H can never be selected together, if two monkeys are selected then G must always be selected). As a corollary, we can conclude that at most two monkeys will be selected (and, from the second rule, we can conclude that at least one monkey must be selected: since N and T cannot be selected together, we cannot form a viable group from just the six pandas and raccoons, and therefore at least one monkey will always be selected).

Second, at the variable level, several more inferences can be drawn. By connecting the second and fourth rules we can infer that K and T can never be selected together. By recycling that inference and combining it with the third rule, we can also infer that H and T can never be selected together.

The last two rules form a chain linking H, K, and N. Consequently, H is an important variable because if H is selected then K and N must also be selected, and once H, K, and N are selected we can conclude from the first two rules that F and T would not be selected. At that point, any of the remaining animals could be selected because all four rules in the scenario would have been satisfied (and, as you might expect, the remaining variables—G, L, V, and Z—are randoms). Hence, the selection of H yields a number of ready-made hypothetical solutions:

$$\underline{\quad H \quad} \quad \underline{\quad K \quad} \quad \underline{\quad N \quad} \quad \underline{(\,G, \quad L, \quad V, \quad Z\,)}$$
$$\cancel{F} \qquad \cancel{T}$$

As with any conditional chain sequence, you should also consider what occurs if the final necessary condition variable is not selected. In this case, if N is not selected, via the contrapositive you know that K and H cannot be selected. At first, this may appear unremarkable, but remember that this is a "9 into 6" grouping scenario, and if H, K, and N are all eliminated, then there are no "extra" variables, and all the remaining variables must be used. This creates the following hypothetical:

$$\underline{\quad F \quad} \quad \underline{\quad G \quad} \quad \underline{\quad L \quad} \quad \underline{\quad T \quad} \quad \underline{\quad V \quad} \quad \underline{\quad Z \quad}$$

Note that you should not just simply assume that such a hypothetical is valid; instead, quickly check the rules to make sure there are no violations (in the above hypothetical, there are no violations). If there was a violation, you would then know that the necessary condition—in this case, N—would have to be selected in every scenario and you would have gained a valuable piece of information (as it stands, since the hypothetical scenario above is workable, N does not have to be selected).

The other variable of note is T. Because T and N cannot be selected together, when T is selected there can be only one solution to the game (because N will not be selected, leading to the hypothetical discussed above).

Question #18: Global, Could Be True, List. The correct answer choice is (D)

Answer choice (A) is incorrect because N and T cannot be selected together.

Answer choice (B) is incorrect because F and H cannot be selected together.

Answer choice (C) is incorrect because if K is selected then N must be selected.

Answer choice (D) is the correct answer.

Answer choice (E) is incorrect because if H is selected then K must be selected.

Question #19: Local, Could Be True. The correct answer choice is (C)

According to the question stem, H and L are selected. From our discussion, we know that once H is selected, then K and N are also selected and F and T are not selected. This leaves the following situation:

$$\underline{\text{H}} \quad \underline{\text{K}} \quad \underline{\text{N}} \quad \underline{\underset{\cancel{F}}{\text{L}}} \quad \underline{\underset{\cancel{T}}{(\text{G, V, Z})}}$$

Answer choices (A) and (B) are eliminated due to the Not Laws. Answer choices (D) and (E) are eliminated because all three pandas must be selected. Consequently, answer choice (C) is correct.

Question #20: Global, Could Be True, Except. The correct answer choice is (C)

From our discussion of inferences, we know that K and T cannot be selected together (the combination of the second, third, and fourth rules makes it impossible). Consequently, answer choice (C) is correct.

Question #21: Local, Must Be True. The correct answer choice is (B)

This is the only question stem to contain a reference to the animal groups. If all three raccoons are selected, then T, V, and Z must be selected. Since T is selected, from the rules and inferences we know that N, K, and H cannot be selected, and therefore F, G, and L must be selected (see the discussion of the inferences if this does not make sense):

$$\underline{\text{T}_{\text{R}}} \quad \underline{\text{V}_{\text{R}}} \quad \underline{\text{Z}_{\text{R}}} \quad \underline{\underset{\substack{\cancel{N}\\\cancel{K}\\\cancel{H}}}{\text{F}_{\text{M}}}} \quad \underline{\text{G}_{\text{M}}} \quad \underline{\text{L}_{\text{P}}}$$

Answer choices (A), (C), (D), and (E) can never be true. Answer choice (B) must be true, and is therefore correct.

Question #22: Local, Must Be True. The correct answer choice is (A)

Similar to question #21, when T is selected, from the rules and inferences we know that N, K, and H cannot be selected, and therefore F, G, and L must be selected:

$$\underline{\text{T}}\quad\underline{\text{V}}\quad\underline{\text{Z}}\quad\underline{\text{F}}\quad\underline{\text{G}}\quad\underline{\text{L}}$$

$$\underset{\cancel{\text{N}}}{}$$
$$\cancel{\text{K}}$$
$$\cancel{\text{H}}$$

Answer choice (A) is therefore correct.

Another way of attacking this question is to eliminate answers that contain a variable that cannot be selected with T: use the rule that N and T cannot be selected together to eliminate answer choice (E); then use the inference that K and T cannot be selected together to eliminate answer choices (C) and (D); then use the inference that K and H cannot be selected together to eliminate answer choice (B).

Question #23: Global, Must Be True. The correct answer choice is (B)

At first glance, this appears to be a difficult Global question. Remember, if you do not have a ready inference to apply to this type of question, prepare to use hypotheticals and previous information.

Answer choice (A) can be eliminated by the question stem to #21.

Answer choice (B) is the correct answer.

Answer choice (C) can be eliminated by the hypothetical produced in #21 (and in our discussion of what occurs when N is not selected).

Answer choice (D) can be eliminated by the hypothetical array we produced when discussing the selection of H, K, and N (when H, K, and N are selected, then any three of G, L, V, and Z can be selected, allowing for a hypothetical with only one monkey).

Answer choice (E) can be eliminated by the question stem to #21.

CONTACTING POWERSCORE

POWERSCORE INTERNATIONAL HEADQUARTERS:

PowerScore Test Preparation
57 Hasell Street
Charleston, SC 29401

Toll-free information number: (800) 545-1750
Website: www.powerscore.com
Email: lsat@powerscore.com

POWERSCORE LSAT PUBLICATIONS INFORMATION:

For information on all PowerScore LSAT publications.

Website: www.powerscore.com/pubs.htm

POWERSCORE FULL-LENGTH LSAT COURSE INFORMATION:

Complete preparation for the LSAT.
Classes available nationwide.

Web: www.powerscore.com/lsat
Request Information: www.powerscore.com/contact.htm

POWERSCORE VIRTUAL LSAT COURSE INFORMATION:

45 hours of online, interactive, real-time preparation for the LSAT.
Classes available worldwide.

Web: www.powerscore.com/lsat/virtual
Request Information: www.powerscore.com/contact.htm

POWERSCORE WEEKEND LSAT COURSE INFORMATION:

Fast and effective LSAT preparation: 16 hour courses, 99th percentile instructors, and real LSAT questions.

Web: www.powerscore.com/lsat/weekend
Request Information: www.powerscore.com/contact.htm

PowerScore LSAT Tutoring Information:

One-on-one meetings with a PowerScore LSAT expert.

Web: www.powerscore.com/lsat/content_tutoring.cfm
Request Information: www.powerscore.com/contact.htm

PowerScore Law School Admissions Counseling Information:

Personalized application and admission assistance.

Web: www.powerscore.com/lsat/content_admissions.cfm
Request Information: www.powerscore.com/contact.htm